OVERLEAF:
Early Christians celebrating the Eucharistic Banquet, or Lord's
Supper, found in the Catacombs of San Callisto.

"Thomas Cahill is taking us on a wonderful ride through Western civilization. . . . The figures in time become real. . . . You can feel the terror and pain when the Romans finally destroy the Temple in Jerusalem in 70. You can sense the enigmatic charisma of Paul. . . . And you get a wonderful sense of the feisty young mother of Jesus." —*Star-Tribune* (Minneapolis)

"Cahill's third offering [in 'The Hinges of History' series] is, if anything, bolder and more engaging than his previous books. . . . Cahill strips away the pious accretions of 2000 years so that a picture of Jesus as an actual human being emerges." —*BookPage*

"Single-handedly reinventing the craft of intellectual history, Cahill struggles 'to make the stick figures of the distant past into flesh-and-blood people with real feelings.' . . . Cahill's Jesus is both unpretentiously down to earth and breathtakingly otherworldly. Instead of a pleasant plaster of Paris divinity, Jesus is a religious radical who comforts the afflicted, afflicts the comfortable and confounds all expectations." —*Religion News Service*

"Cahill . . . has thought vigorously about Jesus. . . . He is clear and consistent . . . but deeply personal. . . . Cahill relies on an excellent group of New Testament scholars." —*Christian Century*

"[Cahill is] a marvelous storyteller who makes Jesus and those who wrote about him very much alive." —*Anniston Star*

"Cahill has created a unique way of writing about history. . . . [He] has rejuvenated and revitalized the historical genre. After reading *Desire of the Everlasting Hills*, many readers may want to pick up the New Testament, which is the primary source of this book, and read it again with fresh eyes." —*Durham Herald-Sun*

"A rich book. . . . Here, at last and at least for our times, is a book about Jesus big enough to contain the world of believers, Christians and Jews, agnostics, skeptics and even scoffers." —*Grand Rapids Press*

Thomas Cahill

Desire of the Everlasting Hills

Thomas Cahill is the author of *How the Irish Saved Civilization* and *The Gifts of the Jews.* He divides his time between New York City and Rome.

BY *Thomas Cahill*

THE HINGES OF HISTORY

Volume I: How the Irish Saved Civilization

Volume II: The Gifts of the Jews

Volume III: Desire of the Everlasting Hills

Four additional volumes are planned.

THE HINGES OF HISTORY

We normally think of history as one catastrophe after another, war followed by war, outrage by outrage—almost as if history were nothing more than all the narratives of human pain, assembled in sequence. And surely this is, often enough, an adequate description. But history is also the narratives of grace, the recountings of those blessed and inexplicable moments when someone did something for someone else, saved a life, bestowed a gift, gave something beyond what was required by circumstance.

In this series, THE HINGES OF HISTORY, I mean to retell the story of the Western world as the story of the great gift-givers, those who entrusted to our keeping one or another of the singular treasures that make up the patrimony of the West. This is also the story of the evolution of Western sensibility, a narration of how we became the people that we are and why we think and feel the way we do. And it is, finally, a recounting of those essential moments when everything was at stake, when the mighty stream that became Western history was in ultimate danger and might have divided into a hundred useless tributaries or frozen in death or evaporated altogether. But the great gift-givers, arriving in the moment of crisis, provided for transition, for transformation, and even for transfiguration, leaving us a world more varied and complex, more awesome and delightful, more beautiful and strong than the one they had found.

—THOMAS CAHILL

Desire
of the
Everlasting
Hills

*The World before
and after Jesus*

Thomas Cahill

NAN A. TALESE
ANCHOR BOOKS
A DIVISION OF RANDOM HOUSE, INC.
NEW YORK

FIRST NAN A. TALESE/ANCHOR BOOKS EDITION,
FEBRUARY 2001

The Library of Congress has cataloged the Nan A. Talese/Doubleday
edition as follows:
Cahill, Thomas.
Desire of the everlasting hills : the world before and after
Jesus/Thomas Cahill. — 1st ed. in the U.S.A.
Includes bibliographical references and index.
p.   cm.
ISBN 0-385-48251-5
1. Jesus Christ Biography.   I. Series: Cahill, Thomas.
Hinges of history; v. 3.
BT301.2.C34 1999b
232—dc21 99-16560
CIP

Anchor ISBN: 0-385-48372-4

Book design by Marysarah Quinn
Maps by Jackie Aher

www.anchorbooks.com

Printed in the United States of America
10   9   8   7   6   5   4   3   2   1

TO JOEY

Christ minds: Christ's interest, what to avow or amend
There, eyes them, heart wants, care haunts, foot follows kind,
Their ransom, their rescue, and first, fast, last friend.

Never have I hoped in any but thee, God of Israel,
who will grow wroth and yet once more be merciful,
forgiving all the sins of human beings
because of our suffering.

—MEDIEVAL CHRISTIAN RESPONSORY
TO THE BOOK OF JUDITH

Christianity, too, is . . . a form of Judaism.

—RABBI SHAYE J. D. COHEN

Contents

VII: YESTERDAY, TODAY, AND FOREVER

The World after Jesus   299

TOMORROW

Introduction

What Do the Everlasting

Hills Desire?

HISTORY HAS MUCH TO DO with hills. From the Hill of Zion on which King David built Jerusalem to the Athenian Acropolis, from Bunker Hill of the American Revolution to Malvern Hill of the American Civil War, from Iwo Jima's Mount Suribachi to Vietnam's Hamburger Hill, the hills of this world have been prized. Much of humanity's recorded story has taken place on their flanks and summits, and how much blood, of both conquerors and conquered, has been absorbed by their accommodating soils no one can say.

In Rome I love to climb the Janiculum, which the ancients called the "Golden Mountain" because of its yellow sand. One of the splendid natural defenses of Rome, it is a ridge that rises steeply from the west bank of the sludge-green Tiber and gives spectacular views of the great city that is spread beneath it. Like other strategic hills, it has known many battles.

It was just a century and a half ago—in 1849—that armies last clashed on its summit around the ornamental Renaissance arches of the Gate of San Pancrazio and in and out of the charming medieval buildings that lie beyond the gate and on whose walls one can still discern the work of bullets. What the bullets did to the men who fought here has long been concealed by earth. The winners were French troops in service to a reactionary pope, outraged that Italians would dare take up arms against him in their attempt to dissolve the Papal States and unite Italy. The losers were boys as young as fourteen, tragically outnumbered but fighting with the insane bravery of youth, inspired by their charismatic leader, Giuseppe Garibaldi, and his no less charismatic wife, Anita. Today, each Garibaldi has a noble equestrian monument on this summit. Garibaldi with his saintly, mild demeanor surveys the city from his lofty marble platform; superwoman Anita, cast in bronze, raises a firearm in her right hand as she suckles a baby at her left breast, all the while urging her horse forward. They lost the battle but won the war; for beneath the hoofs of Anita's advancing charger one can make out in the distance Michelangelo's bone-white dome of Saint Peter's and the lilliputian statelet of the Vatican, to which the pope's vestigial temporal power has been confined since 1870. The dead child-soldiers have no monument in marble or bronze, just a street sign—Piazzale dei Ragazzi di 1849 (Great Square of the Boys of 1849)—but their spirits haunt the slender umbrella trees that cluster mournfully in the Villa Doria Pamphilj, the vast seventeenth-century parkland that runs beside the scene of their deaths, where dirt paths are named in their memory and the boys of contemporary Rome kick footballs and fly kites.

The Janiculum is more than a Roman hill. It speaks to Everyman, for one patch or another of its sloped ascents can serve to remind almost any traveler of his own ancestral history. At the southern end of the hill the alleys of Trastevere wind mazelike in patterns established more than two millennia ago. Until the Tiber silted up, ships sailed upriver from the Mediterranean, depositing exotic cargoes and even more exotic human specimens in the port of Trastevere. From every corner of the ancient world they came here with their strange costumes and peculiar practices, Greeks and Syrians bearing the crushed pride of the vanquished, Gauls and Britons displaying their lately acquired refinements, Oriental merchants speaking languages but dimly understood, Africans of every kind—Egyptians, Berbers, Nubians—and Jews with uncut beards, the whole babble contained within Trastevere's narrow streets whose haphazard apartment buildings, designed to cram in as many souls as possible, leaned over the filthy streets, nearly blocking out the sky. Trastevere (in those days Trans Tiberim, the Place-across-the-Tiber) was exciting and a little dangerous, as it remains today, a place where basic cravings—for food, sex, revenge—can spurt unexpectedly into view.

It is instructive to select one or two of these groups of migrating visitors and see how they fared in subsequent ages. The Jews, for instance, have now been in Rome longer than anyone else, boasting lines of descent far more ancient than any non-Jewish Italian can claim, back to the beginning of the Roman empire and earlier. The first Roman home of the Jews was Trastevere, as memorial fragments found here still testify. These have been mounted in the portico of the Basilica of Santa Maria, where you can identify the shofars and etrogs* that distinguished the graves of ancient Jews, as well as the doves and ships of those Jews—a minority within a minority—who were members of a primitive Christian community, the first to be established at Rome, probably in the fourth decade of the first century.

In the Middle Ages, the community of Jews crossed the river to the huddled quarter that is still called the Ghetto; and from the slopes of the Janiculum there are fine views of the silvery Synagogue, built at the beginning of this century near the site of its several, much smaller predecessors, the four cor-

✠ The shofar is a ram's horn, still used in Jewish ritual; the etrog is a Near Eastern citrus fruit, depicted as a heart shape with a stem to memorialize Jews known for both learning and good deeds.

ners of its dome giving it a curiously Asian appearance and distinguishing it from all the other domes of Rome. During the Middle Ages, the Jews, protected by popes who valued their services, fared better in Italy than in other European countries, though they were subject to punitive taxes and, as early as the thirteenth century, were made to wear a yellow *O,* precursor of horrors to come. Then the retrograde and, at times, paranoid papacy of the early modern period began to insist on marginalizing the Jews in new ways. Locked by night within the Ghetto by order of Paul IV in the sixteenth century, they were dragooned by subsequent popes into listening to Christian sermons and giving up all trades save moneylending, scrap metal, and rag. Forced to be objects of ridicule during carnivals and papal processions, they were periodically barred from owning land or practicing any profession (though they had once been physicians to the popes) and at last banned from any role in public life. Their fellow Romans, however, more *simpatici* than popes generally are, tended to be fond of their Jewish neighbors and to count them as friends and fellow citizens. It is, therefore, considered a terrible blot on the Roman character that the Nazis were able, during their occupation of the city, to round up the Jews of Rome en masse and deport them to Auschwitz on the fateful *16 ottobre 1943,* a date most Romans have committed to memory and which occurred less than a hundred years after Garibaldi's Battalion of Hope had, by its youthful deaths on the Janiculum, won belated freedom and civil rights for all the citizens of Rome.

Shades of my own ancestors haunt the prospect from the Janiculum. Looking out across the valley in the hour before dawn, I can imagine there appearing on the northeast horizon bands of naked, mustachioed Celts, the locks of their limewashed hair standing up on their heads, an "immense host, covering miles of ground with its straggling masses of horse and foot," as the Roman historian Livy described them. Early in the fourth century B.C. they rode their horses into a much smaller Rome, causing panic and flight among the inhabitants. "The air," wrote Livy, "was loud with the dreadful din of the fierce war-songs and discordant shout of a people whose very life is wild adventure." All who did not flee before the marauders hid themselves within the fortifications of the Capitoline Hill, save for the elderly, who could not climb and were slaughtered on their thresholds. Then, waiting for the dead of night, the barbarians almost made it up the Capitoline itself, climbing the stones that face the hill on one another's shoulders in an eerie silence no one thought them capable of. But at the last moment, just when the first of the invaders had reached the summit, the geese of the Capitoline, sacred to Juno whose temple stood on the heights, honked their frantic warnings, and the Celts were cut down. If I could examine the genetic cells of these fierce warriors, I could establish kinship.

7

I can claim even closer kinship with the Irish noblemen Hugh O'Neill, earl of Tyrone, and Rory O'Donnell, prince of Tyrconnel, who lie buried beneath the flagstones of San Pietro in Montorio on the east side of the Janiculum. They fought against impossible odds and almost succeeded in expelling the English occupiers from "Elizabethan" Ireland. Was the prototype of "Tyrconnel's dread war cry, *'O'Donnell Abu!,'* " which rang out in Ireland against the soldiers of Elizabeth I, heard first in the Western world at the gates of Rome on that faraway morning in 390 B.C.?

Beneath the square cobblestones of the Janiculum, who knows whose history remains to be recovered?

THE HISTORY OF THE WORLD, like the history of its hills, is written in blood, the blood of barbaric warriors and bold partisans, of old women and beardless boys, of the guilty and the innocent. And what is the "desire of the everlasting hills"? What could be the meaning of this phrase, taken from the blessing of Jacob on his son Joseph, the last of the patriarchs? Is not the desire of the everlasting hills that they be saved from their everlastingness, that something new happen, that the everlasting cycle of human cruelty, of man's inhumanity to man, be brought to an end?

Two thousand years ago a man was born into a family of carpenters in occupied Palestine. He was a small-town Jew, born in a bad time for Jews. Their land was no longer their own, and they had been made to bow before a succession of conquerors who had diluted their proud culture and, as many would have said, infected it. His name, as everyone knows, was Jesus of Nazareth—or, as the Jews of his own day called him, Yeshua. As everyone knows, he preached a message of mercy, love, and peace and was crucified for his trouble. This unlikely character has long been accounted the central figure of Western civilization. Even now, as we cross to the beginning of the third millennium since his birth, we count our days by his appearance on earth; and, though our supposedly post-Christian society often ignores and even ridicules him, there are no serious suggestions for replacing him as the Icon of the West.

But this book is part of a series on cultural impact. And the great question about Jesus must always be: Did he make a difference? Is our world—in the century that began with the Turkish genocide against the Armenians, reached its nadir with the "scientific" holocaust of six million Jews (and five million others), not to speak of the slaughter by their own governments of Russians and Chinese in the scores of millions, and now comes to its end with genocides in central Africa and "ethnic cleansings" in the Balkans that are still, horribly enough, "in progress"—is our world any better than the one inhabited by the Celts and Romans of twenty-four centuries ago? Did the values preached by Jesus influence the Anglican Queen Elizabeth or her opponent the Catholic Earl O'Neill? Did she ever shudder at the carnage of her battlefields? Did he, even once, as he surveyed the hacked limbs, the gouged eyes, the grisly dying, wonder if there was another way? Do Christian values have any influence on the actions of Christians who on both sides of the English/Irish divide have continued to "fight the old fight again"? Did the life and death of Jesus make any difference to the denizens of first-century Trans Tiberim? Does he make any difference to the residents of today's Trastevere?

9

These are hard questions; some will no doubt label them unfair. But they must be posed at the outset. For if this Jesus, this figure professedly central to our whole culture, has had no effect, he has no place in a history of cultural effects. In the pages that follow, we will look at the phenomenon of Jesus, as experienced by those who knew him best and by the first generations of his followers, who in their surviving traditions, both oral and written, bring us as close as we can get to this often elusive historical figure. When our investigation is completed, we will pose the hard questions again.

But in order to understand Jesus we must begin before his time and strive to appreciate how the world he was born into came to be.

I

Greeks, Jews, and Romans

The People Jesus Knew

THE AXIAL AGE was over. It had lasted three hundred years—from the late seventh century B.C. to the late fourth—a very long time. In Confucian China, it had seen the burgeoning of reasonableness and courtly moderation, as well as the mystical depths uncovered by the Tao of Lao-Tsu. In India, the great age had produced the ineffable example of Gautama Buddha, reforming the chaos of more ancient systems and revealing the steps to personal peace. In Iran, the priest Zarathustra had spoken to the Persians, who carried the fire ceremony and the Zoroastrian vision of a cosmic battle between good and evil beyond the borders of Mesopotamia, situated between the legendary Tigris and Euphrates in the fertile delta where civilization had first shown itself. Just west of Mesopotamia, in the tiny, unstable kingdoms of Israel and Judah, the Hebrew prophets rose, giving to the bizarre monotheism of their singular people an ethical foundation so profound that the Jews could never entirely forsake it. In the isles and peninsulas of Greece, the Axial Age saw the flowering of what would come to be called "philosophy"—love of wisdom for its own sake—and of a noble "politics" (another Greek term) that took the name "democracy." This same time and place saw the invention of drama and its division into "tragedy" and "comedy" in a theater that has never been equaled, as well as the first attempts to write what the Greeks called "history."

These distinct developments within the limits of these ancient cultures certainly showed similarities to one another. In the words of Arnaldo Momigliano, the most learned and nimble interpreter of antiquity in our age: "All these civilizations display literacy, a complex political organization combining central government and local authorities, elaborate town-planning, advanced metal technology and the practice of international diplomacy. In all these civilizations there is a profound tension between political powers and intellectual movements. Everywhere one notices attempts to introduce greater purity, greater justice, greater perfection and a more universal explanation of things. New models of reality, either mystically or prophetically or rationally apprehended, are propounded as a criticism of, and alternative to, the prevailing models."

But these cultural developments proceeded in parallel. They never intersected, never influenced one another save in the most marginal ways, so that the world we find as the curtain rises on the third century B.C. is still a world of separate societies, each enclosed by its own characteristic language and values, each with its own Golden Age to look back on, populated by its own heroes. In the mind of a third-century Athenian, the philosophers Socrates and Plato, the dramatists Sophocles and Euripides, the political leader Pericles, the sculptor Phidias, and the historian Herodotus lived still, and he, living in a lesser age, bore these standards of excellence within him for reference and judgment. He knew nothing of Abraham and Moses, David and Isaiah, Jeremiah and Ezekiel, the figures who lived in the mind of every inhabitant of third-century Jerusalem, just a few nautical miles east across the Mediterranean. But as early as the late fourth century, this cultural exclusiveness was beginning to dissolve; and by the time of Jesus the better part of the ancient world—from Asia Minor to the Atlantic, from North Africa to the edges of the frosty forests that concealed the northern barbarians—had been soldered together by forces so strong that, with only a few notable breaks, the cultural unity has held ever since.

ALEXANDER THE GREAT, the man who would make all the difference, was born in July of 356 B.C., son of Philip II, king of the Greek outpost of Macedon, and a mother who was determined that her child would grow up to be greater than his father. During Alexander's childhood, Philip's ambition made Macedon feared; and he gradually extended its power south into the Greek peninsulas and east through the Balkans, creating a sort of "greater Greece," a unity of politics, language, and culture, where Philip was overlord, the Greek gods were given uniform worship, and Greek culture heroes from Socrates to Herodotus were held in high esteem.

His father's aggressions frightened the child Alexander, but for one reason only: "There will be nothing left for me to conquer," pouted the prince, when news of his progenitor's sensational victories was brought to him. While still a teenager, Alexander successfully acted as regent in his father's absence and at eighteen was given command of the left wing of the Macedonian cavalry at the battle of Chaeronea, which, thanks largely to Alexander's brilliant performance, smashed the combined might of the Greek city-states of Athens, principal city of mainland Greece, and Thebes, chief city of Boeotia and Oedipus's legendary capital. If Chaeronea was decisive for world history, it was also decisive for Alexander's destiny: ever after he was seen as unstoppable. This beautiful boy of the "melting eye," who modestly inclined his head to one side, had overcome the strength of the Athenian federation, even to the extent of crushing the mystical might of the Sacred Band of Thebes, a supposedly invincible posse of superheroes.

It helps to have a mother who believes in you, one who whispers constantly in your perfectly formed little ear that you are the beloved of the gods and your father is just a temporary obstacle. Scarcely a year after the glorious victory at Chaeronea, Philip, full of himself, humiliated Alexander's mother, the meddlesome Olympias, by taking another, much younger wife. It is not surprising that the names of Olympias and Alexander were ever after linked to the conspiracy that all assumed lay behind the savage assassination of the king during the first year of his new marriage.

Alexander found himself at twenty king of Macedon, *hegemon* (or "leader") of the Corinthian League of Greek city-states that his father had formed in the aftermath of Chaeronea, and commander in chief of an army of forty thousand troops and 160 warships that Philip had assembled to challenge the hegemony of the fabulous and detested Persian empire, which lay to the east. Before setting out for Persia, Alexander took the time to put down an annoying little rebellion among the Thebans, unhappy with their reduced status. The young king acted swiftly and with appalling decisiveness: he massacred the Thebans, destroyed their city, and enslaved the survivors. This unrestrained cruelty, carried out with cool calculation and obviously intended as a universal lesson, resounded through the Greek world, and no other city-state dared give trouble during the long absence of the king throughout his coming years of war.

It took Alexander several years to break the power of Persia. In November of 333 at the battle of Issus in the Syrian mountains, Darius III, king of the Persians, himself led his army and was forced to flee the field. In responding dismissively to Darius's subsequent suit for peace, Alexander signed himself "Lord of Asia," giving the first hint that what he had in mind was a prize greater than even greater Persia, in its day the most extensive empire the world had known. During the grueling course of Alexander's seven-month siege of Tyre, the Phoenician port city on the Levantine coast that had supplied the backbone of Darius's fleet, Darius made the desperate offer of half his kingdom. "Heaven cannot support two suns, nor earth two masters," replied the Lord of Asia, who went on to destroy the entire Persian fleet and to make of Tyre the same sort of terrifying example he had made of Thebes. What the Greeks had learned the Asians now knew: do not cross Alexander.

17

He traveled south, captured Gaza, and invaded Egypt, where the charred catastrophes of Thebes and Tyre were not forgotten and where there was now not even a whisper of opposition. There in that archaic land, mysterious even to the ancients, the bulbous crown of Egypt was placed on his golden locks, and he was declared Pharaoh and "Son of God." To Egyptians the god in question was Amon-Ra, the sun; to Alexander's Greek battalions, it was Zeus, the god of gods. And in Egypt, Alexander built at the mouth of the Nile what would become the greatest city of the ancient world for the next two hundred years—Alexandria, the first of dozens by that name throughout the growing empire of the Son of God.

But Alexander had more work before him. Darius had escaped his clutches and was gathering a new army in the heart of Persia. Alexander pursued him, winning the decisive battle of Gaugamela on the Tigris, after which Darius contrived his penultimate escape. Alexander let him go and set his face toward capturing Babylon, Susa, and Persepolis, Darius's capital, where he burned the royal palace to the ground. In June of 330, the Macedonian changed course and set out in full pursuit of the Persian king, who escaped him one last time only because he was stabbed to death by his disaffected deputies. The unfortunate Darius's dying request was for Alexander to avenge him. Kings, even if they are enemies, always have something in common; and Alexander happily hunted down the regicides. After all, the King of Kings, as he began to style himself, cannot allow the murder of his revered predecessor to go unpunished. Alexander, who could now portray himself as Darius's avenger and legitimate successor, also began to assume the elaborate dress, paint, and bodily ornamentation of the Persian royal court—Oriental affectations that did not sit well with his homespun Macedonian guard, the same Macedonians who had been so rigorously trained by his late father. What decorations he did not keep for himself he sent home, along with massive quantities of precious plate and purple, to Mother.

The King of Kings still had plenty of opposition on his hands, obdurate resistance especially in Bactria and Sogdiana, satrapies to the north and east (that correspond roughly to today's Afghanistan and Uzbekistan). His pacification of these difficult areas was aided mightily by his taking in late 328 a Sogdian princess for wife. Her name was Roxane. She was young, she was beautiful, and she seems to have been the unwitting victim of an ancient public relations scheme to give the unpopular new king a better image with truculent ethnics in the far northeast of his domains. The word went out that Alexander and Roxane were madly in love. Of course, the royal marriage, though it produced an heir, didn't mean that the King of Kings had to give up his favorite catamite, who continued to keep his accustomed place in the royal bed. This marriage to a foreign prisoner of war was no more popular with the Macedonians than was Alexander's new wardrobe.

The King of Kings began to establish settlements in the outlying territories, garrisons commanded by his faithful Macedonians. They were labeled new Greek "cities," and the motive ascribed to Alexander in creating them was that he wished to spread the benefits of Greek culture. In reality, these fortifications kept the population quiescent and awarded to fed-up Macedonian warriors the customary spoils of victory—a free hand in the oppression of the local populations and the rape of their economies.

In every age, professional soldiers, especially those engaged for years in combat, have been heavy drinkers, and Alexander and his men were no exception. But Alexander, it was noticed, had begun to drink more heavily than most and to grow unreasonable and violent on such occasions. One night, in his cups, Alexander killed Black Clitus, a trusty old lieutenant of Philip's who had once saved Alexander's life, for deriding the

OVERLEAF: THE EMPIRE OF ALEXANDER THE GREAT

At the time of his death in 323 B.C., the territories under Alexander's sway stretched from the Greek mainland in the west to the east banks of the rivers Indus and Hyphasis in central Asia and as far south as southern Egypt. (The Persian Empire, which Alexander conquered, had also been extensive: beginning in the area of Persepolis, it had stretched far north into the Caucasus on both sides of the Caspian Sea; but it never reached as far as Europe, Africa, or Asia east of the Indus.) The broken line along the Persian Gulf shows the route of the Greek fleet as it returned home from Alexander's last campaign.

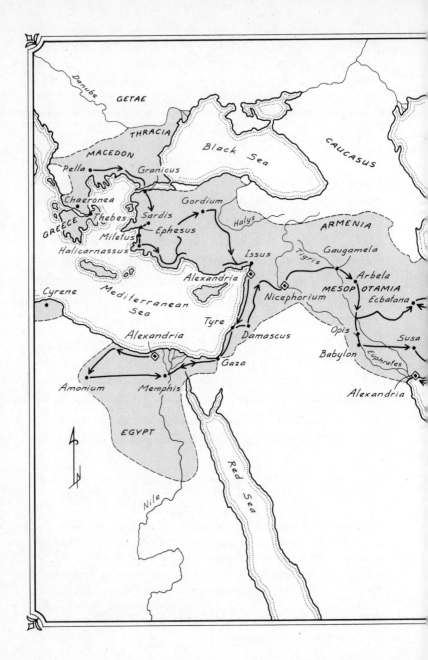

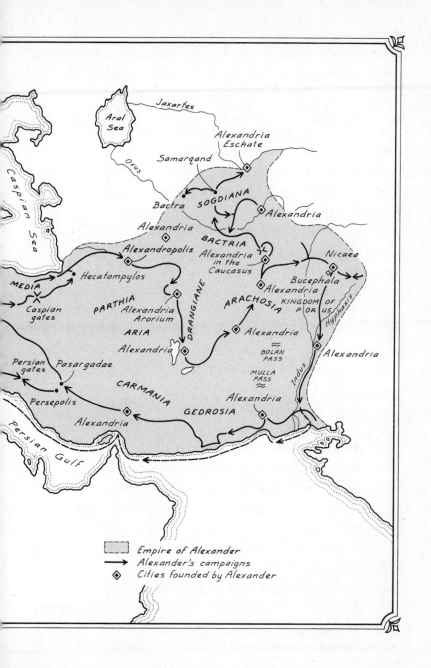

Jaxartes

Aral
Sea

Oxus

Alexandria
Eschate

Samarqand

Bactra   SOGDIANA

Alexandria

Caspian
Sea

Alexandria

Alexandropolis

BACTRIA

Alexandria
in the
Caucasus

Nicaea

Hecatompylos

MEDIA

Caspian
gates

PARTHIA

Alexandria
Arorium

ARIA

Alexandria

Bucephala

Alexandria

KINGDOM OF
P OR US

Hyphasis

DRANGIANE

ARACHOSIA

Alexandria

BOLAN
PASS

Indus

Alexandria

Persian
gates

Pasargadae

CARMANIA

MULLA
PASS

Persepolis

Alexandria

GEDROSIA

Alexandria

Alexandria

Persian
Gulf

Empire of Alexander
Alexander's campaigns
Cities founded by Alexander

increasing "Orientalism" of the Alexandrine court. Alexander had even begun to insist that his subjects approach him by falling forward on the ground in complete prostrations, as Darius's had done, for in the East the king was taken for a god. When the royal pages were discovered plotting Alexander's murder, they were of course summarily executed, but not before giving as the justification for their attempt the king's exceedingly un-Greek behavior. Alexander, increasingly isolated, trusted ever fewer counselors and could no longer treat anyone, even the most belaureled veteran of his father's campaigns, as an intimate. The exception was young Hephestion, his favorite boon companion, who never lost the king's confidence.

22   Alexander, now in command of forces that numbered in the hundred thousands (goodly numbers in a time when the population of the globe was less than two hundred million), continued to look east. Though once Persia was conquered he sent home the troops of the Corinthian League, whom he had never trusted, he did not mean to stop even at the farthest frontiers of the old empire. Ahead lay India and then, so it was thought, the Great Sea—the very end of the earth. What was to prevent him from ruling the world?

The Greek forces entered the mountains of the Hindu Kush in 327 and, with increasing savagery, carved a path for themselves as far east as the River Hyphasis (Beas in modern Pakistan), at which point the unthinkable happened: the army refused to go farther. Alexander had to concede; but he did choose the route home—not the way they'd come but a journey down the Indus, then a forced march west into Persia. It was an insane project, not only because much of the terrain was unknown, but because Alexander's favored route contained highly fortified cities guarded by Indian warriors as adept at warfare as any Macedonian and led by Brahmins, whose fierce ancestors had come from the same stock of marauding Indo-European horsemen as the Greek nobles. Even for Alexander's hardened troops the bloodshed was unparalleled; and then, once they reached the delta of the Indus, Alexander insisted that they make their way across the Gedrosian desert, which was known to have defeated every army that had ever attempted to traverse it. Where all others had failed, even the legendary Semiramis and Cyrus the Great, founder of the Persian empire, Alexander would succeed. If he could not have the whole world, he would at least leave an indelible reputation as the only invincible man.

The Greek army made it through the desert—about a quarter of them, that is. The others, as many as ninety thousand men, were left to die on the desert floor, their bodies sucked dry by a pitiless sun. Along the Persian coast, the soldiers who remained on their feet at last caught sight of the fleet, which managed to sail (the first ships ever to do so) along the coast and up the Gulf all the way from the Indus to the Euphrates. Thence did the creaking vessels bear home not an army of conquering heroes but a motley cargo of bitter and broken men.

This was early in the year 324, and Alexander had but one more year to live. His last days were troubled, not only by the intrigues and corruption of the deputies he'd left behind, but by the refusal of some Greeks to worship him as a living god, an honor he had come to expect in the East. This ruler of the world, who could have anything he wanted by snapping his fingers, seems to have been able to squeeze less and less joy out of life. He took a second wife. His court was crowded with three thousand actors and artists and as many as thirty thousand dancing boys. He was surrounded by soothsayers and priests, sacrificing, purifying, telling the future. Their oracles did not lift the king's spirits. Hephestion's death in late 324 took much of the remaining life out of him. He had the attending physician crucified; then, his grief still unassuaged, he fell upon the pitiable Cosseans, putting their entire nation to the sword—which remedy seems to have improved his humor, for we find him in the spring of 323 in Babylon, restless as ever, gathering a gargantuan force in preparation for invading the Arabian Peninsula. But in Babylon he fell ill, and in early June he died, weeks short of his thirty-third birthday.

The accomplishments of Alexander, fueled by his incomparable daring, inspired ancient writers. Where modern historians count the casualties and detect cruelty and inhumanity, the ancients saw only glory. Public action—that is, by war and conquest—was the most dangerous and, in consequence, the most noble of all human endeavors. Alexander was, therefore, "the Great," the greatest man who had ever lived. If Plato was the measure of all subsequent philosophy and Phidias of all attempts to carve a man in marble, Alexander was the measure of man himself. We may think such a value system outmoded or remote, but it was not so long ago that Napolean enchanted Europe in his quest to be the modern Alexander, nor were such values unknown to the generals and kommandants of the twentieth century, and God knows they continue to infect the brains of all those who take up weapons of destruction in what they believe to be a noble cause. Indeed, down the whole course of history, the invincible warrior with raised sword has been the archetypal hero of the human race.

Wherever one may stand on these matters, in one thing Alexander's accomplishment is unassailable. The man loved Greek, both as a language and as a literature. His love of reading was undoubtedly an inspiration to his successors, who vied with one another not only politically and militarily but culturally, each dynasty meaning to outdo the others in its commitment to learning and literature. In the Great King's eponymous city of Egyptian Alexandria, for instance, there rose ancient civilization's most massive library, containing (or so it was thought) "all the books in the world," a library whose destruction by fire in 47 B.C. is lamented to this day. And though it would be Eurocentrically embarrassing and a little absurd to assert, as was still asserted well into this century, that Alexander succeeded in raising the whole world to the highest standards of civilization (Greek civilization, that is), he did unite the known world by giving it a universal language. Since the racist Greeks believed all languages but theirs defective, they refused to learn the tongues of their conquered neighbors, thus forcing everyone else to learn at least a little Greek. This language as it evolved in popular parlance lacked many of the elegant refinements of Plato, but it was a Greek everyone could learn—a *koine* (or common) tongue, as it was called— and it was serviceable and strong.

Languages bring values with them, and one cannot learn a language without making one's own the things the civilization that developed the language considers important. The warrior as the greatest of all human figures—this was not something confined to the Greeks but enshrined in every ancient language (which is why it still lies hidden in the languages of our day). But the Greeks had their own powerful words and phrases which, once learned, gave the speaker a specifically Greek outlook. One could not learn Greek without reading Homer, and one could not read Homer without encountering the Greek heroes and the Greek gods. Alexander, who slept with his dagger and a copy of the *Iliad* under his pillow, believed himself descended from Achilles, the greatest of all Greek warriors, as well as from Hercules, the god of invincible strength, and from Asiatic Dionysos, the dark, impetuous, havoc-provoking god of wine. In learning to read Homer and the Greek playwrights, one ingested a whole mythology, indeed a whole psychology. In reading Plato and the Stoics, one absorbed a whole philosophy of life. By making use of the rhetorical models of Demosthenes,* the student of Greek learned how to write a letter and to shape a speech—how to argue a point and present his arguments to best advantage.

We needn't imagine that every Iranian garrison commander had studied Demosthenes or that every Levantine merchant could quote Homer to understand that whatever Greek they knew affected their outlook. Similarly, common English words and phrases adopted nowadays throughout the world give even simple people, living in cultures bound by non-Western myths, access to such values as progress, democracy, technology, and capitalism (even if one should see these values through the eyes of inflexible traditionalists: as contempt for traditions of authority and discipline and love of chaos and of self at the expense of the common good).

And just as anyone in our world may turn on a television and see well-stocked refrigerators and family cars as desirable components of the American Way of Life, anyone in the ancient world that Alexander had united could raise his eyes to the horizon and see there the reasonable Greek temple, decorated with the

---

✄ Demosthenes was for the Greeks what Cicero would be for the Romans, the consummate rhetorician. The elder contemporary of Alexander, he had vainly warned the Athenians of the growing power of Philip's Macedon. He considered Philip's son a contemptible parvenu and always referred to him as "the boy." His supple orations, modulated expressions of opinion on political affairs no longer of consequence to us, are virtually unreadable today.

stories of gods and heroes, place of prayers and offerings to the forces of fate. Nearby was the *gymnasion* (from which we derive our word *gymnasium* and the Germans their word for high school), where young male athletes trained in the nude and, after their vigorous workouts, sat at the feet of a philosopher, as Alexander had once sat at the feet of Aristotle, Plato's most famous pupil, whom his father had employed as royal tutor.* (This was not a simple act of paternal affection on Philip's part. The Greeks thought of the Macedonians as shabby cousins at best, and it was essential for the Macedonian royal family to assert convincingly its Greek *bona fides.*) Within the compass of Alexander's far-flung empire, then, Greek was the lingua franca, disseminated first by soldiers and administrators, then by the businessmen, traders, priests, oracles, trainers, and tutors who followed in their wake; and everywhere one was confronted with Greek assumptions, Greek images, the Greek Way of Life.

I T W A S N O T a way of life that everyone welcomed. Like orthodox Muslims of our own time, many of the Jews of the eastern Mediterranean viewed the innovating intromission of foreign values into their society as an infection that might prove fatal. They resented mightily what they took to be these dangerous, exotic fashions that their less thoughtful countrymen were adopting with such gusto. They remembered their own unique history—their forebear Abraham whom their God had called by name to become the father of a great nation, a nation with a salvific role for all humanity; their incomparable leader

⊠ In "Under Ben Bulben," W. B. Yeats, who beat his own son, imagines that "Aristotle played the taws / Upon the bottom of a king of kings," but I doubt that even Aristotle was permitted much whacking of Alexander's precious little bottom.

Moses, who had led them out of cruel slavery in pagan Egypt and given them the Torah, their Law and Way of Life; David, their rocklike poet-king, who had given them the thrilling words of his psalms and, by conquering all their neighbors, had made them safe in the Holy Land that God had said was theirs.

It had been a long time, though, since the Jews had been safe. The happy Davidic kingdom had been torn in two in the generations after David, so long ago that it now seemed a myth. The larger portion to the north—Israel—had then been chewed up by Sargon II of Assyria, who had deported its inhabitants, the Ten Lost Tribes, into slavery and replaced them with his own settlers; the southern portion—Judah—had been wrecked by Nebuchadnezzar of Babylon, who had burned to the ground the wonderful Temple that David's son Solomon had built and where their God had resided invisible above the Tablets of his Law. Like Sargon before him, Nebuchadnezzar had deported much of the population, who languished in Babylon for two generations, till the great Persian king Cyrus, illustrious predecessor of the unfortunate Darius, overcame the Babylonians in the late sixth century and allowed the Jews to return to their devastated homeland. Not that their own prophets hadn't warned them that they faced just such disasters if they didn't amend their evil ways—that is, if they didn't live in the light of God's demanding justice, if they didn't stop worshiping other gods and return to the worship of the God of the Unspeakable Name, the only god who was real.

So now, now that they finally had come to understand the message of the prophets, were they to abandon the living God and run after the dead gods of bronze and wood that these foreigners were setting up? Their God would surely take revenge, a revenge more horrible even than the earlier deportations and destructions. If the Jews forsook the Way of God and once again adorned themselves in the cultural trinkets of the gentiles, the catastrophes of the past would pale before the coming one, the complete catastrophe. And surely such a catastrophe was at hand. As these foreign novelties pressed down upon them and all but a remnant abandoned the ancient ways, how could any sane observer doubt that he was witnessing the steps leading to Apocalypse, the dreadful Day of the Lord?

What the Jews were thinking was of small consequence beyond the borders of their fragment of a kingdom. It is a mark of how unimportant they had become that Plutarch, Alexander's biographer, doesn't even bother to relate that the Macedonian conquered the Jews. He must have, because we know that he marched his army from Tyre to Gaza, and he could not have done so without encountering the Jews, who were certainly in no position to stop him. Perhaps they were relieved to be rid of the Persians, their previous overlords. More likely by this point, one conqueror seemed neither better nor worse than another. In a world that worshiped military might and ever larger spheres of influence, the Jews could not expect to live in freedom, save by a miracle. And a miracle, whether of exaltation or destruction, is just what a people whose day is past, who have been unceremoniously pushed into a confined space at the margins of history, are wont to hope for.

Even if, his sights on bigger game, Alexander immediately forgot the Jews, he did not rule them long. Soon after his untimely death, his son by Roxane was put to the sword, as were Roxane herself, Alexander's half-witted brother, Philip, and at last that skillful survivor, the dowager empress Olympias. No blood relative of Alexander's was left alive. The army, which would have none of them on the throne of Macedon, was taking no chances. Many of Alexander's closest companions-in-arms, those who had survived so many campaigns, were already dead or dying; the others were assassinated. The greatest empire the world had ever seen was broken up among conspiring officers of the second rank: Antigonus II, son of Philip's legendary general Antigonus the One-Eyed, mounted the throne to control both Macedon and Greece; Ptolemy took Egypt, and the Ptolemaic line would last there in its glorious capital of Alexandria, the bones of Alexander interred in the great mausoleum beside the library, till the last of the line, Cleopatra, would end her own life with an asp at her breast; Seleucus took up rule at Antioch in Syria and from there the Seleucids ruled the arc of Asia from the Aegean to the Indus. The Levant, which lay between Syria and Egypt, was at first in vassalage to Egypt. But in 200 B.C., the Seleucid monarch Antiochus III won the Levant from the Ptolemies in battle, after which the Seleucids from their capital of Antioch ruled the entire eastern Mediterranean, including the negligible patch called Judah.

However highly the world may have regarded Alexander and mourned his passing, those perennial outsiders the Jews had a more jaundiced view, which is summed up nicely in the opening paragraph of the First Book of Maccabees:

> Alexander of Macedon son of Philip . . . defeated Darius king of the Persians and Medes, whom he succeeded as ruler. . . . He undertook many campaigns, gained possession of many fortresses, and put the local kings to death. So he advanced to the ends of the earth, plundering nation after nation; the earth grew silent before him and his ambitious heart swelled with pride. He assembled very powerful

forces and subdued provinces, nations, and princes, and they became his tributaries. . . . Alexander had reigned twelve years when he died. Each of his officers established himself in his own region. All assumed crowns after his death, they and their heirs after them for many years, bringing increasing evils on the world.

What is especially impressive about this terse, dry-eyed epitome is its sympathy for the world of fellow sufferers, far beyond the borders of Judah and known to the writer of this chronicle only by report. The growing silence of the earth as nation after nation is plundered and laid low by Alexander, the increasing evils brought on the world by generation after generation of such predatory activity: these are extraordinary images to come upon in ancient records, which seldom waste space on the sufferings of losers. But, then, it is seldom people at the invigorating center of events—the ones who normally write the first drafts of history—who see clearly what has happened, especially the "increasing evils" wrought by those who blindly pursue their own wealth and power. Rather, it is the dispossessed, the ones who have been relegated to the margins, whose eyes are open and who know what wounds they bear.

A decade or so before the end of the sixth century B.C., the Jews had completed the rebuilding of their Temple, ever after called the Second Temple. But the Holy of Holies was empty. According to the Talmud, several important things were missing, most notably the Ark of the Covenant—which had contained the Ten Commandments, the very heart of the Law of Moses—and the Spirit of God, who had fled with the destruction of the Ark. Without God's living presence, prophecy, which depended on the Spirit, must necessarily dwindle; and by the time the First Book of Maccabees was written (at the end of the second century B.C.), its author had reason to lament that there were no longer any prophets about that one could count on to settle difficult matters definitively and give the sort of advice one might act on with confidence.

The First Book of Maccabees lives in a kind of canonical limbo: considered an inspired book of the Bible by most Christians but, since we no longer have the Hebrew original, only a Greek translation, never accepted by the rabbis into the canon of the Hebrew Bible and relegated to an appendix of "apocrypha" by Martin Luther and subsequent Protestants. It certainly reads nothing like the Torah, the normative Five Books of Moses, to which Judaism gives its deepest reverence. Nor is there anything of prophetic ecstasy and terror in it. It isn't even much like the Bible's primitive "historical" books, which chronicle in saga-like form the exploits of such outsized figures as David and Solomon. It is, even if the original was written in Hebrew, a species of Greek history. For, though it takes a sober view of Alexander and all his ilk, it reads very like Plutarch's and all the other histories that were churned out regularly by authors throughout the Greek world. Just as Plutarch depended largely on the correspondence contained in Alexander's archive and on diaries of eyewitnesses, the author of First Maccabees has reviewed the correspondence in the royal archive of the Seleucids and eyewitness accounts kept in the Temple at Jerusalem. Like Plutarch, he is interested in phenomena, like dreams and visions, to which a modern historian would be unlikely to devote so much attention; and, like historians in every age, he is looking for a meaning beneath the chaotic surface of events. But he understands that he is bound by rules of evidence, research, and fact checking: he is a scholar, using the Greek methods of scholarship that were current in his day.

But if he borrows Greek form, the content of his story is decidedly Jewish. Its hero is Judas Maccabeus, known to the world not only for his appearance here but because Dante in the *Divine Comedy* discovers him in Paradise, because he is the title character of Handel's stirring oratorio, and because the story of Hanukkah, the Jewish Festival of Lights celebrated each December, is largely a celebration of Judas himself.

The Seleucids were engaged, like all successful successors to Alexander, in actively Hellenizing their conquests. After all, uniformity of culture and standardization of its procedures made governing so much simpler. When toward the end of the third century B.C. the Seleucid king Antiochus Epiphanes proposed a *gymnasion* for Jerusalem, all too many Jews were eager to imitate their betters by taking out gym memberships and running around naked (a practice alien to the modest Judeans, among whom public nudity, so prevalent in the ancient world—at least among males—was quite unknown). Because the perfect male body was for the Greeks a kind of physical expression of spirit—the harder the pecs and the tighter the buns the more spiritual you were—any deformity or deviation from the norms of perfection (ideally expressed in the work of sculptors like Phidias and Praxiteles) was viewed with repugnance. If a missing ear or toe rendered one an object of derision, imagine what circumcision did. So the Jews who were especially eager to be Greek began to "disguise their circumcision," as First Maccabees puts it discreetly—that is, they underwent epispasm, a painful (and often unsuccessful) exercise in ancient plastic surgery.

But circumcision was not for the Jews an arbitrary or optional practice: it was the sign of the Covenant between them and their God, the seal that told that God had chosen them from among the nations. It was the very thing that separated them from all the others—the confirmation of their Jewish identity. Without it, they were no longer a people.

By giving his encouragement to the Hellenizing party among the Jews, Antiochus was merely laying the groundwork for more appalling schemes. Empires need cash, and Antiochus's was no exception. What he really needed to get his hands on was the Temple treasury. He occupied Jerusalem and built there a typical Greek Acra (or citadel of military administration), which towered over the Temple, a message for all to see and understand. As First Maccabees tells it, the Greeks "installed there a brood of sinners [the occupying Greeks], of renegades [the Hellenized Jews], who fortified themselves inside it, storing arms and provisions, and depositing there the loot they had collected from Jerusalem. They were," as First Maccabees puts it mildly, "to prove a great trouble."

The initial Hellenizing, promoted as a generous cultural outpouring on the part of Antiochus and anxiously received as such by many of Jerusalem's citizens ("He built us the *gymnasion* and now the lovely Acra"), was but the first step. Having softened up the citizens and sown cultural confusion, Antiochus could now proceed as he liked. Wouldn't it make sense, in the interests of unity, for all the king's subjects to become "a single people," giving up their peculiar ethnic customs, which only militate against harmony? Shouldn't—oh, to take one example—the Temple of Jerusalem be open to all, as are all Greek temples in all the cities of the empire, open for all to worship whichever god they wish? Why should the city's central house of worship be closed to all men of goodwill and open only to this odd little sect within a sect? Why, isn't it plain that most of their compatriots long for an open Temple that allows complete freedom of worship, as do all proper temples through which the breeze of reason blows?

Within Hellenistic religious culture, there was always room for one more god. Athens was Athena's city, but of course all the gods were welcome there—no point in narrowing one's options; better to hedge one's bets. In any case, no one but the simple took the gods en masse too seriously, and those who studied philosophy had come to understand that the pantheon of gods was but a metaphor for higher things. The real purpose of religion—at the popular level—was to unify the populace. Let everyone worship his favorite god in some niche or other, but let's all sacrifice at the same altar, climb the same steps, and wander through the same colonnades. Let the Jews have their god, by all means—who's stopping them?—and let us all have ours. And no provincial exclusiveness, please.

From one perspective, it sounds so reasonable, not unlike the "patriotic associations" that China insists all churches be controlled by. To a party apparatchik, what could be wrong with patriotism, with insisting that Chinese churches be free of foreign interference? But if you believe that the Church is universal and cannot be confined within one country, such patriotism will "prove a great trouble." Similarly—but even more fundamentally—for the core of Jewish believers, there was but one God, who could not be depicted in stone or set beside the dead gods of the pagans because he was the living God, the Creator-beyond-all-creation. To the Greek mind, the unwillingness to compromise in religious matters—which were not all *that* important, anyway—was impious, unpatriotic, maybe even seditious. For the Jews, religion was the Way of Life; it had nothing in common with the empty rituals of the Greeks.

Then, "on the fifteenth day of Chislev in the year 145"— in the reckoning of the Seleucid dynasty (that is, in late December of 167 B.C.)—"the king set the Abomination of Desolation on the altar of holocausts," according to the horrified chronicler of First Maccabees. This thing was a statue of Olympian Zeus, king of the Greek gods (also known in Asia Minor as Baal, for the Greeks were happy to have their gods take local names), now given pride of place in the Temple of the living God and defiling both the Temple and the Jewish people with unimaginable sacrilege. Whoever objected, whoever persisted in the old, exclusive ways, whoever had her children circumcised, whoever refused to perform his civic duty and make sacrifices in the customary manner to the pantheon of gods was put to the sword—mothers with their circumcised infants "hung round their necks." The new order was publicized as the triumph of reason over backwardness and superstition. And the current Lord of Asia at last controlled the Temple treasury, as he did all other treasuries in his domains, as was his right.

But there are humiliations a proud people—even one oppressed for generations—cannot abide. Judas Maccabeus ("Hammer-like") rose and, calling to himself all those who loved the Law, made war upon the gentiles. This man, one of five brothers inspired by their dying father, energized his outraged troops and won battle after battle. Judas understood that, even if they are outnumbered, those who fight for a cause can overcome those who, like many of the Greek troops, are mercenaries fighting only for a pay packet or hapless ordinary men drafted against their will. "It is easy," cried Judas to his partisans, "for a great number to be defeated by a few. . . . They are coming against us in full-blown insolence and lawlessness to destroy us, our wives, and our children, and to plunder us; but we are fighting for our lives and our laws, and he will crush them before our eyes; do not be afraid of them." By this point in Jewish history, the reverence accorded the Name of God was so great that all references were indirect. None of Judas's troops required any instruction in who "he" was.

Antiochus's rage at this rebellion and his subsequent mustering of an overwhelming force made clear to the partisans that their defeat would spell the end not only of their lives and those of their families but of Judaism itself. They had no choice but victory. Judas's army stealthily left its position at Mizpah, eight miles north of Jerusalem, while the Greek general, who bore the unfortunate name of Gorgias, intending a surprise attack, advanced by night upon the now-empty Jewish camp with a handpicked force of six thousand men. But the Jewish army, some three thousand in all and lacking "the armor and swords they would have wished," moved simultaneously toward the royal base camp at Emmaus, closer to Jerusalem. When they beheld it, the Jews were astonished by the gentile encampment, fortified and surrounded by cavalry—"clearly people who understood warfare." But the guerrillas had not forgotten the stirring words of their general, the Hammer of God.

Morning was just breaking and the Greek soldiers were still rubbing their eyes when the Jews fell on them, precipitating confusion, easy slaughter, and flight. The Jews set fire to the camp and pursued the Greeks across the plain, hacking all the way and severely compromising the opposing army, which lost as many men as Judas had been able to muster. Gorgias and his

37

handpicked force, returning just in time to see the fires rising from their ruined camp, the backs of their companions in flight, the bodies of Greeks scattered across the plain, and Judas's troops drawn up against them, fled to Philistine territory, beyond the reach of the Jews.

In the following year, Judas, now with ten thousand at his side and invoking the great name of David, Jerusalem's beloved warrior-king, defeated a Greek force that was more than six times the size of the Jewish army. Then, keeping the army of the Acra at bay, he entered Jerusalem to undo the blasphemy. The sanctuary of the Temple was deserted, the altar horribly desecrated, the gates burned down, the courts as filled with vegetation "as it might in a wood or on some mountain." The Jews "prostrated themselves on the ground, and when the trumpets gave the signal they cried aloud to Heaven." Priests who were "blameless and zealous for the Law" removed the "stones of the Pollution" to a cesspool. The Jews pulled down the profaned altar of burnt offering and "deposited the stones in a suitable place . . . to await the appearance of a prophet"— sadly, there was none—"who should give a ruling about them." They made a new altar from unhewn stones, restored the Holy of Holies, forged new sacred vessels, lit the lamps of the great menorah, and made an eight-day celebration, singing psalms and playing music "with rejoicing and with gladness." This is the Feast of Hanukkah (or [Re]Dedication), to which the pleasant legend later attached that there was found in the Temple a cruse of oil sufficient for only one night's illumination, but the miraculous oil burned for eight nights, inspiring the Jewish domestic custom of lighting lamps during the eight nights of the commemoration.

This festival marks an extraordinary moment in the history

of the ancient world, a triumph over the prevailing religious indifferentism and over the tyrant's assumed right to regulate the heart as well as the realm. What is most inspiring about Hanukkah is that it memorializes the first clear victory in history for freedom of worship, a celebration that, as contemporary rabbis point out, belongs to all religious people.

THE STORY OF THE MACCABEES (Judas's nickname was eventually used of his whole family) has more to impart to us than a simple tale of victory over tyranny. The chronicler's exacting Greek method of approaching his material shows how far alien techniques and ideas had penetrated Jewish society by the end of the second century B.C. and that, no matter the vigilance of any ethnarchy, it cannot withstand the siren song of the larger society that encompasses it. Even the most faithful Jews were now part of the Greek world; and, like it or not, by adopting its techniques, they were adopting at least some of its values.

Judas, though he created a new balance between believing Jews and their Greek overlords, did not succeed in wresting the Acra from the Greeks and could not, given his limited resources, overcome Greek power permanently or establish a new political order. His later campaigns, however, which broadened the territory under direct Jewish control, grew more savage, taking up the Alexander principle of putting whole cities to the sword and dealing mercilessly with whoever dared defy him. The militancy of the Maccabees not only divided Jewish society but led to the rise of the Zealots, the armed revolutionaries who would at last draw upon Judah the unwonted attentions of an empire far more powerful than even the Greeks could have imagined, an empire that would in A.D. 70 crush Jerusalem like a gnat, leaving "not a stone upon a stone." The leveled city would not again know Jewish ownership till our day, when the Maccabees were "rediscovered" by Israeli Zionists, who made them culture heroes once again and gave them new legitimacy.

Ironically, however, the later Maccabees would hardly join the revolution their ancestors inspired. Instead, they became the disappointing Hasmoneans, a dynastic family whose predecessors sprang from an unimportant line that had made no mark on Jewish history prior to the Maccabees. Thus, they had no legitimate claim to the offices they came to occupy—of local ruler and high priest, both offices at times devolving on one man—because they descended neither from the seed of Aaron, Moses's brother and the first high priest, nor from the seed of David, the champion who had once united the Twelve Tribes of Israel into one great kingdom. The "legitimacy" of the Maccabee-Hasmoneans rested rather on their complicity with the monarch of the moment. Judas had taught the king a lesson that subsequent Greek and Roman leaders did not forget. Future rulers would normally come to the sensible conclusion that it is better not to stir the pot of Judah unnecessarily but to put a Jew in charge, especially one as accommodating—and enthusiastic about imperial taxation—as the Hasmoneans gradually became. The majority of Jews came to view these Jewish overlords as oppressors. The last and least distinguished of the line are well known to us: the Herods.

This sorry state of affairs poisoned even the atmosphere of the holy Temple, held hostage to a gang of priest-pretenders who, like so many Renaissance cardinals, had little interest in God or prayer, whose interest in wealth and ignorance of religion led them to take rigidly conservative positions, and whose piety was not so much suspect as nonexistent. But a people so absorbed with God cannot be left so spiritually poor. In reaction to the Hasmonean dilution of Judaism, countermovements developed.

The members of one of these movements abandoned the Temple and took to the desert. They were called Essenes,* and we knew little about them before 1947, when the Dead Sea Scrolls were discovered by a Bedouin shepherd boy who, idly throwing stones into a dark cave near Qumran, south of Jericho, heard an unexpected clunk—the sound of his stone fracturing an ancient urn, which turned out to be one of scores of such urns filled with hundreds of scrolls. Almost all scholars now agree that these scrolls (and fragments) of papyrus and leather are the remains of an extensive Essene library, squirreled away for safekeeping in eleven separate caves during a time of civil unrest (perhaps in Jerusalem's last hour) and successfully hidden from view for nineteen hundred years. The scrolls, containing biblical books in versions far more ancient than anything we previously possessed, have also yielded documents unknown till now, giving rich evidence of the elusive community that preserved them.

To all intents and purposes, the Essenes were celibate Jewish monks, permanently severed from a society that had grown degenerate, and they were a

✳ The Essenes may have risen out of an earlier movement, the Hasidim (or Saints), who were scrupulous about the Law, had already removed themselves to caves beyond the city in the time of Judas Maccabeus, and temporarily allied themselves with him in the early stages of the Maccabean-Hasmonean movement. Some scholars are of the opinion that the Hasidim were also forerunners of the Pharisees and even of the Sadducees. Such speculation lies outside our story. The Hasidim of our day, who first appeared in southeastern Poland in the mid-eighteenth century as followers of the Baal Shem Tov, have no direct connection, apart from their name, to the ancient Hasidim.

shocking development within a religion that had come close to worshiping generativity and worldly involvement. Abraham had been promised progeny; and all the promises God had made to the Jews revolved around the ultimate success of "their seed" within the confines of this world. How, then, could a movement of pious Jews forsake the obligation (and concomitant pleasure) of sexual reproduction and the joys of material life? If this strikes one as grotesque, almost as remarkable is the evidence, contained in the scroll entitled *The Manual of Discipline,* that in addition to chastity, the Essenes were effectively vowed to poverty (or the community of goods) and obedience, submitting to near-military control by the Essene leaders.

Because God's Temple, now in the hands of time-servers and worse, had been irreparably compromised, there was only one course the righteous could take: to withdraw from the world, since it must be coming to an end. The high priest of the Temple, the "Wicked Priest," though "called by the name of truth when he first arose," had betrayed God and built "with blood a city of vanity," a city that robbed the poor to fatten the rich. There is good reason to identify this priest with Jonathan Maccabeus, Judas's younger brother, who was appointed high priest after Judas's death and played footsie with the Seleucids. His opposite number in the Dead Sea Scrolls is "the Teacher of Righteousness," a kind of abbot of the community, of whom we know nothing outside the Scrolls. All indications pointed in the direction of a final battle, which the Essene community believed would soon be waged, between "the Sons of Darkness and the Sons of Light," who would have the archangel Michael as their champion. It was this proximate apocalypse that supported the Essenes' radical lifestyle: if the world was about to end, generativity, property, and personal freedom were beside the point. What evidence we have also suggests that John the Baptizer, Jesus's immediate predecessor, whom the gospels locate in the same Judean desert that the Essenes called home, was once part of this community and shared its vision of a coming conflagration.

The underlying reason for the exclusion of the Maccabean material from the canon of the Hebrew Bible was not that the Jews lacked a version in Hebrew. At least in the case of First Maccabees, they once possessed the Hebrew original. The reason it was lost is that the early rabbis did not value the material, which glorified the exploits of the Maccabees, because they had no use for the Maccabees' descendants, the Hasmonean dynasty. The rabbis—or "teachers" of Israel, who are first mentioned in this post-Alexandrine period and who are with us to this day—tried in many ways to steer a middle course between the absolute purity of the Essenes and the smarmy pragmatism of the Hasmoneans. They loved the Law in all its details; and this was their focus, not fanciful predictions of apocalypse. They would not be pushed out of society; they would live normal lives as normal men but with a reverence for the Law more elaborate than anyone had ever attempted before them. Paradoxically, they were called "Pharisees" (or "Separate Ones"), but this may be a name given them by enemies. It is among their ranks that we should probably seek one of their less distinguished (and abnormal) colleagues, Jesus of Nazareth, whose followers called him "rabbi."

The world in which this Jesus grew to manhood, a world of now-extinct "Judaisms," was not very like any Jewish environment that we know of in more recent times. After all, the ancient Temple cultus and its priesthood, however compro-

43

mised, were destroyed completely in the catastrophe of A.D. 70—about four decades after Jesus. The Essenes disappeared about the same time beneath the desert sands. Of all these divergent "Judaisms" the one we know least about is Sadduceeism. The Sadducees, who seem to have departed the scene about the same time as the Essenes and the Hasmonean high priests, had links to the priesthood and appear to have been, in the main, wealthy, influential men. Almost the only things we know for certain about them are that they some-times clashed with the Pharisees over interpretation of the Law and that they did not believe in an afterlife.

The idea of continued life for human beings after physical death is unknown in the earliest—and most important—doc-uments of Judaism, the Torah and the Prophets. Enslaved Israel's brush with Egyptian religion, when the Israelites in the second millennium B.C. were forced to build mausoleums for dead pharaohs, may have been enough to keep the Jews away from all that woo-woo "spirituality" about the Mummy's Curse and the floating and immortal souls of dead kings and their retinues. Israelite religion was about land and progeny, thank you all the same—not the unreal realms of the dead, backed up by creepy movie music. But it was also about good and evil actions, about justice to the poor, and fidelity to God. The Ten Commandments, which came to the Jews through Moses, but ultimately from God, give scant promise of reward for doing right. One must love justice and mercy for their own sake—and for God's—not because one receives heavenly up-grades for good behavior. Of course, leading a good life, a life in accordance with God's justice, will normally lead to all the good things: children, honor, prosperity, and serene old age.

But what of those who suffer? What of those, like Job, who

44

lose everything despite their faithfulness? Are their lives merely evidence that God is not the God of Justice but of Injustice? Such thoughts troubled the Jews (as they still trouble us); and in the later writings of the Hebrew Bible, as well as in the writings of this period that were not accepted into the Hebrew canon, they worried over this dilemma.

One solution was, as we have seen, Apocalypse: a universal Dies Irae that would get the wicked and vindicate the good guys. The later chapters of the Book of Isaiah—which do not come from the pen of the prophet but from an unknown writer who lived after the return of the Jews from Babylon in the period before the Hasmoneans—begin to speak of the re-demptive power of suffering and of a "suffering servant" who will in his meekness redeem his people, that is, ransom them from slavery and sin. The Book of Daniel contains a prophecy about "one like a Son of Man"—that is, a human being—al-most certainly an image of Israel, rescued by God from its suf-ferings and exalted among the nations after the successive collapse of each of the world's empires. All these prophecies are couched in ambiguous symbolic language, and all seem to as-sume that the coming Good Time must be preceded by the Day of God's Wrath.

The Second Book of Maccabees, which covers much the same material as First Maccabees but in a far more florid style, recounts the Gothic tale of a woman who, during the perse-cution of Antiochus Epiphanes, was made to watch as her seven sons, who had refused to taste pork, were whipped and scourged. Antiochus (who would hardly have been present in a sordid Jerusalem torture chamber but would rather have been found far from this scene in one of his palaces at Antioch or Babylon) is depicted as mad with rage, ordering that pans and cauldrons be heated till they are red-hot. He commands that the spokesman for the brothers have his tongue cut out, his head scalped, and his extremities cut off. What is left of the poor man is then fried in a pan. His brothers know that the same fate awaits them if they again refuse the forbidden food. "The Lord God is watching," encourages their mother, "and certainly feels sorry for us, as Moses declared in his song, which clearly states that 'he will take pity on his servants.' "

You can almost hear the writer's mental gears turning: if good people, the best people, are made to die in this way, death cannot be the end of everything. The saints must prevail—but how? The mother, as she witnesses successively the torture and death of each son, does not try to intervene but encourages each "in their ancestral tongue," a telling detail, because by this time the Jews no longer spoke Hebrew but Aramaic, the dominant tongue of the Near East, which the Greek Seleucids had grudgingly adopted as their language of administration after they became the kings of Alexander's Asia. Antiochus, who is counting on at least one recantation to make his day, is distraught when he finds he is now down to the youngest son, who is proving as inflexible as his freshly executed brothers. The king appeals to the mother to give her one surviving son some sensible, motherly advice. But the mother, leaning over her son, "fooled the cruel tyrant with these words," uttered, of course, in excellent Hebrew, which the king, nodding his enthusiastic assent, could not understand: " 'My son, have pity on me; I carried you nine months in my womb and suckled you three years, fed you and reared you to the age you are now, and provided for you. I implore you, my child, look at the earth and sky and everything in them, and consider how God made them out of what did not exist, and that human beings come into being in the same way. Do not fear this executioner, but prove yourself worthy of your brothers and accept death, so that I may receive you back with them in the day of mercy.' " The last son is slaughtered, and then the mother.*

The saints will prevail "in the day of mercy." But all these images and prophecies of eventual victory seem to require a preliminary "judgment on the wicked" (as the last son prophesies)—a prior cataclysm, something that more moderate believers were, understandably, loath to entertain. (I recall a zonked British rocker in the late sixties urging me to cancel a trip to California because, according to the prophecies of Nostradamus, that state was about to be divided from the mainland and slip into the Pacific. Well, perhaps Nostradamus was merely off by a few decades or—more likely, in my opinion—true prophets are few and far between and, in any case, notoriously unreliable when it comes to actual dates.) Balanced believers who had productive lives and investments in family and property and who did not especially welcome the fiery end of everything found a variant way to answer the question of how the suffering of good people can be justified, a way that did not insist so extravagantly on universal destruction: the just—those who had lived by the Word of God and treated their fellow man fairly and mercifully—would live forever with God, so their earthly suffering was but a prelude to their everlasting glory.

It is often asserted that this idea of

* This rather chilling woman was hailed not only by unyielding Jews of late antiquity but by early Christians who took her as a model of martyrdom and built churches in memory of her and her sons. The legend of this mother and her sons is, in fact, our first recorded "martyrology" (or inspiring record of religious witness in the face of certain torture and death at the hands of a cruel public official) and provided the pattern that all subsequent examples of the genre would follow. The Greek word *martyr* means "witness."

everlasting life is a borrowing from the Greeks, who thought the body but a prison that enclosed the immortal butterfly of the soul. But the Greek idea of immortality was very different from the evolving Jewish idea that there must be life beyond this life—if life is to make sense. For one thing, the Greeks imagined that the soul had existed forever, prior to its imprisonment in a body. The Jews could never countenance such ethereal blather. God had created each individual at one particular time as a body born of woman; there could be no possibility of anything like preexistent spirit. Each person was exactly what you saw and smelled: a body of flesh and blood.

48

Job, at the lowest point of his hideous suffering, his children dead, his property gone, his body covered in sores, screams out his justification:

> *This I know: that my Avenger* lives,*
> *and that he, the Last, will take his stand on earth.*
> *After my awaking, he will set me close to him,*
> *and in my flesh shall I see God!*

On earth. In his flesh. Within the classic Jewish worldview nothing else is possible, no merely spiritual vindication. "Heaven," boasted the third son of the mother of Second Maccabees, "gave me these limbs; for the sake of his laws I have no concern for them; from him I hope to receive them again"—not float around as a disembodied soul.

But, gradually, even this possibility of

✶ This passage has many translations, the most famous being "I know that my Redeemer liveth . . ." in the King James Version. But the Hebrew *goel* is not "redeemer" but a technical legal term meaning something like "public defender" or "ombudsman"—though with a more aggressive nuance. However one translates it, it appears to refer to God.

"resurrection to new life," as the fourth son termed it, gave way to a more nuanced interpretation, based neither on Platonic metaphor nor on Jewish theological speculation, but on what the Jews had always relied on, their faith in their God. Someday, *somehow*, there will be a final accounting, which must, of necessity, include a resurrection of the bodies that have turned to dust—a resurrection "in my flesh." Beyond the grave, the good will be rewarded as they never were in life; and the evil ones, who seemed to own the world, will be hurled into unimaginable perdition. But there must be a place—outside time—where the souls of the just are kept, awaiting their final resurrection and vindication. We cannot understand these matters, for they lie beyond our ken. But we believe that God is just and that even after death we are, as we have always been, in his hands. Thus, this passage from the Book of Wisdom, written by a Jew of Alexandria in the decades just before Jesus and so hopeful that it has been read at funerals ever since:

49

> *The souls of the just are in the hands of God,*
> *and the torments wrought by evil-doers*
> *can never touch them again.*
> *It is true that they appeared to die—*
> *but only in the eyes of people who cannot see*
> *and who imagined that their passing away was a defeat,*
> *that their leaving us was an annihilation.*
> *No, they are at peace.*
> *If, as it seemed to us, they suffered punishment,*
> *their hope was rich with immortality;*
> *slight was their correction, great will their blessings be.*
> *God was putting them to the test,*
> *and has proved them worthy to be with him;*

he has tested them like gold in a crucible,
and accepted them as a perfect holocaust.
In the hour of judgment they will shine in glory,
and will sweep over the world like sparks through stubble.
They will judge nations, rule over peoples,
and the Lord will be their king forever.
Those who trust in him will come to understand the truth,
those who are faithful will live with him in love.
Only grace and mercy await them—
all those whom God, in his compassion, has called to himself.

50 "KNEW YOU NOT POMPEY?" exclaims Marullus, a tribune of the people* and supporter of the popular Roman general, at the start of Shakespeare's *Julius Caesar.* The Jews, who by the summer of 63 B.C. had lived under the heel of successive conquerors for more than half a millennium, knew neither Pompey nor his Rome. They were about to learn.

The Alexandrine empire, significantly weakened by its division into parts, was, by the early first century B.C., ripe for plucking. The energies of the founder had long been squandered in ceaseless competition among the leading dynasties, led by ever less distinguished scions. The Hasmoneans, who were but an instance of local resurgences throughout the lands of Alexander's conquests, were particularly

* Tribunes were elected by the people to protect their interests. The office was one of several of the Roman Republic designed to achieve a careful balance of powers among competing forces and to keep political chaos at bay. The two consuls, elected to serve but one year's term, were the executive pinnacle of government. There were two of them in order that they might keep each other honest, and they served but one year so that they could not amass undue power. The office of senator was either hereditary or bestowed for exceptional distinction (as in the British House of Lords). But all the rhetoric

successful in establishing first a measure of local rule, then gradually something approaching independence—though it should not be forgotten that much of what they accomplished was at the expense of Jewish identity. In the end, they were even affecting Greek names.

The Jews of Palestine* knew almost nothing of Rome but its name and that it was a newly expanding power, situated in far-distant Italy. Though Judas had entered briefly into alliance with the Romans, First Maccabees makes clear how vague and naive the Jews were about these Romans: "Now Judas had heard of the reputation of the Romans: how strong they were, and how well disposed toward any who made common cause with them, making a treaty of friendship with anyone who approached them." Yeah, sure. Judas also thought he had an alliance with the strange, militaristic, xenophobic Greek city-state of Sparta, the North Korea of its day, because for some reason the Jews imagined they were kin to the Spartans.

Rome, the far-distant, was in its expansiveness drawing near. Having begun in the seventh century at a bend in the Tiber as a settlement of Latin-speaking farmers, it came to master the Italian

about "Republican" Rome hid the truth that Rome was an oligarchy, arranged to protect the interests of its wealthiest families. Once the empire was established, supposedly as a temporary measure during an emergency, there was no longer any need to uphold the fiction of the Republic (*ResPublica,* "the Common Good"), save as vestigial decoration.

✉ The Holy Land, or Canaan, as it is called in Genesis, was gradually colonized by the Israelites under Joshua (and later), though it was never without other colonizers, such as the Philistines. Under Kings Saul and David, the federation of Israelite tribes united as the Kingdom of Israel. Under David's knuckleheaded grandson Rehoboam, the kingdom was sundered in two: Israel in the north and Judah in the south. Israel was subsequently destroyed as a separate political entity by the Assyrians, its principal families scattered and replaced by Aramaic-speaking colonizers, who intermarried with the remaining peasant stock to become the Samaritans of Samaria. The people of Judah, now the Jews, though they suffered the Babylonian Captivity, were allowed to return to their devastated country by the Edict of (the Persian

51

peninsula by a combination of military acumen and what it thought of as moral superiority. Romans were, by their own lights, a frugal, plainspoken people who put security first, prosperity second, and pleasure far down the list. They had nothing in common with the sybaritic, effeminate East that had so attracted Alexander; and while they admired the Greeks for their unparalleled intellectual accomplishments, they wanted no truck with their effete self-indulgence and inability to form a cohesive society. Despite Alexander's formal uniting of the known world, the traditions of the independent Greek city-states, each with its cherished and eccentric sensibility—democratic, indifferent, philosophical Athens, for instance; fat, artistic, fornicating Corinth; brutish, lockstep, homosexual Sparta; erudite, airy, esoteric Alexandria—were too ingrained to be dislodged. If all this made for variety, excitement, and life, to the self-denying Romans such quirkiness invited centrifugal fragmentation; and it was no way to run a society or an army, both of which require the upholding of inviolable laws of consistency, uniformity, and order—the preeminent Roman virtue. The Greeks thought they were the most intellectually discerning; and the Romans, arriving late to the fountains of self-conscious culture, were happy to hand them the palm in this regard. But the Romans prided themselves on having crucial talents that the Greeks, for all their complexity, lacked: realism and practicality. By the time their general, Pompey, invaded Palestine, the Romans had come to believe that, since they knew best, they would rule best. To implement their purposes, they had created a military

king) Cyrus in 538 B.C. Many remained abroad, creating the Jewish diaspora, but some returned. From this time on, the land was designated by the Greeks as "Palestine" (from "Philistine"). The reduced Jewish homeland of Judah would be called "Judea" by the Romans, who would sometimes use this name to refer to all of Palestine.

machine that, like a universal steamroller, could flatten the world and re-create it according to Roman specifications.

Pompey was an old warhorse who had put down a rebellion in Spain, helped extinguish the slave revolt led by Spartacus, and served as consul in 70 B.C., having pressured the Roman Senate into giving him this highest executive honor even though he was only thirty-six at the time and had held none of the required prior offices. Thereafter, he was allowed much leeway in his successful campaign to rid the Mediterranean of pirates (piracy being just the sort of thing Romans found intolerable) and to settle matters in Pontus on the south shore of the Black Sea, where the local king had a misconceived ambition to rule the Balkans and Greek Asia. While Pompey was putting paid to that bit of business, civil war broke out most opportunely in Judea between the forces of two opposing candidates for the kingship—brothers and Hasmoneans—giving Pompey the excuse to intervene in the year 63. Judea, as well as all of Palestine, Syria, and North Africa, would remain in Roman hands till it would fall to the Muslims in the seventh century of the Christian era.

Pompey was one of three eminent Romans—the others being Crassus and Julius Caesar—whom Caesar would shortly bring together to form the First Triumvirate, whose public mission was to solidify Rome's political order (always an admirable Roman objective) while furthering Caesar's unannounced political ambition to become Rome's dictator. Pompey took Jerusalem after a three-month siege and entered the Holy of Holies—which the high priest alone was fit to enter, and that but once a year. You can almost hear Pompey's gruff "What the hell d'ye suppose they have in there?" as he, mounting the steps of the sanctuary, noted the growing alarm

53

of the priests. But, his curiosity satisfied, he otherwise left the Temple alone. It would fall to the well-named Crassus to plunder its treasury to finance his military campaign against the Parthians. The Parthians (today they are Iranians), however, were tough nuts whom the Romans never cracked. Apart from the Scots, they were the only people ever to stop the Romans, who were made to halt their eastward expansion at the Euphrates, where Crassus was cut down at ancient Harran, from which a man named Abraham had once set out on the journey of a lifetime.

Crassus's quaestor (or quartermaster), one Cassius, became Rome's proconsul for Syria (and, incidentally, Judea), soon after which civil war broke out in Rome between Caesar, who had added the conquest of Gaul to his résumé (and immeasurably increased his fame by writing a book about it), and sour old Pompey, who'd had enough of Caesar's strutting about. Pompey lost and was assassinated by the Ptolemies on fleeing with his army into Egypt. Caesar followed and quickly found himself outnumbered and in trouble, from which he was rescued—by Jews! Hyrcanus II, the Hasmonean priest-ruler whom Pompey had set in place, persuaded the Jews of Egypt, who were considerable in number, especially in Alexandria, to fight for Caesar. Antipater, influential king of the Idumeans, a mixed population of Jews and Arabs who lived south of Jerusalem between the Judean hills and the Negev desert, sent troops and supplies. Caesar, triumphing once again while carrying on a torrid affair with Cleopatra, the teen queen of Egypt, was grateful for such surprise support. He gave Hyrcanus the official title "ethnarch of the Jews"; to Antipater he gave Roman citizenship, exemption from taxation, and the procuratorship of Judea. Obviously, he valued Antipater's contribution more highly than Hyrcanus's, and he was right to do so: the Idumean king was the real power propping up the Hasmonean priest. Antipater was a crafty desert chieftain who had converted to Judaism and had ambitions far beyond the desert. His son Herod was appointed about this time military prefect of greater Syria and would soon become a Hasmonean by marriage.

Just three years after his victory in Egypt, on the Ides of March 44 B.C., Caesar was assassinated by conspirators who included Cassius, the proconsul for Syria-Judea. The following year, Caesar's great desert supporter Antipater was murdered; and Mark Antony and Octavian, Caesar's nephew and adoptive heir, defeated Caesar's murderers at Philippi, where Philip of Macedon had long ago begun his conquests. The Parthians entered Jerusalem, elevating their own candidate as king and high priest. But Herod escaped to Rome where, with the help of Antony and Octavian, he was declared by the Senate to be "King of the Jews." Hard fighting lay ahead; but the Parthians were pushed back, and by the summer of 37, after a successful three-month siege of Jerusalem, Herod could claim his land as well as his title. He would sit for thirty-three years on the Judean throne, dying in 4 B.C., a year or two after the birth of Jesus.*

Mark Antony divided the emerging Roman empire with Octavian (and—for a short while—Lepidus, another of Caesar's allies). Mark Antony's share was Asia, which included Egypt; and it was there he met Caesar's old mistress Cleopatra, with whom he fell desperately in love, quite forgetting his mar-

* It is one of the ironies of calendrical history that Jesus was born between 6 and 4 B.C. (before Christ). Dionysius Exiguus, or Denis the Short, the sixth-century monk who created our dating system of B.C. and A.D. (*anno Domini,* "in the year of the Lord") on the basis of earlier rabbinical models, made a miscalculation.

riage to Octavian's sister. In his ardor, he began to make presents of vast territories under his command to Cleopatra and her children, leading Pascal to remark many centuries later that "had Cleopatra's nose been shorter [it was quite long], the whole face of the world would have been changed." But however decisive details such as nose length may be to the outcomes of history, time had run out for Cleopatra. Octavian prevailed upon the Senate to declare war on this unwholesome twosome; and the once-stalwart Roman tribune and the sultry Egyptian queen were defeated at the sea battle of Actium, after which each committed suicide. Octavian returned to Rome, now the only claimant to the authority of Caesar. A grateful Senate, filled with his supporters, greeted him as Rome's deliverer, the man who had restored its precious peace and order. Octavian, who had already assumed the name of Caesar on his adoption, now received his new name of Augustus ("Exalted One") and the title Imperator ("Commander-in-Chief"), which was soon to have the force of Emperor.

The year was 31 B.C. The Roman Republic, with its elaborate consultative mechanisms of Senate, consuls, and tribunes of the people, was drawing to its close. Though no one had quite noticed as yet, the empire had been born, and it would grow ever more extensive and absolute in the years to come. Octavian Caesar Augustus would reign for forty-five years. In 31 B.C., when he was barely thirty, no one could be sure what kind of ruler he would make; but Augustus would prove a proper emperor—an excellent administrator, a politician of labyrinthine cunning, difficult, delusional, and cruel. Those who knew him hated and feared him. He was approaching his fourth decade on the imperial throne when a male baby of uncertain paternity was born to a rural Galilean girl in the emperor's province of Syria, in the bothersome subdivision the Romans called Judea.

The Waiting Game

By the year of Jesus's birth, the Jews, long familiar with Greek language and culture, had adopted many of the ways of their overlords for many reasons—to survive, to do business, to fit in. They had even, like the Irish in the wake of the nineteenth-century potato famines, abandoned their ancestral language, the Hebrew in which all their sacred books were written, and adopted the common Aramaic of the eastern provinces. This shift in language gives us a better sense of their dispossession than almost anything else. What does it take for a whole people to give up their language, their mother tongue, the original nourishment received along with breast milk, the medium of their hopes and dreams? Does it not mean that their common hopes and dreams have already been shattered and that they have seen their inheritance so devalued that it no longer counts for much of anything?

Of course, beneath the surface of such a devastating situation, there live the dreams no one wishes any longer to give name to, the dreams we can no longer recount even to ourselves. These dreams had been expressed by the prophets, who initially had warned the people that their apostasies would bring catastrophe, then subsequently tried to comfort them with visions of a time when God would come to save them from their miseries and grant them peace, prosperity, and mastery once more under a salvific leader:

57

"Comfort ye, comfort ye, my people,"
saith your God.
"Speak ye comfortably to Jerusalem
and cry unto her
that her warfare is accomplished
and her iniquity is pardoned." . . .
The voice of him that crieth in the wilderness,
"Prepare ye the way of the Lord!
Make straight in the desert
a highway for our God.
Every valley shall be exalted,
every mountain and hill laid low,
the crooked straight and the rough places plain.
And the glory of the Lord shall be revealed
and all flesh shall see it together
for the mouth of the Lord hath spoken it."

Drop down dew, ye heavens from above,
and let the clouds rain down the Just One.
Let the earth open and the Savior blossom forth.

Thus the anonymous prophet, known to scholars as Deutero-Isaiah (or the Second Isaiah) and whose prophecies are collected in the last third of the Book of Isaiah. The historical Isaiah, whose oracles are collected in the other two-thirds—the first thirty-nine chapters—wrote in the late eighth century B.C., before the fall of Jerusalem to the Babylonians. Deutero-Isaiah, writing at the end of the Babylonian Captivity, does not wag his finger as his predecessor did but caresses his people and weeps with them, speaking in chapters 40–55—often called the Book of the Consolation of Israel—

about a coming era of fulfillment. But even the original Isaiah was full of mysterious prophecies of comforts to come:

> Behold, a virgin* shall conceive
> and bear a son
> and shall call his name Immanuel [God-with-Us].

> The people that walked in darkness have seen a great light;
> they that dwell in the land of the shadow of death, upon them
>   hath the light shined. . . .
> For unto us a child is born, unto us a son is given:
> and the government shall be upon his shoulder:
> and his name shall be called Wonderful, Counsellor, The mighty God,
> The everlasting Father, The Prince of Peace.

59

> And there shall come forth a rod out of the stem of Jesse
>   [progenitor of the Davidic dynasty],
> and a Branch shall grow out of his roots:
> And the spirit of the Lord shall rest upon him,
> the spirit of wisdom and understanding,
> the spirit of counsel and might,
> the spirit of knowledge and fear of the
>   Lord.

One of Isaiah's most memorable passages is his vision of the Peaceable Kingdom:

> The wolf also shall dwell with the lamb,
> and the leopard shall lie down with the
>   kid;

✻ In the Septuagint, the Greek translation of the Hebrew Bible that was read throughout the ancient Jewish diaspora, the word *parthenos,* or "virgin," is used. The Hebrew original has simply *alma,* or "young (unmarried) girl," though, given the rigid sexual conventions of the age, *alma* pretty much shades into "virgin." Hebrew does have a separate word, *betula,* for "virgin" in the technical sense.

and the calf and the young lion and the fatling together;
and a little child shall lead them. . . .
And the suckling child shall play on the hole of the asp,
and the weaned child shall put his hand on the cockatrice' den.
They shall not hurt nor destroy
in all my holy mountain:
for the earth shall be full of the knowledge of the Lord,
as the waters cover the sea.

So often these prophecies read like daydreams. A time is envisioned in which all wrongs shall be righted, the land once promised by God to his people shall know everlasting peace, and a second David, anointed by God himself, will sit upon the throne of Israel. This figure, the Anointed One, is called *Messiah* in Hebrew, *Christos* in the Greek translations of the Hebrew scriptures made for Jews living in cities throughout the Greek world who could no longer comprehend Hebrew.

This longing in the midst of present suffering for an impossibly happy outcome is a phenomenon by no means limited to Jews or even to the ancient world. Who hasn't had such feelings? But beyond the Jews, such longings were almost always thought delusions. The Sibyl of Cumae, a shadowy figure who lived in a cave near the Greek city of Neopolis (modern Naples) about 500 B.C., prophesied doom and death and the cyclical nature of all reality. "As time pursued its cyclic course," she is made to say in Book 3 of the Sibylline Oracles, "the kingdom of Egypt arose, then that of the Persians, Medes, and Ethiopians, and Assyrian Babylon, then that of the Macedonians, of Egypt again, then Rome." The succession of empires is without end, all part of the turning of the wheel of time and the infinite procession of worlds (the thought of which made young Alexander weep because he had not conquered one). The message of the Sibyl, who continued to reappear in later periods, haunting various shrines and caves throughout the Greco-Roman world, seems to have been that, though some times are better and some worse, there can be no permanent safety. Peace will be followed by war, prosperity by poverty, happiness by suffering, life by death. This was indeed the constant message of all ancient literature and its principal insight into human existence.

We actually have no unadulterated Sibylline Oracles left. The perspective of the fragment just quoted (with its two mentions of Egypt) gives indication of having been composed by a Greek-speaking Egyptian, and other portions of the book betray its provenance in Alexandrian Jewish circles of the second century B.C. The work is a pastiche of pagan and Jewish attitudes, alternating between cyclical cynicism and prophetic expectation. But whereas Greeks and Romans and all other ancient peoples tended to see history as an ultimately empty succession of triumphs and tragedies—and human beings as evanescent phenomena appearing briefly on the surface of historical events—the Jews believed that history had a beginning (in God's act of Creation) and would have an end and that each human being, created by God, had an individual destiny to fulfill and was not merely a momentary glimmer on the ever-recurring waves of fate. And as in so much material written by Jews in the disappointing centuries after the Babylonian Captivity, there is even in this peculiar collection of oracles the assertion of a promised Messiah, a king sent from God:

And then God will send a king from the sun
who will stop the entire earth from evil war . . .

61

and he will not do all these things by his private plans
but in obedience to the noble teachings of the great God.

For many readers in the late first century B.C. and early first century A.D., verses like these brought Augustus to mind. The emperor had created peace without end, Pax Romana (which in fact would last a very long two hundred years). That he had done so by merciless policies would not have given ancient readers pause. After all, how else could you create peace save by unswerving military imposition?

The historian Tacitus, describing the fall of Celtic Britain to Roman forces in A.D. 60, would put this apostrophe to the Romans on the lips of a conquered Celt:

> Harriers of the world, now that the earth [the continent of Eurasia] fails their all-devastating hands they probe even the sea [the Atlantic island of Britain]; if their enemy has wealth, they have greed; if he is poor, they are ambitious; East and West have glutted them; alone of mankind they behold with the same passion of concupiscence waste alike and want. To plunder, butcher, steal, these things they misname Empire; they make a desolation and call it peace. Children and kin are by the law of nature each man's dearest possessions: they are swept away from us by conscription to be slaves in other lands; our wives and sisters, even when they escape a soldier's lust, are debauched by self-styled friends and guests: our goods and chattels go for tribute, our lands and harvests in requisitions of grain; life and limb themselves are used up in leveling marsh and forest to the accompaniment of gibes

and blows. Slaves born to slavery are sold once for all
and are fed by their masters free of charge; but Britain
pays a daily price for her own enslavement, and feeds
the slavers.

Seldom has an imperialist seen so clearly the cost of imperialism on "lesser breeds" as the mordant Tacitus does here. But even Tacitus, who aimed to write *sine ira et studio* ("without passion or partisanship"), thought conquest inevitable.

On his victorious return to Rome from his provinces of Spain and Gaul, Augustus personally dedicated the exquisite Ara Pacis Augustae, the Altar of Augustan Peace, on the Campus Martius, the Field of Mars, the Roman god of war. Peace grew out of war: that was how things were. That the Roman empire was, like all its predecessors, a form of extortion by force, an enriching of well-connected Romans (who "make a desolation and call it peace") at the expense of hapless conquered peoples, would also not have carried much weight with most readers. Hadn't Philip of Macedon's first conquest been the seizure of the Balkan gold mines? Hadn't Alexander's last planned campaign been for the sake of controlling the lucrative Arabian spice trade? How could anyone demur over such things? What would be the point of holding out against the nature of man and of the universe itself? Augustus set up in the midst of the Roman Forum a statue of himself that loomed eleven times the size of a normal man,* and similarly awesome statues were erected in central shrines throughout the empire. Augustus was not a normal man; he was a god, deserving of worship. And, like all gods, he was terrifying.

63

---

* Of this colossus only a finger remains, still to be seen in the Forum.

If the emperor had many apologists, none did him greater honor than Virgil, who wrote the stirring national epic, the Aeneid, in Augustus's honor, connecting the emperor (as did the reliefs that decorated the Ara Pacis) to Aeneas, Rome's legendary founding hero. In the famous "Fourth Eclogue," Virgil assumes the prophetic mantle and, giving the Sibylline prophecies a wildly optimistic interpretation, uses the old technique of pretending to anticipate what had already come to pass:

> *Now comes the time sung by Cumae's Sibyl,*
> *when the wheel of the ages starts afresh.*
> *Now is the Virgin herself made known*
> *and the reign of Saturn on earth;*
> *Now is a child engendered by heaven.*
> *Smile, chaste Lucina, at the birth of this boy*
> *who will put an end to our wretched age,*
> *from whom golden people shall spring.*
> *Now does your own Apollo reign!*

If Jews might be pardoned for thinking that Virgil was writing of their Messiah, or Christians their Christ (as was imagined to be the case throughout the Middle Ages), the educated pagan reader took Virgil's *parve puer,* his "baby boy," to be the young Augustus, who would go on to bring about a peace so extensive that it would affect even nature:

> *Without being called, the goats shall return,*
> *their udders swollen with milk.*
> *The herds shall have no fear of lions. . . .*
> *The serpent shall be no more,*

and the poison-plant shall perish,
but Assyrian spice shall spring up everywhere.

Despite the remarkable affinity of these lines with Isaiah's prophecy of the Peaceable Kingdom, Virgil knew nothing of Isaiah or any of the Jewish holy books. How, then, explain the striking similarity of images—the response of nature, the favor of God that rests upon the child, the "gift of divine life" *(ille deum vitam accipiet),* even the seeming allusion to a virgin birth? One may chalk it all up to coincidence. Or one may say that, beneath the surface differences of each culture—whether of cynical Romans, theoretical Greeks, fantasizing Jews, cyclical Orientals, or post-Christian Occidentals—there beats in human hearts a hope beyond all hoping, the hope of the hopeless, the hope of those who would disclaim any such longing, the hope of those who like the two tramps in *Waiting for Godot* seem to be waiting in vain, a hope—not for an emperor, not for an Exalted One—but for a Just One.

65

II

The Last of the Prophets

The Jesus the Apostles Knew

❧

T HE TIME HAS COME: the Kingdom of God draws near. Open your hearts and believe the Good News."

These are the first words that Jesus speaks in Mark's Gospel, which—at least in the form that we now have it—is the most primitive of the four canonical accounts of Jesus's life. There is scarcely a word of this proclamation that does not call for explanation, though in Jesus's day each word would have carried a clear, if surprising, meaning to the Galilean peasants who heard it. The "Time" that has come is the time of the fulfillment of Jewish dreams, the time when God will show his special love for the Jews by breaking the bonds of their servitude and exalting them among the nations. It is the time they have been waiting for—waiting so long that they had almost ceased to believe that it could ever come to pass, so long after the destruction of ten of the Twelve Tribes, so long after the disaster of the Babylonian Captivity, which had been followed only by further oppression, so long after the drying up of prophetic inspiration had left them without direction. The "Kingdom" that they will participate in will be God's Kingdom, as he promised.

They are invited to shake off their worldly preoccupations and "open [their] hearts." The Greek imperative is *metanoeite,* which means literally "change your minds." It is usually translated as "repent" or "convert," both more harsh than the Greek. The word certainly refers to a spiritual turnaround, but the change that is looked for here is an openness to something new and unheard of. This "something new" is *to euaggelion,* not simply "good news" but *"the* good news," the best news ever. Our word "go'spel," an Anglo-Saxon elision of "good spell" (meaning "good word" or "good news") is the Old English translation of the Greek *euaggelion.**

Jesus's idea of the Time-That-Has-Come has no suggestion of catastrophe, no smell of fire and brimstone in it. Though present in his announcement is a challenge, his words caress the listener with welcome possibility. He does not threaten or condemn; he opens his arms to invite and encourage. The gentleness of this prophet is as unexpected as his message.

This does not mean that Jesus did not know the apocalyptic tradition. His precursor, John the Baptizer, stood squarely within that tradition, which was, in any case, in the air that Jesus breathed. And Jesus, by beginning with the normally dreadful words "the Time has come," is making direct reference to this tradition of expectation. But the surprise is that this Time-That-Has-Come is to be Apocalypse without Armageddon.† Jesus takes the tradition and gives it a twist, develops it beyond what might have been thought possible, and transforms it into something new. It is a method we will see him use repeatedly throughout his short life.

* The Greek prefix *eu-,* meaning "good," becomes in Latin *ev-*. The Greek stem *aggel-* becomes the Latin *angel-* (and direct source of the English *angel*). The Greek ending *-os* and the Latin ending *us* indicate a (male) person; the Greek ending *-ion* and the Latin *-ium* indicate a thing. Thus, *aggelos* and *angelus* mean "messenger," while *euaggelion* and *evangelium* mean "good message," this last giving us such English words as *evangelize* and *evangelist*.

† Armageddon, though it has entered many languages as the site of the final battle between good and evil, appears in the Bible but once: in the final book, Revelation. It means "the mountain of Megiddo." Though Megiddo in north-western Palestine was a crossroads in ancient times and the scene of many battles, there is no mountain there, so we must take the term, as I have here, as broadly symbolic.

70

There is perhaps no more important word in this brief formula, remembered from Jesus's early preaching, than the word *believe*. No news is good news, as we know even today and as the ancients knew in their bones. But Jesus's audience is invited to allow themselves to experience an inner change, so that they may put their trust in this Good News—so that they may believe, despite the ingrained presuppositions of the ancient world, that news *can* be good.

What made this man think that he could get away with this—this patent nonsense that went so directly against the grain of ancient society? For an answer we may turn to the first figure to present himself in Mark's Gospel—not Jesus but an even more marginal character, the wild and (literally) woolly John the Baptizer, who inhabited the deserts south of Jerusalem, lived off locusts and wild honey, clothed his loins in camel skin, and could be counted on to put the fear of God in people. He, too, told them that "the Time has come" and that they'd better get themselves ready. He was a man removed from ordinary human commerce, a desert crazy quite outside the life of society, one probably associated with the exceptional community of Essenes, but people sought him out and submitted to his baptism* because his predictions of the coming retribution both thrilled and terrified them. Having been cleansed with water while confessing their sins, they thought themselves ready for the coming Time. Mark connects the Baptizer to the prophecy of Deutero-Isaiah: this John is "the voice of [one] that crieth in the wilderness, 'Prepare ye the way of the

71

* *Baptism* means "immersion." Lustral bathing was a common practice not only among Jews, for whom it was chiefly a purification after sex or contact with a corpse, but also among Greeks, Romans, and many other peoples, who associated it with release from ritual sin (that is, sin incurred by transgressing some taboo) and new health or wholeness.

Lord,' " who "make[s] straight in the desert a highway for our God."

Then Jesus arrives on the scene and allows John to immerse him in the Jordan. As he breaks the surface of the water, he sees the heavens torn open and God's Spirit "like a dove, descending on him"; and he hears a voice, saying: "You are my Son, the Beloved One. You delight me." Mark fails to tell us if anyone but Jesus saw and heard these marvels. But there can be no question that this moment is central to Jesus's life. Like all the prophets before him, he has received the Spirit, lamentably absent during the preceding prophet-less centuries. Henceforth, the words that come from his mouth, like those of Isaiah and all of Jesus's prophetic predecessors, will be the words of God himself.

This is a difficult scene for modern readers to take seriously. Despite the fact that many of us secretly harbor uncanny experiences that have helped us lead our lives, the tenor of our age encourages us to brush these off as "coincidences," and we don't talk about such things lest everyone think we're nuts. Instead, we—publicly, at least—relegate all such experiences to the dustbin of pathology and speak dismissively of narcissism, Messiah complexes, and delusions of grandeur. The trouble with this response is that it fails to explain the rest of Jesus's life, including what happens next.

Returning to his native Galilee, he calls out to two fishermen (whom we may presume he knew previously) to "follow me and I will make you fishers of men." These two, Simon and his brother Andrew, surnamed bar-Jonah,* two rough, down-

to-earth laborers unlikely to follow a madman, "immediately dropped the nets [that they had been casting into the Lake

---

* The Hebrew patronymic *ben* becomes *bin* in Arabic and *bar* in Aramaic.

of Galilee] and followed him." Even if these two had been un-usually suggestive, it's unlikely that any self-enclosed whacko could have pulled off this trick a second time—but this is what Jesus proceeds to do. "And when he had gone a bit further," Mark tells us, "he noticed James son of Zebedee and his brother John, sitting in their boat and mending their nets. Straightaway, he called them to him; and they left old Zebedee behind in the boat, along with the hired men, and they too followed him." A single loner might have heeded this call, but surely not two separate sets of brothers, the second two over-seeing employees at their father's behest.

The next scene goes to the heart of the extraordinary im-pression that Jesus's presence made on his contemporaries and relieves us of any lingering suspicions about his sanity. Jesus and his four fishermen travel on to Capernaum, where the bar-Jonah brothers live. On the Sabbath, Jesus enters the local synagogue, reads aloud a passage from the scroll of scriptures, and then begins "to teach. And everyone was amazed at his teaching, because he taught them with authority, unlike the scribes." We all know what this means, for we have all en-countered people who instill confidence in others by the air of authority that issues from them. The other teachers (scribes or rabbis, to use the usual appellations) could not compare.

What did Jesus teach? Recent, and highly publicized, argu-ments among scholars (and some who just parade themselves as such) concerning this question have left many with the im-pression that there is no scholarly consensus on this issue. Jesus was a peasant revolutionary. No, he was an urbane wise man, something like an Eastern sage—no, more like a Greek skep-tic. It's all in the Dead Sea Scrolls and the Vatican is trying to keep it quiet: Jesus didn't actually die on the cross; he managed to escape, marry Mary Magdalene, and move to southern France (as who would not if he could?). Well, actually, we know almost nothing about him, because nearly all the sayings attributed to him were invented by his followers after his death.*

Amidst this cacophony of competing theories, the press tends to give the most attention to the loudest voices and the most sensational hypotheses. So it may come as a surprise to the common reader that there *is* a broad scholarly consensus about what Jesus taught (as there has been now for nearly half a century), even though inventive new theories do keep popping up, a tribute (as much as anything else) to the intense, metahistorical interest that Jesus continues to generate after two thousand years. Certainly, it would be hard to imagine such a plethora of theories sprouting around the life of any other ancient historical figure, even one as important as, say, Julius Caesar.

But before investigating what Jesus taught, let's step back a bit and take a look at the origins of Mark's Gospel, as well as at Matthew's, since these are the gospels that bear the closest resemblance to each other. According to a tradition established by the second century, Matthew, a tax collector (employed by the Romans to dun his own people)

✴ John Dominic Crossan, the leading proponent of the theory that Jesus was a peasant revolutionary, is a reputable scholar, if rather on the edge. Jesus as a sage (of one cultural variety or another) was widely proposed earlier in the century (by Albert Schweitzer, for instance) but has now fallen somewhat out of fashion. The fantasy about Jesus coming down from the cross etc. has been most recently proposed by an Australian writer named Barbara Thiering. Her theory rests on a reading of the tiny scraps of papyrus (many containing a single character or less, only one a full word—*kai,* meaning "and" in Greek) found in Cave 7 at the Dead Sea. These "documents" are so uninterpretable that they might as well be tea leaves. The theory that only a minority of Jesus's sayings can safely be attributed to him is proposed by the Jesus Seminar, a self-appointed California group of scholars and others (such as Hollywood movie directors) who meet occasionally to vote (!) on such matters.

who left his profession to follow Jesus as the fishermen had done, wrote the first gospel "in the Hebrew tongue"—probably the same Aramaic that Jesus and all Judea spoke as their daily language. But we have lost this Aramaic Matthew,* and what we have bears evidence of having been lifted from Mark and mixed with another source, which, because Matthew's Gospel contains many more of Jesus's words than does Mark's, must have been a collection of the sayings of Jesus. This collection, now also lost, may well be the original Aramaic Matthew. Since scholars can no longer consult it, they have given to this putative source the name "Q" (short for German *Quelle,* or "source," as modern biblical scholarship got under way among German scholars). Matthew's Gospel, at least as we have it, could not have been written directly by Matthew, the Jewish tax collector who abandoned his careful ledgers to follow Jesus. It was written rather by someone who had a Greek-speaking audience in mind (and, therefore, one outside Palestine), an audience that included at least some gentiles, who needed explanations of Jewish customs that would need no explaining to Jews. But this does not mean that this gospel has no connection to Jesus's truant tax collector. Its origins, especially its meticulous preserving of Jesus's sayings and discourses, may well lie with such an eyewitness.

75

Mark is traditionally remembered as an "interpreter" for Simon Peter, an Aramaic-speaking fisherman and Jesus's first follower, who would certainly have required interpretation when he arrived, as we know he did in later life, in Greek-speaking cities, such as Antioch, and Latin-speaking cities, such as Rome,

✻ The names of the four evangelists (or gospel writers), Matthew, Mark, Luke, and John, are also used of their work, so that phrases like "in Matthew" or "the original Matthew" should normally be taken as referring to Matthew's Gospel, not directly to the author himself.

where he was crucified in the seventh decade of the first century by Augustus's notorious successor, Nero, as part of an evening's entertainment. If Mark was Simon's amanuensis and this is his gospel, it is unlikely that he could have written it before Simon Peter's death, for in such a case it would almost certainly have borne the fisherman's name. As with Matthew, close analysis of the text reveals that this gospel came into existence over time—starting from oral testimony, advancing to written drafts and then to its final form—a process that cannot now be reconstructed exactly. But there is no compelling reason to doubt that at the beginning of the process stands the apostle* Simon Peter, just as the apostle Matthew may stand as the ultimate source of the gospel that bears his name.

Matthew's account is considerably more developed than Mark's—which makes sense if the origin of Matthew's Gospel lies with a fairly sophisticated Roman official, used to keeping accounts and comfortable in passing from one culture to another, while the origin of Mark's Gospel, written in all likelihood after 63 but before 70, lies with a fisherman. Matthew's Gospel, as we have it, must have been written after Mark's—probably in the 70s or early 80s—which suggests that both gospels, dependent ultimately on eyewitness (and earwitness) accounts, were committed to the written page within a few decades of Jesus's death. And though Jesus certainly speaks in Mark, it is Matthew to whom we must look for an elaboration of Jesus's teaching.

❧ The evangelists use several terms to describe the followers of Jesus. The "crowds" that run after him are not quite followers, but exhibit the fickleness and fascination with novelty that we expect of crowds. The "disciples" are all those who take the new teaching seriously. The "apostles" (from the Greek *apostolos,* meaning "envoy") are designated spokesmen and -women. "The Twelve" are Jesus's inner circle, made up of the five apostles already named—Simon Peter, Andrew, James, John, and Matthew (Levi)—plus seven more, including Thomas the Doubter and Judas, Jesus's eventual betrayer.

Jesus, attracting crowds to himself by his authoritative explications of the scriptures and his unusual power to heal those who suffer, sees a large multitude headed his way. He trudges up a mountainside and addresses the crowded valley (which must have had very good acoustics) thus:

> *Happy the poor in spirit, for theirs is the Kingdom of Heaven.*
> *Happy the afflicted, for they will be comforted.*
> *Happy the undemanding, for they will inherit the earth.*
> *Happy the hungerers and thirsters for justice, for they will be filled.*
> *Happy the merciful, for they will be given mercy.*
> *Happy the pure in heart, for they will see God.*
> *Happy the peacemakers, for they will be called God's children.*
> *Happy the persecuted for justice's sake, for theirs is the Kingdom of Heaven.*
> *Happy are you when they abuse and persecute you and tell all evil against you because of me. Rejoice and be glad for your reward is great in heaven: so did they treat the prophets before you.*

Well, with one or two possible exceptions, this doesn't seem a happy lot. What's happy about the poor ("in spirit" or otherwise), the afflicted, and the persecuted? Empty stomachs that hunger and dry throats that thirst don't sound so happy; peacemakers usually get their comeuppance; and is anyone more persecuted than "the pure in heart"? "Happy the unhappy," we might say in summary. But these are the Beatitudes, as central to Jesus's teaching as the Lord's Prayer will be and—for Matthew, at least—Jesus's basic program.

Once again, we see the apocalyptic imagination at work, concentrating on a future of rewards beyond earthly time, but—as is becoming part of Jesus's signature approach—not bothering to mention the destruction of the wicked persecutors or to emphasize some coming conflagration. Some of the "happy" ones are clearly miserable for the moment—the afflicted (or, in another translation, "those in mourning"), the undemanding ("the meek" being the usual translation), the pure, and the persecuted—all of whom are persecuted in one way or another and appear to have had their way of life thrust upon them. Others—the poor in spirit, the champions of justice for the downtrodden, the merciful, the peacemakers—seem to have chosen their way. The division points to Jesus's two audiences: the powerless, who need to be reminded that God loves them and will see to their ultimate triumph, and the powerful, who need to be goaded by the example of those who have abandoned their comfort for the sake of others. The purpose of the Gospel is to comfort the afflicted and afflict the comfortable.

There courses through the Beatitudes the strong current of Jewish ethics, that countercultural tendency so opposed to the majority societies of the ancient world. Like the prophets before him, Jesus wants justice. Even if he does not harangue as they did, there can be no doubt of his profound commitment to their ideals. As Amos had warned the people of Israel, they were all about to be destroyed because they ignored the poor; as Micah told Judah, the only things necessary to avoid the coming catastrophe were to "do justice, love mercy, and walk humbly with your God." Jesus does not speak of destruction or enslavement. Instead of lashing out with threats, he holds up an ideal—or rather ideals, which are all humbly concrete: become one with the poor, defend their undefended interests, be sympathetic and forgiving toward others, make peace wherever you can. If you do these things, you will be happy. Indeed, these are the only ways to happiness. Power is an illusion and its exercise an excuse for cruelty. It is the misuse of power that is responsible for poverty, oppression, injustice, war, and torture. Not exactly inspiration for Alexander, Augustus, or their admiring biographers.

Jesus does not mention Alexander or Augustus. His references to oppression, war, torture, and the poverty created by military conquest are indirect. But within a world that worshiped the emperor and his sword (not to speak of his armies of soldiers and bureaucrats), this bold challenge to the existing mindset was unmistakable and arresting. People stopped and listened. Matthew tells us that news of this new preacher spread all over the province of Syria, and, besides the small band of companions he had already attracted, "large crowds followed him, coming from Galilee, the Decapolis, Jerusalem, Judea, and Transjordan."

The discourse at the beginning of which Matthew sets the Beatitudes is always called the "Sermon on the Mount," but we know that the author (or, better, the final editor) of this gospel is not recounting here a single event but has arranged much of the material he found in Q into a digest of Jesus's essential message. Having enunciated his basic program, Jesus is now depicted by Matthew as going on to provide a commentary on the Torah, the Law (or, better, Way of Life) of the Jewish people as outlined for them in their most sacred texts, the Five Books of Moses. This commentary is so important within Matthew's framework that it is worth quoting in its entirety:

> Do not imagine that I have come to abolish the Torah
> or the Prophets: I have come not to abolish but to
> complete. I tell you solemnly: till heaven and earth

disappear, not one jot or tittle will disappear from the Torah—not till everything has come to be. So whoever breaks even one of the least of these commandments and teaches other human beings to do likewise will be called least in the Kingdom of Heaven; but whoever keeps them and teaches them will be called great in the Kingdom of Heaven. (For I tell you: unless you do more justice than the scribes and Pharisees, you will never make it into the Kingdom of Heaven.)

You have heard that it was said to our People long ago: *Thou shalt not kill;** and whoever does must face judgment. But I say to you: Whoever is angry with a brother must face judgment; whoever calls a brother *"raqa"* [Aramaic for "moron"] must answer to the Sanhedrin [the Jewish high court]; whoever calls him "traitor" is in danger of the fire of Gehenna.† Let's say that you are bringing your offering to the altar and remember that your brother holds something against you: leave your offering before the altar and go first to reconcile yourself with your brother; then return and make your offering. [Similarly,] come to terms with your accuser before you reach the court, lest he hand you over to the judge,

א This sentence, which is the Sixth Commandment, is found first in Exodus 20:13 in the narration of God's giving of the Commandments to Moses and the Chosen People at Mount Sinai. Whenever a passage from the New Testament contains a quotation from the so-called Old Testament, that quotation is set in italics. For readers who wish to pursue such quotations to their original source, *The New Jerusalem Bible* (New York, 1985) provides complete marginal citations that unfortunately cannot be reproduced here.

† Gehenna—in the prophetic literature it is called "the Valley of Hinnom"—was a hideous place south of Jerusalem where Canaanites once made holocausts of living children to the god Moloch and where pyres were kept burning for this purpose. Jesus uses it as an image of the ultimate horror.

and the judge to the warden, and you be thrown into prison. Solemnly I tell you: you will not get out till you have paid the last penny.

You have heard that it was said: *Thou shalt not commit adultery.* But I say to you: Whoever looks on a woman with lust has already committed adultery with her in his heart. If your right eye is your downfall, tear it out and throw it away; better you should lose one of your members than that your whole body perish in Gehenna. And if your right hand is your downfall, cut it off and throw it away; better to lose one of your members than that your whole body go down to Gehenna.

And it has been said: *Whoever divorces his wife must give her a writ of dismissal.* But I say to you: Whoever divorces his wife, unless the marriage is already spoiled,* makes her an adulterer; and whoever marries a divorced woman commits adultery.

Again, you have heard that it was said to our People long ago: *Thou shalt not swear falsely, but keep the oaths that you have made to the Lord.* But I say to you: Do not swear at all, either by heaven, since that is God's throne, or by earth, since that is his footstool, or by Jerusalem, since that is the City of the Great King. Do not swear by your own head either, since you cannot turn a single hair white or black. Say "yes" when you mean "yes," and "no" when you mean "no." Anything more than this comes from the Evil One.

⚜ The phrase that I have translated "unless the marriage is already spoiled" is often called "the exception clause"; it may refer to marriage within an illicit degree of kinship or to marital infidelity, in which case it would be better translated as "except in the case of her adultery."

You have heard that it was said: *Eye for eye and tooth for tooth*. But I say to you: Do not resist the evildoer. If someone strikes you on the right cheek, turn the other to him; if someone sues you for your shirt, give him your coat as well; if someone makes you go one mile, go with him an extra mile. Give to everyone who asks; and from anyone who wants to borrow from you do not turn away.

You have heard that it was said: *Love your neighbor* and hate your enemy. But I say to you: Love your enemies and pray for those who persecute you, so that you may be children of your Father in Heaven—for *he makes his sun to rise on the evil and the good, and sends his rain to fall on the just and the unjust.* For if you love those who love you, what reward can you expect? Don't even the tax collectors do as much? And if you save your greeting for your brother, what are you doing that's so wonderful? Don't even the gentiles do as much? You must, therefore, include everyone, just as your heavenly Father includes everyone.

It is one thing to tell people that they may not murder one another without losing their own lives; but it is quite another to say that we may not even dress someone down or make fun of him or exclude him from our midst—or hellfire may be the consequence! What would happen if men could not divorce their wives? (Among the Jews, a man could obtain a *get,* or "writ of dismissal," for as trivial a reason as bad cooking. But there were no grounds under which a woman could obtain a *get* against her husband—and it is the sexual injustice of such procedures that Jesus is principally objecting to.) And don't look on a woman with lust? Earth to Jesus: Hel*lo!* (Of course, what Jesus is objecting to here is not spontaneous arousal but sexual oppression—the ease with which any man of the ancient world, especially a well-connected one, could arrange to satisfy himself on any woman he wished, her wishes in the matter being beside the point.) In a world where Alexander the Great was the supreme icon, ideas like "turn the other cheek" and "love your enemies" must have struck many as positively hilarious. Certainly, in the atmosphere of first-century Judea, where the brutal examples of the Seleucids, the Caesars, and the Hasmoneans held the cultural spotlight, this advice would have sounded even more unrealistic than it does to us.

There is no question that Jesus is using metaphor and exaggeration to make his points. Judgment by the Sanhedrin, being thrown into jail, exile to Gehenna are metaphors. He is not really urging that you should slice off your testicles to stop unwanted erections (though in the third century, poor, humorless Origen, taking this passage literally, will do great damage to himself). I do not mean to make Jesus the first stand-up Jewish comedian; but to get the tone here, one must hear the irony (and something close to self-mockery) in Jesus's voice—he knows perfectly well that he's asking the impossible—and one must see the great crowd, buzzing with confusion, and observe the light dawning in some faces as they come to realize what he is *really* talking about.

It is precisely the entitlement of the powerful and the disfranchisement of the powerless that make life so unlivable. And whether this enshrined and permanent injustice, taken for granted by all, issues in war, torture, and all the grand oppressions to which the Beatitudes allude or just in the petty tortures that we visit on one another—the casual oppression of women by men, the interior wounds caused by quotidian mean-spiritedness, exclusiveness, and theatrical mendacity—spirit is crushed and ordinary life is made a torment.

Whereas Mark's Jesus speaks in blunt staccato phrases ("The Time has come")—not unlike a certain inspired fisherman—Matthew's subtle, balanced Jesus exhibits mastery of intellectual discourse, an attention to detail that verges on the legalistic, and a profound reverence for the godliness of Jewish tradition, all of which are likely to have been heightened by the mind and memories of Matthew, the well-schooled Jewish tax collector and Roman employee. However that may be, each portrait of Jesus has been given its peculiar style by the hand, personality, and life experiences of the artist who stands behind the portrait. And yet, both portraits are patently of the same Jesus, who preaches prophetic justice—that unique, inflexible ethic of Jewish religious tradition which insists that the poor, the downtrodden, and the marginalized be taken care of—but graciously encloses his words in a gentleness that was hardly the hallmark of the old Hebrew prophets. This is Jewish justice, all right, but justice tempered by an affectionate mercy.

JESUS KEEPS TWO AUDIENCES clearly in view: the poor and miserable; and those who, because they are neither poor nor miserable, have a religious obligation to stand in solidarity with those at the bottom of the sociopsychological heap. For those at the bottom, their only "obligation" (if that is not too strong a word) is to trust in God's mercy. But the obligation of those on top is to exhibit God's mercy toward those who have nothing. Mark, Matthew, and Luke all recount the story of the young man who runs up and kneels before Jesus, pleading:

> "Good rabbi, what must I do to inherit eternal life?"
>
> Jesus replied, "Why call me good? No one is good but God alone. You know the Commandments: *Thou shalt not kill; thou shalt not commit adultery; thou shalt not steal; thou shalt not bear false witness;* thou shalt not defraud; *honor thy father and thy mother."* *
>
> "Rabbi," said he, "I have kept all these since I was a child." Jesus looked searchingly at the young man and, loving him well, said to him: "You are missing only one thing: go, sell everything you own and give the proceeds to the poor, and your treasure will be in heaven. Then, come, follow me."

The young man rejects this loving invitation, not to the Kingdom which Jesus has already promised him on account of his good life, but to something more—the high honor of service to the poor and companionship with Jesus. "His face fell," Mark tells us, "and he went away sad, because he was very rich." This exchange alerts us to the fact that Jesus is not so much issuing "commandments" as offering invitations. And however uninviting some of these invitations may appear, Jesus insists that, if only we would look at the world through his eyes, we would see that even the harshest life can be full of comfort and the mercy of God.

✱ The idea that "only God is good" and human beings are evil was a commonplace not just among the Jews but throughout the ancient world. Polytheistic societies tended to imagine that only their far-off high god was truly good. "Thou shalt not defraud" is not actually one of the Ten Commandments, but Jesus cites the scriptures loosely and with the confidence of one who views the Hebrew texts as family documents—as does the entire rabbinical tradition.

The truth is that no one is permanently on top of the social heap. All of us from time to time find ourselves in misery, pain, and (at least) spiritual poverty. But, Jesus insists, the ultimate answer is a simple one:

> Come to me, all you who labor and are weighed down with burdens, and I will give you rest. Take my yoke upon you and learn from me, for I am gentle and humble in heart, and you will find rest for your souls. For my yoke is easy and my burden is light.

The care that Jesus takes in approaching others and making them comfortable is phenomenal; there is nothing like his modus operandi in any other literature of the ancient world. Almost his first miracle in Mark's Gospel is a homely, unspectacular one, the cure of Simon's mother-in-law, whom Jesus finds sick with fever on his arrival in Capernaum. This is healing that does not mean to advertise itself but takes place in a little house* at the bedside of an otherwise unknown woman, whom Jesus happens to encounter—healing for the sake of healing. Another cure, the raising of Jairus's twelve-year-old daughter—whom everyone thought dead but who Jesus insists is alive—ends with Jesus enjoining her open-mouthed relatives to silence about his success and reminding them that a twelve-year-old who has just been through such an ordeal needs not their astonishment but "something to eat."

Food will play an important role throughout Jesus's life. He feeds a vast throng by miraculously multiplying a few loaves of bread and some fish that his disciples happen to have with them. These ever-increasing mobs that followed him

86

✠ The remains of Simon Peter's modest home may still be seen at Capernaum.

about would become a real headache for his regular disciples, especially for the ones Jesus counted on to play a strategic role in the more practical aspects of his ministry, such as crowd control. Sometimes Jesus and his disciples would just have made it to "some lonely place all by [themselves] in order to rest for a while," get a bite to eat, and have a little conversation, when the groupies would descend "from every town." But Jesus would "take pity on them because they were like sheep without a shepherd"; and he would "set himself to teach them at some length." When at last the irritated disciples would urge Jesus to send the mob on its way, we learn that his pity extends not only to the spiritual but to the physical nourishment of these "sheep"—and this is what prompts the miracle of the multiplication of the loaves and fish, a miracle that Jesus may have performed more than once.

87

But these extraordinary moments aside, Jesus was known as someone who hugely enjoyed a good dinner with friends; in fact, his reputation in this regard was manipulated by less successful rabbis to suggest that Jesus was nothing but a sot. Jesus finds their green-eyed characterizations ludicrous: "When John [the Baptizer] came, neither eating nor drinking, these same people said, 'He is possessed!' [I arrive], eating and drinking, and they say, 'See, he's nothing but a glutton and a drunkard, an intimate of tax collectors and an habitué of whores!' " Hostile rabbis continued their attack: why did his disciples eat without washing their hands first? didn't they even pluck corn on the Sabbath? Jesus throws their objections back at them: "You set aside the Commandment of God to observe man-made traditions [about hand-washing]"; and "The Sabbath [the weekly day of rest enjoined by the Fourth Commandment] was made for man, not man for the Sabbath."

At the end of John's Gospel, Jesus, as almost his last act on earth, cooks an aromatic lakeside meal of grilled fish for his friends. And the singular Seder, or Passover meal, which Jesus celebrated with his closest associates on the night before his crucifixion, has been reenacted almost every day for the last two thousand years.

Jesus was no ivory-tower philosopher but a down-to-earth man who understood that much of the good of human life is to be found in taste, touch, smell, and the small attentions of one human being for another. His disciples, raised to a new level of perception by their contact with him, begin to take themselves quite seriously, so that Jesus must constantly remind them of simple truths. When they begin to imagine that their operation is far too important to be interrupted by children, Jesus is forced to reprimand them: "Let the little children come to me—and don't ever stop them—for it is to just such little ones that the Kingdom of God belongs." He thanks God for revealing the secrets of the Kingdom only to people who are able to retain the forthright outlook of children: "I bless you, Father, Lord of heaven and earth, for hiding these things from the learned and the clever and revealing them to little children."

Sometimes the stolid dimness of his most intimate friends necessitates that he speak to them with unadorned bluntness. While other teachers warn his audiences to obey rabbinical proscriptions and not eat with unwashed hands, Jesus counters by telling the crowds that "nothing that originates outside a man can make him 'unclean' by going into him. Rather, it's what comes out of a man that makes him 'unclean.' " Later, in private, his closest disciples admit that they don't quite get that bit. "What don't you get?" wonders the exasperated Jesus. "Don't you see that nothing that enters a man from the outside can make him 'unclean,' since it doesn't go into his heart but into his bowels and then passes out into the shithole?* What comes out of a man's mouth is what makes him 'unclean.' For it is from within—from the human heart—that evil intentions flow."

Jesus was a first-century Jew, a rural rabbi from Galilee, the Bumblefuck of its day. As Cajun Country is to New Orleans and Kerry is to Dublin, the Galilean hills were the ultimate Boonies, the archetypal setting for all of arch Jerusalem's hayseed jokes. In a time of many Judaisms, originating in a contentious urban atmosphere, Jesus is not easily placeable in any of them. Like other rabbis, he read the scriptures aloud in the synagogue† and gave a commentary on the reading. Even though rabbis, or teachers of the scripture (unlike the prophets, priests, and kings, who had a long lineage through Israelite history), were a fairly new grouping among the Jews, commentary, or midrash, had a most ancient pedigree. The words of the prophets were commentary on the Torah, for they interpreted the Books of the Law for new generations and new situations. Even within the Torah itself there was midrash. The second half of the Book of Exodus, for instance, was largely commentary on the first half, especially on the Ten Commandments; and the rabbinical interpretations of the "laws" of the Jews were midrash on midrash. Jesus's midrash

✠ Usually translated "privy" or "sewer," the word that Matthew chooses is *aphedron*, Macedonian slang that would have sounded barbarous to Greek ears. Jesus was not bashful about referring to bodily functions, even if his translators are.

† The picture of Jesus actually reading "from the scroll" of the scriptures comes not from Mark or Matthew but from Luke (4:16–22). This has led some scholars to wonder if Luke, whose gospel is probably later than Mark's and may be slightly later than Matthew's, has wrongly assumed that Jesus was literate. But the preponderance of the evidence suggests strongly that Jesus could read Hebrew and was extensively educated in the Jewish scriptures.

on the Commandments and other "laws," as presented in Matthew's Gospel, fits squarely within this tradition.

But in another way Jesus could have been closer to the Sadducees and the Temple priesthood, who seem to have favored a freer interpretation of Jewish law than did the rabbis. Jesus, however, was hardly a member of the establishment and clearly believed in life after death—which set him far from the priests and Sadducees of his day. That he shared with John the Baptizer and the Essenes an anticipation of Apocalypse is undeniable, but just as undeniable is his uniquely gentle sense of expectation. His many references to peace and the implicit antiviolence of so much of his teaching would make it hard to place him among the Zealots, though his family, as we shall see, may have had a little Zealotry in it.

Almost all these ancient movements died within a few years of Jesus's time. Only Pharisaism, which would gradually turn into normative rabbinic Judaism, has lasted to our day. In effect, ancient Judaism, which in the first century of our era was represented by a broad spectrum of emerging "Judaisms," had two children that survived: rabbinic Judaism and the Judaism we have come to call "Christianity." To appreciate the atmosphere of first-century Judea we must understand that the "religion" that Jesus preached was, in its time, one of many alternative Judaisms. The word *Christianity,* which appears nowhere in the New Testament, is a term that would not be invented till a hundred years after Jesus's time (and then by Roman enemies of the Jewish followers of Jesus). "We Jews must . . . recognize," Shaye Cohen, Ungerleider Professor of Jewish Studies at Brown, has remarked, "that Christianity, too, is (or at least once was) a form of Judaism." Far more urgently must Christians come to the same understanding, if they are to know who they are.

In his most engaging book, *A Rabbi Talks to Jesus,* Jacob Neusner claims to show that Jesus was not really a good Jew because he took exception to the Torah. Certainly, he would take exception to Rabbi Neusner's neo-Orthodox interpretation of the Torah. But Jesus's critique is no more radical than that of many Conservative and virtually all Reform Jews, who make up the considerable majority of American Jewry: the heart of Torah is not obedience to regulations about such things as diet—what one may eat, whom one may eat with, how one must prepare oneself beforehand—but to *tzedakka,* justice like God's Justice, justice toward the downtrodden. The majority of the world's Jews* could hardly find fault with Jesus's midrash in Matthew's Gospel according to the norms that they themselves would use to articulate a contemporary interpretation of God's Word. If any-

thing, they might, like the rest of us, find him just too zealous, pushing us to a level of "observance" far more onerous than food and Sabbath regulations. Must we really "love our enemies"? How is it possible to live in this world while lending to anyone who asks, always walking the extra mile, always turning the other cheek? Isn't the observance of the Law on a literal level of interpretation a considerably more possible and practical "Way" to follow than this unrealism?

It is exactly this extremism that confirms Jesus's credentials as a prophet. He was, in the minds of his followers and in his own view, "a prophet mighty in deed

✄ Popular opinion among Israeli Jews is more ambiguous than among American Jews. Though observant, Orthodox Jews number no more than twenty percent or so of the Israeli Jewish population, the rest ("secular," or nonobservant) tend to the opinion that only the Orthodox way represents "real" religion and that the Conservative and Reform movements are forms of self-deception. But the mental gymnastics of these secular Jews—who defend the Orthodox way as the only one while steadfastly refraining from it themselves—suggest an ambiguity born of Israeli history, rather than a considered, logical position.

and word before God and all the people," the last of the prophets, the direct inheritor of the mantle of Amos, Isaiah, Jeremiah, Micah, and the whole long train of terrible figures who had demanded the impossible—all of whom were shown to have been, in hindsight, far more realistic than their supposedly saner, more balanced contemporaries.

But why is Jesus "the last"? Because this is "the last age of the world," the Time of the drawing near of the Kingdom of God* at the end of which we will surely witness the transformation of reality, the end of all things as we have known them. If Jesus's Apocalypse is a gentle one, it is still Apocalypse. When the Pharisees and the disciples of the Baptizer were keeping a fast, some pious souls approached Jesus to inquire why he and his disciples were not keeping the same fast, a fast that was meant to bring Apocalypse nearer. Jesus replied:

> How can the wedding guests fast while the bridegroom is with them? They cannot, as long as he is in their midst. But the Time will come when the bridegroom will be taken from them, and on that day they will fast.

✎ "The Kingdom of God" is Mark's phrase; Matthew, more alert to Jewish sensitivities about "the Name" and therefore less willing to seem to speak casually of "God," uses instead "the Kingdom of Heaven," obviously with the same intent as the less polished, more spontaneous Mark. This is a good example of how the two evangelists differ from each other.

Jesus is the bridegroom, but who is the bride? Present happiness is to be followed by suffering: Jesus will be taken from them. This saying does not properly address apocalyptic expectations, in which suffering is to be followed by happiness. The sequence is off. Jesus, the last of the prophets, sounds more and more like his prophetic predecessors, obscurely predicting unavoidable calamity. One thing is clear: something horrible is going to happen.

His Mother's Son

Everybody has a mother. As Phyllis McGinley put it:

> *A mother's hardest to forgive.*
> *Life is the fruit she longs to hand you,*
> *Ripe on a plate. And while you live,*
> *Relentlessly she understands you.*

93

Love of one's mother is so often accompanied by a wish that she would be blown away to an outer galaxy. This is especially true if one's mother is of the relentlessly understanding type who wants only the best for her child. But mothers, of whatever variety, tend to have an influence on their children that exceeds that of father, siblings, town, and school—that, in fact, exceeds everything but (perhaps) genetic makeup or the mother's own early death. No wonder that she should be "hardest to forgive."

What was Jesus's mother like? It is often said that her appearances in the gospels are so infrequent and fragmentary that we can know nothing substantive of her from these sources and that the mythical Virgin Mother of medieval piety has so overshadowed the real woman that there is now no way of reaching any solid conclusions about the historical Mary. Despite these formidable caveats, I tend to the idea that a real woman is concealed in the partial, pointillist portraits of the gospels and that we can find her there if we are willing to connect the dots.

Two of the gospels—Matthew's and Luke's—open with what scholars have come to call "infancy narratives," stories that begin not long before Jesus's birth and take us through his first days and years. Matthew's Gospel, which grew out of intensely Jewish concerns about patriarchal transmission, gives Joseph, Mary's betrothed, the central role in the story of Jesus's birth: he is "of the house and family of David" from which the Messiah must come; and he is the one who "in a dream" is let in on the real identity of Jesus—Immanuel, born of the virgin foreseen by Isaiah. In Matthew, Mary has nothing to say for herself.

Luke is an evangelist of a different color, whose gospel as a whole we shall consider later. But his infancy narrative is so intriguing that I would like to borrow from it here. In Luke, who is more painterly and lush than Matthew, an angel arrives named Gabriel—

> sent by God to a town in Galilee called Nazareth, to a virgin engaged to a man named Joseph, of the House of David, and the virgin's name was Mary. And he came to her and said, "Greetings to the Graceful One! The Lord himself is with you." She was decidedly put off by these words and asked herself what kind of hello this was supposed to be. But the angel had more to say: *"Fear not,* Mary, for you have found favor with God. Look, you will conceive in your womb and bear a son, whom you are to name Jesus. He will be great and will be called the Son of the Most High God. The Lord God will give him the throne of his father [or ancestor] David, and he will reign over the House of Jacob forever; and his Kingdom shall have no end."

Mary said to the angel, "This doesn't make any sense. I haven't had sex yet."

The angel replied, "The Holy Spirit will come upon you and the power of the Most High will overshadow you. So the child to be born will be the Holy One and will be called the Son of God. One thing more: your cousin Elizabeth has conceived a son [who will grow up to be John the Baptizer] despite her age, and she is in her sixth month, the very one people called sterile, *for nothing is impossible with God."*

Mary said, *"Here I am,* the Lord's servant. Let's get on with it." And the angel was gone.

95

In traditional sermons, Mary is presented as a shy child-bride, espoused but not yet living with her husband, mystified and trembling before the unheard-of responsibility she is being asked to take on. But I read her reactions, especially her words of challenge to the angel (however one translates them), to be down-to-earth and peasant-sensible, almost an exasperated "Get serious." She was indeed a girl—no more than fourteen or so—but she was a smart Jewish girl. Like Abraham, Moses, and so many of the great figures of Jewish tradition, she argues with God (here represented by his messenger), objecting to God's unfortunate lack of realism, but in the end she responds as they did: *Here I am.* She doesn't see this unexpected turn of events as unalloyed good fortune but rather seems to have some premonition of what it will cost her. At the same time, she doesn't tremble, even once. Like Job, who uttered the famous words "The Lord gives and the Lord takes away: Blessed be the Name of the Lord," she is more resigned than anything else.

Her mood seems to shift somewhat by the time she comes to visit her pregnant cousin Elizabeth in the Judean hills, for it is to Elizabeth that Mary speaks her Magnificat, the most muscular poem of celebration in all of ancient literature:

> *My soul extols the Lord*
> *and my spirit rejoices in God my Savior,*
> *because he has acknowledged his servant's humiliation.*
> *Look: from now on will all ages call me happy*
> *because the Almighty One (holy his Name) has done great things*
>   *for me!*
> *His mercy falls on every generation that fears him.*
> *With his powerful arm he has routed the proud of heart.*
> *He has pulled the princes from their thrones and exalted the*
>   *humble.*
> *He has filled the hungry with good things and sent the rich away*
>   *empty.*
> *He has come to help his servant Israel, remembering his mercy,*
> *in accordance with the promise he made to our fathers—*
> *to Abraham and his seed forever.*

Mary's "humility" in this poem is hardly the humility of the meek and unassuming. This is a larger-than-life song of triumph, thanking God for righting all wrongs by making a definitive choice in favor of the powerless over the powerful. No one knows it yet, but the poor, the hungry, and the humiliated have won!—and this unknown fourteen-year-old is their unexpected representative.

If it is unlikely that Mary was a poet, it is even more unlikely that she wrote this poem, full of literary allusions to Samuel, Isaiah, Habakkuk, Genesis, Job, and the Psalms. The

Magnificat is either Luke's own composition or, more likely, a song in circulation among first-century Christians. It sounds very like the songs of the Anawim (or the Poor in Spirit), yet another Jewish movement of this time that emphasized that the poor and dispossessed were God's real friends, rather than those who paraded around in the trappings of wealth and power. To emphasize their point, the Anawim dressed shabbily (though they came from education and affluence), befriended the actual poor, and lived among them. But there is no reason to think that Luke has given Mary lines that are at odds with what her own sentiments were known to be. Rather, a common practice among ancient biographers was to put on the lips of a historical character an expression of the sort of sentiments he or she was known to harbor—even if they had no record of the character's actual words at a particularly crucial moment. (Thus did Tacitus give speech to his Celtic commentator.) One needn't be a Freudian to spot the aggression implicit in Mary's words: my Son will triumph, reversing all our previous humiliations; our whole People will be exalted in him—and I will be seen as the source of it all.

97

However one may receive the news of Mary's virginity and miraculous parthenogenesis,* there can be little doubt that she was not the Ever-Virgin of subsequent popular piety (a piety later raised by the Greek church to the level of doctrine). The gospels mention that Jesus had "brothers and sisters," who were not (despite the best efforts of apologists) "cousins." At any rate, the case for Mary's supposed "perpetual virginity" required, as the fathers of the Eastern church understood these mat-

---

✂ *Parthenogenesis* (literally, "virginal conception"), or reproduction from an unfertilized ovum, is not unknown in nature, though scientists tell us it is impossible in the higher forms of life, such as mammals. But it is probably no more impossible than the exaltation of the humble.

ters, that her hymen not be broken in giving birth—since an unbroken hymen is what makes a virgin a virgin. This realization led them to the conclusion that Baby Jesus had appeared suddenly in his mother's arms without ever having passed through the birth canal. Just about the only people who have been able to swallow this one are males sequestered in desert monasteries at an early age without the opportunity to ever witness an actual birth, whether animal or human. The rest of us are left to wonder what happened to the placenta, which kills a woman if it remains in the uterus: did it conveniently disappear, or was it also delivered into Mary's arms, making for a rather messy miracle? Jesus, who in his teaching referred explicitly to the terrible pain endured by women in labor, no doubt had his information from witnessing his mother's subsequent pregnancies and labors—and could hardly imagine her an exception to the ordinary human lot.

98

The totality of the mise-en-scène, as Luke unfolds it, forbids our ascribing to Mary anything but a very down-to-earth character. Between the angelic entrances and exits, he gives us Mary and Joseph trudging along the road to Bethlehem, unable to get out from under a most inopportune tax problem (though tax problems are never opportune):

> Now it happened that at this time Caesar Augustus issued a decree that a census should be taken of the whole Roman world [for the sake of more accurate taxation]. This census, which was the first, was made while Quirinius was governor of Syria, and everyone went to be registered, each to his own town. So Joseph set out from the town of Nazareth in Galilee for Judea, to David's town called

Bethlehem, since he was of David's House and lineage, in order to be registered, along with Mary, who was pledged to him in marriage and who was already expecting a child. Now it happened that, while they were there, the time came for her delivery, and she gave birth to a son, her firstborn. She wrapped him in swaddling clothes and laid him in a manger because there was no room for them in the living-space.*

Mary and Joseph are not relegated to a romantic stable "because there was no room for them in the inn," the old, inaccurate translation. What is far more likely is that they were relegated to an unused room, originally set up for domestic cattle, because there was no room for them in the crowded family quarters of Joseph's poor Bethlehem relations, who could no doubt count to nine and may have relegated them to the worst room because they disapproved of such an embarrassing pregnancy. First, the tax man descends at the worst possible moment, forcing a most untimely journey; then you end up on your sister-in-law's uncomfortable old pullout; then, believe it or not, the contractions begin.

What we have here, it seems to me, is a picture of Jesus's parents bearing up under the very oppressions that their son will later rail against: political injustice—the grand and arbitrary gestures, made in flagrant disregard for the deep concerns of ordinary human beings (who cut no figure on the world's stage), that so

✠ Luke does not use here *pandocheion,* the Greek word for "inn," which he *does* use in the parable of the Good Samaritan, but *kataluma,* which means a "room (occupied by human beings)." Many contemporary scholars have questioned whether Jesus was born in Bethlehem, as both Matthew and Luke have it, or whether this is an assumption these two evangelists made because one of the Messianic prophecies (Micah 5:1) so predicts. But the questions about Bethlehem hardly constitute proof that Jesus was not born there.

facilely issue forth from Caesar and all his presumptuous ilk—as well as petty, person-to-person stinginess, the low-level withholding of generosity that can make such a burden of daily life. At its profoundest, our celebration of Christmas, which continues to maintain such an inexplicable hold on our whole culture, is not "good news" about material acquisitions (as everything from department stores to television commercials proclaims to us): it is, rather, a dramatization of the simple triumphs of common humanity, in which joy at a baby's birth can overcome the most grievous official oppressions, and even the pedestrian aggravations, of ordinary life. "When a woman is in labor," the adult Jesus will remind us in John's Gospel, "she suffers all the pain that is necessary to this experience. But then her baby is born; and the intensity of her sufferings is wiped from her memory—because of the joy she possesses in having brought a new human being into the world."

The Mary of the gospels is a tough little survivor, who keeps on coming. Given her high expectations for her firstborn, she is bitterly disappointed at the way he actually turns out. When he comes home to preach in the small-town Nazareth synagogue, the audience is exceedingly unimpressed, and she must endure the shame of her neighbors' rejection of her pride and joy. ("Where did this guy get all this stuff? . . . Isn't this the carpenter, Mary's son?") The unexpected strangeness of Jesus's teaching finally prompts Mary to round up Jesus's brothers and set off to bring him home from his travels for a good rest (and maybe a little chicken soup). He is plainly, as they say to one another, "out of his mind." Here is this child, who was supposed to pull the princes from their thrones and restore the fortunes of Israel, talking about loving the enemy and turning the other cheek. Mary, with her keen sense of retributive justice, had been counting on something with more testosterone in it. But it is also this same Mary who, when Jesus is completely disgraced and undergoing the ultimate public degradation—naked, nailed to a pole, and bleeding to death—sticks by him (though Simon Peter, Matthew, and similar supporters are nowhere to be seen), even if it means keeping company with some of her son's more unconventional friends, like that tramp from Magdala. In the iconographic tradition, Mary is shown as the one who cradled Jesus's dead body after it was taken down from the cross. In Michelangelo's best-known *Pietà,* she is depicted as a virginal girl, but larger than her son's corpse, and her nurturing breasts are emphasized. All this to move the viewer to *pietà* (pity), because for the son the mother was always young and vibrant, and for the mother this was always her little boy.

The mothers of firstborn sons who go on to do great things are often of the Mary variety, pushing their kid to do what he doesn't want to do (like the miracle at Cana),* expressing withering dissatisfaction on inappropriate occasions, but being there when all is lost. Jesus was a man and he had a human psyche, a psyche formed largely by his mother's extraordinary nurture. However much he, as a reflective adult, modified her attitudes and diluted her prejudices, much of his instinctive outlook was formed by this fierce, unbending woman, so that in many ways Jesus's worldview is already spelled out in the Magnificat, the most obvious model for which was Hannah's triumphant song (more than a thousand years earlier) on the birth of her son, the prophet Samuel. But then, everybody has a mother.

✠ During the wedding reception at Cana, Mary asks Jesus, who has not yet declared himself publicly, to do something about the fact that the hosts have run out of wine. Jesus objects to her noodging ("Woman, my Time has not yet come"), but in the end he acts spectacularly to head off the bridal couple's embarrassment (John 2:1–11).

III

The Cosmic Christ

Paul's Jesus

THE HORRIBLE THING that was going to happen, which Jesus told his closest followers about—at first gently and indirectly, then by ever stronger and more troubling allusions—was his own hideous execution, carried out in the Roman tradition of exquisite cruelty for all Jerusalem to see. This was no way for a prophet to end. Except for a few women, courageous to the point of foolhardy loyalty, his followers—the tax collector, the fishermen, the crowd-control experts, indeed the whole raft of self-important male strategists and thunder-thinkers who had attached themselves to the prophet—fled as far from the scene as their uncertain legs would carry them.

Simon Peter's betrayal carried special opprobrium, because he had been the friend of Jesus's heart. Jesus, knowing well what a tinderbox Jerusalem was, had never openly claimed to be the Messiah, only "a prophet"—and, most commonly, "the Son of Man," that ambiguous title borrowed from the apocalyptic passages of the Book of Daniel. But he was delighted to hear Simon the Fisherman say the dangerous word out loud. Drawing near the Roman city of Caesarea Philippi, the name of which was meant to call to everyone's mind both the emperor Caesar Augustus and the local tetrarch Herod Philip, Jesus had asked the disciples who surrounded him: "Who do people say the Son of Man is?" They answered variously John the Baptizer come back to life (John had been executed by Herod Antipas), Elijah, Jeremiah, or one of the other prophets.

"But you," asked Jesus, "who do you say I am?" Simon, always the one to blurt things out, spoke up immediately, seeming to speak for all: "You are the Messiah, the son of the living God."

Jesus replied, "Simon bar-Jonah, happy man. Flesh and blood could never have told you this, only my Father-in-Heaven. You, too, have a part to play, for you are Rock,* and on this rock will I build my synagogue, which the gates of Hades will never conquer. To you will I give the keys to the Kingdom of Heaven. Whatever you bind on earth will be bound in heaven; whatever you loose on earth will be loosed in heaven."

The strong bond of affection between the two men is palpable; and because of this, Jesus's heart was heavy when, his arrest but an hour away, he told Simon Peter of his impending betrayal: "I tell you solemnly, this very night before the cock crows, you will have disowned me three times over." The impulsive fisherman swore up and down that this could never happen: "Even if I have to die with you, I will never disown you!"

An hour later, when the Roman guard arrived at the little olive grove outside the city where Jesus had gone to pray, their clanging metallic entrance and the invincible brutality of their faces drained all courage from even his best friends, who took off quickly enough, leaving Jesus alone in custody. Peter did try for a while to follow at a distance, loitering in the courtyard of the high

---

✠ There are three words in this saying of Jesus that present special difficulties. The word "Rock" (petros in the evangelists' Greek, but kepha in Jesus's Aramaic) was not a normal proper name, any more than "Messiah" or "Christos" was; but from this moment Simon became "Simon Rock," as Jesus would become "Jesus Christ." In English we translate petros as "Peter," though the English (unlike the French "Pierre") carries no special connotation. What Jesus means to build on this human rock is his ekklesia—in the evangelists' Greek—but the word he would actually have used was qahal, which has a long and distinguished pedigree, referring in the Hebrew Bible to the desert assembly

priest while Jesus was interrogated, till, because of his Galilean accent, he was identified as a follower of Jesus by serving girls and other bystanders. As they pressed him to own up, Peter became more and more indignant, at last cursing Jesus in order to make his denials credible. "And at once the cock crew," and Peter recalled Jesus's words to him, "and he went outside [beyond their scrutiny] and wept his heart out."

Peter, like all the disciples, was traumatized by Jesus's sudden reversal of fortune. Less than a week before, Jerusalem had given him a royal reception, welcoming him as the true "king" of the Jews. Now, in short order, he was flogged, pushed derisively through the same streets that had so recently exulted in him, stripped naked, nailed to some boards in a public place, and left to bleed to death in slow agony.

Pontius Pilate, the Roman governor who condemned him after a hasty "trial," meant to have a little fun of his own with this execution and so had ordered a trilingual sign affixed to the top of Jesus's cross, proclaiming him to be "The King of the Jews." Yes, smirked the prickly governor, here was as much of a king as the annoying Jews would ever get: a pitiable, shuddering worm of a man, covered in bruises and rivulets of his own blood, his silly circumcised penis swelling for all to see, as he moaned incomprehensibly and died. The Temple priests, who had collaborated in the tortured man's condemnation, were not amused by Pilate's joke. The inscrip-

of God's People and, after their settlement, to their regular meeting, both a civic and religious occasion. The word is usually translated in English as "church," but "synagogue," which like *ekklesia* simply means a "gathering of human beings," is probably closer to the flavor of Jesus's original. "Hades" was the Greek underworld, where the souls of the dead led a shadowy, fitful existence. Jesus would have used the Hebrew-Aramaic *sheol,* which carries the same force. It is not clear that "hell," the usual English translation, is what is meant, because Jesus's sense seems to be not that evil will never conquer his assembly (which it has many times over) but that it will not know death.

tion only inflamed the crowds (who can always be expected to gather for the gorily diverting spectacle of a public execution): they spat on the dying man and mocked him, making lewd references to his sexual inadequacies and to his parentage, and generally convinced themselves that this thing they were ridiculing had never really been a man, only the ugly deformity that he now appeared to be.

The psychology of crucifixion had a profound political purpose. This was the end that awaited every enemy of the absolute Roman state: the opposite of the peaceful death that all good men hoped for at the last; instead, an end in which one's dignity and pride were torn away, then all shreds of one's identity in life, and finally the last semblance of one's humanity till one died the comic gargoyle of the moment. For Jesus's disciples, the crucifixion hit like an earthquake, destroying in a moment their entire world. No matter how many times he had told them that the Son of Man would have to suffer and die, they had not really listened: they had pushed it aside as the one part of Jesus's message they didn't want to hear.

If the crucifixion left the disciples utterly desolate, the news that Jesus was risen came on them like a tidal wave following an earthquake. They knew, as do we all, that death is the end and that there is no possibility of reversing its finality. If their world had been destroyed, would nature now play tricks on them, upending the only things they still knew to be true, the constant and reliable laws of the cosmos? If one has just suffered a tragic loss that sucks life dry of all its joy, one may somehow find the dull courage to go on—but one doesn't want to open one's door two mornings after such a tragedy to find that earth and sky have changed places.

This is what happened to the disciples, which is why they

were not so receptive to the seemingly meaningless news that "he is risen." For the first disciples to hear this, the loyal women who had stood by him in his final agony, these words constituted one shock too many. Mark, in the most primitive account left to us, paints a vivid picture, despite his wobbly grammar:

> Having bought new linen and taken [the corpse of Jesus] down [Joseph of Arimathea, a wealthy member of the Sanhedrin and a secret follower of Jesus] wrapped him with the linen, put him in a tomb hewn from rock and rolled a stone across the entrance of the tomb.
>
> Mary the Magdalene and Mary the mother of Joses watched where he was put.
>
> When the Sabbath passed Mary the Magdalene, Mary the mother of James, and Salome bought spices so they could come and anoint him. Very early on the first day of the week they came to the tomb as the sun was rising. They said to each other "Who'll roll the stone off the tomb door for us?" and looking up they [were surprised to see] that the stone had been rolled back for it was huge. Entering the tomb they saw a young man sitting on the right dressed in a white robe and they were much stunned.
>
> But he said to them "Don't be stunned. Are you looking for Jesus the crucified Nazarene? He was raised. He isn't here. Look, the place where they laid him. But go tell his disciples and Peter 'He's going ahead of you to Galilee. There you'll see him as he told you.' "

> Going out they fled the tomb—they were shud-
> dering and wild—and they told no one nothing for
> they were afraid.

I took this passage from Reynolds Price's fine translation, which has the rough, unrehearsed quality of Mark's Greek. Even readers long familiar with the gospels may themselves be stunned to learn that Mark's original ends right here with the shuddering and wild fear of the women. (A later scribe, feeling that this was no way for a gospel to end, added to one manuscript of Mark's text some resurrection appearances borrowed from Matthew, Luke, and John; Mark's Gospel is usually printed with these additions.) Some scholars have seen this abrupt ending as proof that Jesus was not "raised" and that Mark is merely recounting a wild rumor. But it would make no sense for Mark, having so painstakingly assembled a story that presents Jesus as a true prophet, indeed the promised Messiah and God's "beloved son," to pull the rug out from his entire narrative with a final "Fooled ya!" Mark means rather to depict for us the utter confusion and even terror that the news of Jesus's resurrection evoked in his dejected, disoriented disciples. As Nick Cave, lead singer of the Australian rock band Nick Cave and the Bad Seeds, has written: "Mark's Gospel is a clatter of bones, so raw, nervy, and lean on information that the narrative aches with the melancholy of absence." This gospel's open-ended conclusion should invite the psychologically astute reader not so much to skepticism as to credence: the shuddering women, afraid to tell anyone what they've seen and heard, make for a far more likely story than would some bogusly triumphant finale.

From the other gospels, however, we do learn of Jesus's

post-resurrection appearances and last teachings to his disciples, which included the promise of "the Spirit" of God, the divinely prophetic presence that will remain with them after Jesus leaves them and returns to his "Father." Certainly, after Jesus's final disappearance the disciples felt themselves imbued with a courage they had never known before, a courage that enabled them to communicate to their fellow Jews a new vision of a Judaism that no longer awaited an unknown Messiah but that had already received God's Anointed One in the fullness of time and that now, living in the last age of the world by the breath of the Spirit, awaited only the end-of-time return of this Son of God and Man. This new Judaism traveled from Jerusalem along the many trade routes of the ancient world, so that within a few years of Jesus's death, groups of his followers could be identified as a subset within many of the communities of diaspora Jews that were to be found in major cities throughout the far-flung Eurasian empire of the Romans.

J E R U S A L E M, where several of the chief witnesses to Jesus's life and teaching had taken up residence—men like the repentant Peter and Jesus's brother James—became the obvious hub for broadcasting the Good News. And it was at the door of Peter's humble house in Jerusalem that a man knocked one evening about seven years after the tumultuous events of Jesus's last days. He was a smallish, balding man in his late thirties, as intense, lean, and quick as the curly-haired Peter was tender, bearlike, and lumbering. Though both men were of an age, Peter appeared the older because his hair and beard had gone white as the result of a sudden shock; and with his hulking fisherman's frame, his wide shoulders, and pronounced upper-body musculature, he towered over the man at the door, whose neat figure, tight muscles, and corded forearms gave him the appearance of a gymnast or even a long-distance runner. Peter had good reason to be suspicious of the fellow before him, whose Jewish name was Saul, though he was also called by his Roman name, Paul.

Saul-Paul was a Pharisee, one of the party of rabbis who had gradually grown suspicious of Jesus and set themselves against his teaching on the Law and who were now beginning to speak of him not as the promised Messiah but as an unworthy renegade from authentic Judaism. Some of their number had gone from public opposition to Jesus's followers in the synagogues to active persecution, attempting to have the Messianists expelled from the synagogues, shunned by other Jews, and, when possible, arrested (and sometimes even executed) by local Jewish authorities. Some Pharisees seem to have tried to get the Messianists in trouble with the Romans, who were always on the lookout to eradicate any group that might be about to foment political instability.

Paul was known to be one of the persecutors and relentlessly effective. How far he went—whether he simply hounded the Messianists out of the synagogues or collaborated with the hated Romans—is not clear from the records of the New Testament, but we know from Paul's own words that he "persecuted God's Gathering [or Church]" and that he did not confine his efforts to Jerusalem but, in his zeal, pursued the new sect as far and wide as the limitations of ancient travel permitted. So the man was a constant worry to the leaders of the Messianic movement and had among them the reputation of a canny enemy whose sharp vigilance made him hard to outwit. Now the enemy himself stood before the Rock asking acceptance.

Word of unlikely occurrences had preceded Paul's knock at the door. This Pharisee, riding his horse hard toward Damascus in hot pursuit of his favorite prey, had been knocked from his mount by—what? By what the man himself had come to call an intervention of God. As he scrambled in the dust of the road, overcome by a blinding light, a Voice asked a question that the dismounted rider could not have found more unexpected or unwelcome: "Saul, Saul, why do you persecute me?"

Forever after, this would be for Saul the moment at which his life took a completely new direction: God cared about him in the same way he had cared about the great figures of Israel's past. Only a few men had heaven ever addressed by name— and always with their name spoken twice: "Abraham, Abraham"; "Moses, Moses." God himself was telling his child that his road was a mistaken one and giving him a new direction. The identity of the Voice was evident: it was the same Voice that had spoken to the patriarchs and prophets, but the meaning of its words would take the fallen rider many moons to ponder. In persecuting "God's Gathering," Saul-Paul had been persecuting Jesus, the discredited prophet, who had died so ignominiously. But if the Voice of God now spoke on behalf of this prophet—indeed, so identified with him that the Voice could say "me" of Jesus—then this Pharisee who had been so certain of the righteous godliness of his course must come to discover that the hated Messianists were, collectively and in some mysterious sense yet to be fathomed, the Body of Jesus and that the dead Jesus, now exalted by God, was somehow identifiable with God himself. From then on Paul would speak of his overthrow on the road to Damascus, the blinding light, and the questioning Voice as his encounter with Christ, his own belated "resurrection appearance." Jesus risen had come to him just as surely as he "showed himself to the disciples"—to Peter and the others—so that Paul, who had not known Jesus previously, ever after thought of himself as one "born out of time."

This dismounting on the Damascus road was just as disorienting to Paul as the empty tomb had once been to the little embalming party organized by Mary Magdalene. According to Luke, Paul, temporarily blinded, had to be led "by the hand" into Damascus, where he found himself unable to eat or drink for several days. His sight, as well as his appetite, returned after an encounter with a Damascene disciple of Jesus named Ananias, who, already aware that Paul was to be God's "chosen instrument," laid healing hands on the stunned man. In Luke's theatrical account of these events, Paul, now feeling course through him that infusion of courage characteristic of so many of these early "conversion" experiences, stands up and asks to be baptized.

Our two sources for Paul's story are his own words, as preserved for us in his surviving letters, and the evangelist Luke's second work, the Acts of the Apostles, which recounts the early years of the Jesus Movement and in which Paul figures as the central character. To the ear of most scholars, Paul, who is remarkably cut-and-dried about his extraordinary experiences, is much more trustworthy than the literary Luke, who, anxious to present the movement to his readers in the most favorable light, tends to smooth over all rough edges and, in highly colored presentations, to dramatize events that must originally have appeared more commonplace. But whatever the actual, physical details of Paul's Damascus experience, there can be no doubt that the man himself saw it as the turning point of his life, the moment in which he went from being a devout per-secutor of a movement that he thought a tremendous danger to Judaism to becoming the most arresting advocate of this movement in his day. Following what can only be described as his "meeting with Jesus," Paul spent the remainder of his life preaching that Jesus, crucified to death and now risen, was the long-awaited Messiah of the Jews and the fulfillment of all their hopes.

For Paul, it will become extremely important that this Gospel he will come to preach far and wide is "no human message, for I did not take it from any man, nor was it taught me: rather, it was revealed to me by Jesus Christ himself!" *115* Given this stress, it is no surprise that Paul never makes men-tion of Ananias (who, unless he is Luke's literary invention, must have taught Paul *something*). In Paul's brief account of the period of his conversion in his letter to the Galatians, he will insist that the revelation he was given at Damascus is not in any sense secondhand, so much so that "I was in no hurry to con-fer with anyone, nor to run up to Jerusalem to see those who were apostles before I was. No, I went off immediately to Arabia and later came back to Damascus."

Luke, who may have known nothing of this Arabian ad-venture, omits it altogether; and we can only wish that Paul had more to say on the subject. His "Arabia" would have been the kingdom of the Nabateans, whose fabulous capital was the desert city of Petra, carved from the pink rock of the Great Rift Valley and looking today in its uninhabited state like the unreal movie set it has become. What must it have been in Paul's day when it was still a bustling capital? But Paul, who will in his zeal visit many of the great cities of the ancient world, traversing its roads and sea-lanes and encountering many of its most exotic wonders, has no time for tourism. He is a man with a mission; and every ounce of energy will be directed toward his goal—the divine commission given him on the Damascus road—of spreading the Gospel as far as possible.

According to Luke, Paul had to quit Damascus for good because his uncompromising preaching in the synagogues there "threw the Jewish community . . . into confusion" and even invited their murderous attention, which Paul escaped in the knick of time by being lowered from the city wall in a basket by his new Messianist friends in the dead of night. If it doesn't take much imagination to see the confusion of the Jewish community, who had so recently known the preacher as the implacable foe of the Jesus Movement, it takes only imagination to appreciate the Scheherazade-like detail of Luke's basket. Whatever the real reason for Paul's exit, we can more securely trust Luke's information that Paul's appearance in Jerusalem (where he went next) alarmed "the disciples," who "were all afraid of him" and that it took them some time to cool down and find him credible. According to Paul himself, by the time he arrived in Jerusalem, three years had elapsed since his conversion, and the express purpose of his visit was "to meet the Rock," with whom he "stayed fifteen days."

If readers can only be curious about where Paul went in "Arabia" and what he did there (probably a novice's unsuccessful attempt at preaching), what would we not give to know something of the conversations that passed between the relentless former Pharisee and his host, the formerly faithless fisherman, during Paul's two-week sojourn? The Voice that spoke to Paul from heaven (or from within himself) had such personal impact that it reoriented his whole course, but it could hardly have filled in for him all the events of Jesus's earthly life. For this, he had no doubt the stories already circulating in the communities of Jesus's disciples, stories that would eventually attain written form in the four gospels. But who could give Paul a sense of Jesus—what he looked like, how he sounded, how he moved, what he meant—more palpable than Peter? Surely, a fortnight with this principal friend of Jesus was worth a lifetime of gathering stories from here and there. So, though we have no record of their conversations, we can take it for granted that they did not waste their time on pleasantries and that at the end of those two weeks the insatiable Paul had as much information on his new Lord as one man could impart to another.

But Paul also had something of importance to impart to Peter, who though faithful to Jesus (after his one night of betrayal) had a naturally muddled mind. Peter, the bighearted friend, was not the sort of fellow you would wish to rely on for drafting a difficult document, whether of science, law, or theology. In the gospel stories, he is full of generous intentions and can-do attitudes, but woefully short on self-knowledge, analysis, and follow-through. Paul, angular, tense, and hardly anyone's ideal buddy, possessed nevertheless the very qualities that Peter lacked.

Paul was born in Tarsus, by his own description "no mean city" but rather the cosmopolitan capital of the Roman province of Cilicia, a great crossroads where Asian and European, Jew and Greek met in often fruitful intercourse. He had received two very different kinds of education. Within his family circle, which was Pharisaic and devoted to the Mosaic Law, he had learned biblical Hebrew in order to study the sacred scrolls. As a young man (or perhaps even earlier as an adolescent), he was sent by his pious father to study in Jerusalem with the most learned rabbis. According to Luke, Paul's teacher was Gamaliel himself, remembered in subsequent Jewish literature as the most renowned rabbi of his time. It is obvious from Paul's self-descriptions in his surviving correspondence that he gloried in his lineage: "An Israelite am I, of Abraham's seed, of Benjamin's branch"—the same tribe to which Saul, Israel's first king, belonged. If he boasts of his descent, even more does he glory in his commitment to Judaism: "If anyone has cause to be confident in his body, I have more: circumcised on the eighth day; a member of the people of Israel; . . . a Jew of Jews; as regards the Law, a Pharisee; . . . as regards righteousness before the Law, blameless." Elsewhere, he makes the claim that "I, in Judaism, outstripped most of my peers because of my zeal for the traditions of my fathers."

This athletic metaphor—in which the young man's advance in his understanding of Judaism is remembered as his distinguishing himself in a race—betrays something of Saul-Paul's other world: besides being a yeshiva boy, he was also a *pais gymnasiou,* a gymnasium boy, a prep school kid. His father wished him not only to know thoroughly the world of his pious ancestors but to be able to negotiate the "modern" world that he would have to live in. Thus did he need to attain mastery over the exceedingly un-Jewish environment of Greek athletic competitions and Greek education. The *agon*— the Greek athletic contest—is one of the few reliable metaphors in the repertoire of this sparingly metaphorical author. (Not surprisingly, the strongly physical image of the living human body—its parts and unitive movement—underlies many of Paul's other essays into metaphor.) Paul's Greek flows from his pen with a facility far beyond that of Mark (or even

Matthew) and is obviously shaped by his knowledge of the models of classical rhetoric, disputation, and diatribe; and there is more than a hint that he was widely read in Greek literature and had read at least some Greek philosophy.

In their different ways, both Jewish and Greek intellectual traditions laid great stress on breaking things down into their component parts for the sake of minute analysis—what contemporary literary critics might call "deconstruction." For the Jews the objects of analysis were halakha and haggada, the laws and stories inscribed in their holy books; for the Greeks the objects to be parsed were ideas about the nature of the universe. But both traditions prized serious reflection, careful analysis, and the ultimate fruit of these mental processes—understanding. Paul, the inheritor of both traditions, was able to bring to the somewhat amorphous enterprise of the Jesus Movement intellectual tools beyond the scope of its relatively uneducated devotees, such as women and fishermen (even if spiked with the sophistication of the occasional tax collector).

Over the last century much has been made of Paul as the inventor of Christianity, the man who took the unfocused, anti-intellectual messianism of the bubble-headed followers of Jesus and constructed it into an effective theological weapon, which Christians would eventually use to beat not only the Jews but the whole of the ancient world. This is only partly true. Paul did not *invent* the faith of the early Church in the continuing reality and presence of Jesus. If Paul became in his own lifetime the most articulate spokesman for this faith, he was never much more than an articulator who knew how to zero in on the most essential elements of his argument and could thread his discourse with the welcome colors of his own very personal experience. If Paul had never left the Pharisaical school, the Jesus Movement that became Christianity would have survived and probably even prospered (if with a more limited scope), but it would have been a Christianity that lacked (at least for some time) Paul's intellectual edge as well as his emotional edginess.

For beyond his education, by which he intertwined antiquity's most rigorous intellectual traditions, we cannot neglect to consider the man's natural temper: neither flatterer nor diplomat, neither charmer nor salesman, Paul was not the sort of man you would immediately associate with the effort to pitch a new idea, let alone a whole new worldview and way of life. Devoid of small talk, anecdotes, and the sort of chatter that puts people at their ease, Paul was an either/or kind of guy, an absolutist for whom the matter under discussion would always be All or Nothing. An intellectual overachiever, pushed repeatedly to success by a keenly competitive father, Paul had no time for ordinary social niceties and neither gave nor expected to receive normal social comforts. One can imagine him sitting uncomfortably in some conventional parlor, staring penetratingly at his hostess while trying to find some Meaning in her inquiry as to whether he took one lump or two.

But the combination of intellectual and emotional relentlessness that constituted Paul's personality made this unlikely man the perfect vehicle for this moment in the development of the Jesus Movement. Had he appeared a little earlier—say, soon after the "raising" of Jesus and the descent of the Spirit—his intellectual ardor would probably have been too much for an inchoate community of simply educated disciples who were just beginning to get their minds around these inexplicable events. Once they had got their bearings again, come to understand what had happened as a coherent story, and begun to give voice to their unique experiences, they were—whether they knew it or not—ready to hear from someone more intellectually incisive than they, someone who could give a more precise formulation to these experiences, someone who was part of them but also part of the larger world of which they had only limited knowledge. Had Paul arrived on the scene much later than he did (when the movement, settling down as an elaborated organization with defined structures, had become the Church it would become), his emotional edginess—his intolerance for muddleheadedness, his knowing when he was right and you were wrong, his essential abstraction from the details of ordinary life—would have made him a poor candidate to be an organization man; and he would soon have been isolated and eventually cast aside.

121

WHAT DID PAUL CONTRIBUTE substantively to the development of the Jesus Movement? Though—from Peter, Ananias, and who knows how many oral "memoirists"—he must have known thoroughly the major events of Jesus's life (and many of its minor anecdotes as well), Paul, unlike the four evangelists (who finished their work a decade or more after his time), never set himself the task of collecting and anthologizing the oral tradition. These stories, which when Paul began to write (about the year 50) probably seemed so fresh that no one had yet thought to write them down, were the meat and drink of the Jesus Movement: they were talked about endlessly and retold in "improved" versions by travelers from other communities; they provided illustrations for sermons in Jesus-centered synagogues, where the incidents and prophecies of the Jewish scriptures were read as foreshadow-

ings of the life of the Messiah; they were extolled and summa-
rized in new hymns devised by the more creative members of
the Messianic assemblies. And the central events of the Jesus
"reality"—his death and resurrection, his sending of the Spirit,
his hoped-for coming again—were memorialized in ritual
baptisms and in "the breaking of the bread," the haggadic reenactment of the Last Supper which took place not in the synagogue but in some private home where the disciples
consumed bread and wine as Christ's body and blood, according to his own instructions.*

Paul, building on all this information (and doubtless some
misinformation), already in general circulation among the
small Jesus-centered communities of the Roman empire, sets
himself the task of being not another storyteller but a theolo-
gian—that is, someone who can articulate clearly the intellectual affirmations that lie behind the stories. Of course, some
theologizing was already under way. Peter and the others had
constructed a simple thought-structure, which came to be
called the *kerygma* (or "proclamation") and which served as a kind of intellectual container for the stories. But it was primitive and—from the vantage point
of the complicated Jewish and Greek intellectual systems—underdeveloped:

The man Jesus's teaching and all the acts of his life (such as his healing miracles) had been given definitive approval by God himself, who has raised this Jesus from the dead. Jesus is, therefore, not only the promised Messiah of the Jews but has shown forth in the words and deeds of his life what God ex-

---

❉ We should not overlook how closely these most basic of Christian rituals adhere to Jewish models. Proselyte baptism was practiced within orthodox (i.e., non-Christian) Judaism as early as the first century A.D., but rites of immersion for the sake of purification from sin are at least as old as the Book of Leviticus (see 15, 16:4, 24). That the rite of the Eucharist is a form of the Seder cannot be doubted, which of course makes the Missal a form of the Passover Haggada.

pects of each human being. He is the model whom we all must imitate. The proof that Jesus is risen is the living testimony of eyewitnesses, whose credibility may be established by meeting and questioning them, people such as Mary Magdalene ("Come over and say hello to these people, Mary; they're interested in hearing what you saw"), Peter and the Twelve, and now—as one "born out of [the proper sequence of] time"—Paul.

Paul had not been called mildly from his nets by Jesus, as had Peter, Andrew, James, and John. He had not been invited to leave his counting table, as had Matthew. He had not been gently healed from psychological torments, as had Mary Magdalene. He had been knocked off his horse and blinded, forced to stop and reconsider—everything. His theology would be as startling and overwhelming as his conversion experience.

123

"Saul, Saul, why do you persecute me?" said the Voice, and we can believe that these words were burned into the rider's memory for the rest of his life, capable of rising to awful consciousness and shocking him anew when he least expected it. But these words must also have presented him with a conundrum: in what sense is Jesus to be identified with his followers? Paul the Pharisee already possessed rich models of identification on which he could draw. All Jews were "the children of Israel," Abraham's grandson, who had engendered twelve sons, who in their turn had engendered the Twelve Tribes. But Jews were also, collectively, "Israel," as if they were part of the patriarch Israel's body (which, in a sense, they were). All Jewish males, by virtue of their circumcision, were no longer merely single individuals but a kind of organic collectivity: they *were* the Circumcision. But if Jesus had come as Messiah, God's Promised One, had he not completed Israel by bringing all the longings of the Jewish people to fulfillment? Were not the followers of Jesus, in effect, Israel renewed, Israel fulfilled, the Promise completed?

Beyond Jewish confessional considerations, were not all human beings descended from the original man, the *adam,* the mud-man of Genesis, raised by God from among unthinking creation to a new, a godlike level? And did not all descend, because of his disobedience, to the bent and broken world beyond the gates of Paradise, the world of disease, death, and disharmony, the world that we all inhabit? Did not Jesus, by his resurrection, by this startling proof of life beyond death, set this process of decay going in the opposite direction? Did he not, in effect, by his resurrection (and the promise of ours) reinstitute the Creation? Is he not, therefore, the New Adam, and are we not the New Creation?

Slowly, asking himself such questions as these, plumbing all his rabbinic lore and learning, bringing to bear the precision instruments of Greek ratiocination, concentrating all his considerable energies on these thorny matters, does Paul begin to give shape to his theology. He does not do this as one might today while strolling through a university garden. He does it while walking great distances as fast as he can under a merciless sun, while being tossed about the Aegean or the Mediterranean in sickeningly unreliable vessels, while (once more) setting up his portable canvas- and leather-mending shop* in the mobbed bazaar of a strange city. For Paul was only an accidental

124

✠ Luke gives Paul's profession as "tentmaker," i.e., one who had skill in using special implements for making and mending tents, awnings, pavilions, and similar protections against sun and weather that were erected throughout Mediterranean lands at open-air markets, fairs, regional athletic competitions, etc. Since the materials were supplied by the customer, Paul needed only the tools of his trade (sickle, awl, needles, and waxed thread) to open shop in any population center. Paul was writer. His letters, collected in the New Testament, are almost all to the many Jesus communities that he established in his extensive travels, encouraging, admonishing, instructing them further. Before all else Paul was a relentless man with a relentless mission: to preach the Gospel—"in season and out"—to anyone who would listen, and to many who would not. Though others (probably many others) in this early period traveled to bring the Gospel to distant cities, it is Paul who, because of the sheer magnitude of his activities, is remembered as the world's first missionary.

For his pains, he is arrested at Macedonian Philippi, Alexander's old capital, for daring to proselytize Roman citizens,* stripped, and publicly flogged. In the Athens marketplace, where he had hoped to cut a figure as a wise philosopher, they make fun of him and hoot him down; others merely yawn. At Corinth, he is hauled before the Roman proconsul by Jews determined to get him in trouble (though the proconsul, unwilling to be drawn into a purely sectarian matter, dismisses the tiresome charges as "quibbles about words and names"). At Ephesus he is imprisoned for a time and, according to his own words, made to "fight wild

certainly not brought up to this trade as Jesus was to carpentry. Pharisees, who were members of the leisured class, shared with all the wellborn of the ancient world an abhorrence of manual labor. But we may presume that after his conversion Paul could no longer avail himself of the customary Pharisaical subventions and may even have been disinherited. By taking up a craft that was welcome everywhere, Paul was also less dependent on handouts from the communities he established.

125

❈ Paul might have been all right had he stuck to proselytizing Jews (since there was no law against Jews proselytizing one another), but the Roman citizens who brought charges were actually upset about something else: "It happened," says Luke, who seems to have accompanied Paul on this trip, "that as we were going to prayer [at the Jewish prayer service where Paul would preach], we were met by a slave girl who had a Python-spirit [i.e., was an oracle] and made a lot of money for her masters by fortune-telling. This girl started following Paul and the rest of us shouting: 'These men are the servants of the Most High God! They have come to tell you how to be saved!' She did this day after animals." His preaching there becomes so successful that it sets off a riot among the silversmiths, who made little statues of the many-breasted goddess Diana of Ephesus for the throngs of pilgrims (flocking to the shrine of the Great Mother at Ephesus) and who were afraid that Paul's preaching would depress their trade. The scene, as depicted for us by Luke, is like a Shakespearean crowd scene (a mass of confusion, with the silversmiths shouting over and over "Great is Diana of the Ephesians!"), but the upshot is that Paul has to depart the city in haste. Before his life is over Paul will endure additional imprisonments (one lasting two years at Caesarea Maritima because of his refusal to bribe the procurator), house arrest, shipwreck, and who knows how many physical illnesses brought on by the harshness of his travels. In his own words to his converts at Corinth: "Five times have I had thirty-nine lashes from Jews, three times been beaten with rods, once stoned, three times shipwrecked, adrift on the open sea for a night and a day; always traveling on, in danger from rivers, in danger from brigands, in danger from my own people, in danger from the gentiles, in danger in the towns, in danger in open country, in danger at sea, in danger from false brothers. I have worked unstintingly, gone many nights without sleep, gone hungry and thirsty, often without anything to eat or drink; I have been cold and naked. And, besides all this, I face day in, day out, my anxiety for all the churches. Who among you feels any weakness that I do not feel? Who among you stumbles, and I do not burn inwardly?"

This driven man (driven by his zeal for the Gospel), this caring man (attempting to sympathize with all his

126

day till Paul, exasperated, turned and said to the spirit [who possessed the girl]: 'I order you in the name of Jesus Christ to come out of her.' The spirit left her then and there. When her masters saw that there was no hope of making more money out of her, they seized Paul and Silas [another of Paul's companions] and dragged them into the marketplace before the authorities" (Acts 16:16–18).

charges, perhaps even with everyone he met), is remembered today not so much for the effectiveness of his preaching, the warmth of his sympathy, or even the extent of his labors as for the words he left behind in his surviving letters, which are still read each Sunday in churches throughout the world—all those churches for which he felt such anxiety. Dimly, we can see him entering a new marketplace for the first time, setting up his modest booth, engaging in conversation whomever he can— potential customers, their servants, his fellow merchants. We can see him taking a room in the tiny house of some merchant from a neighboring booth, gradually gathering a small community around him, instructing them in the Gospel and watching it take root among them. Then far into the night, sometimes with the help of a friendly scribe, sometimes alone, he scratches his letters to the church-communities he has had to leave behind, trying to find the right words, the words that will catch fire in their hearts and enable them to keep going. If nothing else, the overwhelming loneliness of this man—always beginning again, always "a stranger in a strange land," always opening and closing his letters by naming distant friends, always recalling his ties of affection to those he has had to leave behind—should impress us.

OVERLEAF: THE ROMAN EMPIRE
IN THE AGE OF AUGUSTUS

Though the Romans, forced to stop at the borders of Parthia, could not hold as much of Asia as Alexander did, they extended their empire west through North Africa and southern and central Europe, finally conquering as far west as southern Britain in A.D. 60, forty-six years after the death of Augustus. Their empire lasted much longer than Alexander's, in part because it was geographically fortunate: the Mediterranean served as its unifying medium of trade, communication, and control.

GERMANIA

LUGDUNENSIS BELGICA

GAUL

RAETIA NORICUM PANNONIA

AQUITANIA ILLYRICUM

Ravenna DALMATIA

NARBONENSIS

TARRACONENSIS

CORSICA — Rome ITALIA

LUSITANIA

SARDINIA

BAETICA

SICILY

MAURETANIA Carthage
NUMIDIA MALTA
AFRICA

Mediterranean

▭ The Roman Empire
⊙ Principal Places of Paul's Apostolate

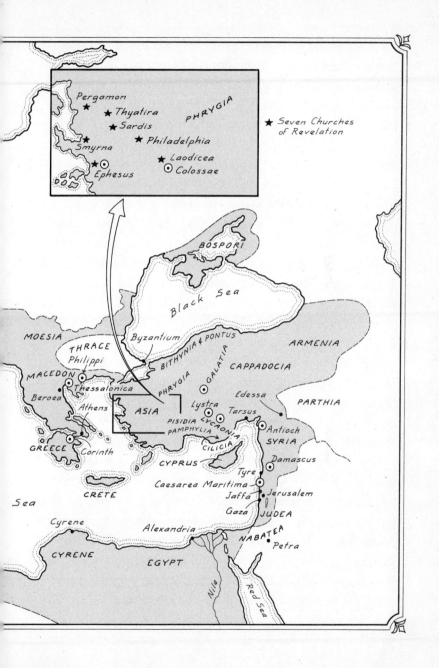

Seven Churches
of Revelation

★ Seven Churches of Revelation

Pergamon
★ Thyatira
★ Sardis
★ Philadelphia
Smyrna
⊙ Ephesus
★ Laodicea
⊙ Colossae
PHRYGIA

BOSPORI

Black Sea

MOESIA
THRACE
Philippi
MACEDON
Thessalonica
Beroea
Athens
GREECE
Corinth
CRETE

Byzantium

BITHYNIA & PONTUS
ARMENIA
PHRYGIA
⊙ GALATIA
CAPPADOCIA
ASIA
Lystra
PISIDIA
LYCAONIA
Tarsus
PAMPHYLIA
CILICIA
Edessa
PARTHIA
Antioch
SYRIA
Damascus

CYPRUS
Tyre
Caesarea Maritima
Jaffa
Jerusalem
Gaza
JUDEA

Sea

Cyrene
Alexandria
NABATEA
Petra
CYRENE
EGYPT
Nile
Red Sea

If the image of Paul bent over his page, filling it with inky letters, illuminated by a flickering oil lamp, is a judgment on anyone who has ever claimed to have "no time to write," it is also a reminder of how few of us would wish to be remembered for our letters, those peculiar documents written for particular occasions, gaining only in obscurity through the passage of time. Given such circumstances, the theology that shines forth from Paul's letters is amazing for its clarity, profundity, and even (with a few lapses) consistency of development.

Paul begins where all the early believers in Jesus begin—with Jesus crucified and risen. This Jesus, who lived an ordinary human life, is the medium through which God has fulfilled his promises to Israel. This God, who has done these things, is the same God he has always been—the Creator of all that is (and, therefore, not just Israel's God but everyone's) and the Lord of history (which, in his mysterious wisdom and despite all appearances to the contrary, he is bringing to its proper conclusion). At every turn, he has entered history and transformed human possibilities: by creating the universe, by raising mankind, by choosing Abraham, by liberating Israel from Egyptian slavery, by sending the prophets. But in Jesus's death-and-resurrection (the one cannot be separated from the other, since there is no way to have a resurrection without a death), we see God's definitive intervention on mankind's behalf—the great anti-tragedy. In all the tragic dramas of antiquity, whether lived or staged, we detect the same pattern: the hero, be he Alexander or Oedipus, reaches his pinnacle only to be cut down. Only in the drama of Jesus does the opposite pattern hold: the hero is cut down only to be raised up.

This is literally marvelous and, from the viewpoint of all previous human experience, completely unexpected. The terrifying trauma of those first witnesses to the resurrection has been transmuted, upon reflection, into the very surprise we were all waiting for without knowing it or being able to articulate it. For "in Christ," writes Paul to the Corinthians, "God was reconciling the world to himself, holding no one's faults against them, but entrusting to us the message of reconciliation." What are the particulars of this reconciliation? "In the fullness of time," writes Paul to the Galatians, "God sent his son, born of a woman, born a subject of the Law, to redeem the subjects of the Law, so that we could receive adoption as his children. As you are his children, God has sent into our hearts the Spirit of his son crying, *'Abba!'* (that is, the Father).* So you are no longer a slave but God's child; and as his child his heir—and this by God's own act."

Jesus, who referred to himself by the (at least retrospectively) ironic title "the Son of Man," has been proved to be also "the Son of God" by virtue of his resurrection. But how do we—all the rest of the sons and daughters of Man—get to tag along in his train as the Sons and Daughters of God? How does Jesus, born of woman, redeem us (that is, buy us back from slavery), so that we can "receive adoption" as God's children? To work this out, we have to take humanity and human flesh as seriously as Paul (and all the Jews) did. The human race—"all flesh," as it is called repeatedly in the sacred scriptures of the Jews—is a unity. Just as all Adam's descendants were subject to the blight of his disobedience, the advent of a perfectly obedient man—

* This language of "Father" and "children" creates translation difficulties. *Abba* is Hebrew/Aramaic not for "Father" but for a more familiar term of endearment, such as "Papa" or "Daddy." It was the word Jesus used when addressing God in prayer. Paul then calls Jesus God's "son" and us God's "sons" by adoption. The wordplay is lessened by translating our status as "his children," but it is preferable to "his sons," which in English refers only to males. The Greek original—*huioi*—can refer to issue of both sexes, and there is no question that Paul means to include females.

"obedient unto death, to death upon a cross"—raised "all flesh" with him. Adam—the name means "earthman," thus signaling that he is symbolic of mankind—could not content himself with human status but wished to be "a god," and so brought on himself and all his descendants the fall from grace and "the heartache, and the thousand natural shocks that flesh is heir to." Jesus, by accepting his creatureliness and all the severest limitations of fallen human status, including suffering and death, has reversed that fall. "As it was because of one man that death [and all the lesser forms of disaster, decay, and disharmony] came," wrote Paul to his Corinthians, "so because of one man has come the resurrection of the dead. Just as all die in Adam, so in Christ shall all be revived."

Like all the early believers in Jesus, Paul knew better than to imagine that Jesus's resurrection had brought about the end of suffering. They were living at the *beginning* of the end-time that Jesus's victory had initiated, but of the actual end they "knew not the day nor the hour." Though they would certainly be surprised to be informed that two thousand years would pass without a sign of Jesus's return, they were not crackpot millenarians who thought they could calculate exactly what would happen next and when it would happen. The majority of early converts came from the same stratum of society that Jesus had come from: they were working-class artisans and had neither the leisure nor the inclination to imagine themselves exempt from any of the ills "that flesh is heir to." They would be "in the world but not of it": they would continue to occupy whatever position was their lot, cheerfully accepting its sufferings, but they would not allow themselves to be infected by the cynical, self-serving values of the world they found themselves inhabiting.

They would live in this world and share its sufferings, as Jesus had done. These sufferings, however, were not merely to be endured but welcomed as if they were each individual's share in the sufferings of Jesus, in whose sufferings, because he is the new Adam, we all have a share. "All of us," writes Paul in his final epistolary instruction, "when we were baptized into Christ Jesus, were baptized into his death." In baptism, in our immersion, we descend, as Jesus did, to the depths of human misery. But our trajectory, like his, is opposite to the movement of classical tragedy. For we, like Christ, arise from the depths of our baptism to new life: "Thus, by our baptism into his death we were buried with him, so that just as Christ was raised from the dead by the glory of the Father, we too should begin to live a new life. For if we have been joined to him by dying a death like his, we shall surely be joined to him in his resurrection; realizing that our old self was crucified with him, so that the self that belonged to sin might be destroyed and we should be freed from the slavery of sin. . . . If we died with Christ, then it is our belief that we shall live with him, too. We know that Christ has been raised from the dead and will never die again. Death no longer has dominion over him. For by dying, he is dead to sin once and for all, and now the life that he lives is Life-with-God. In the same way, you must see yourselves as being dead to sin but alive to God in Christ Jesus."

133

Baptism, as presented by Paul, has none of the magic power of automatic salvation that it would come to have for medieval and many modern Christians. It does not *effect* the inner transformation that only God's grace and individual human response can effect. Baptism is an outward symbolic ritual that dramatizes the inner transformation—the conversion or turnabout that Paul experienced on the road to Damascus, the *metanoia* or opening of the heart that Jesus asked for. For each human being, this "death" comes in a different guise. The sin that I must die to if I am to live God's life will be quite different from the sin that you must die to.

It is interesting to consider how, even in my truncated quotation about baptism's symbolic death (taken from Paul's letter to the Jesus community in Rome, a community he did not found), Paul circles around his own thought, repeating himself with variations, straining to get his meaning across. This is because he is trying to get his audience to go deeper. He is elaborating on the primitive *kerygma*—the simple sentences that constituted the creed of the early Jesus Movement—and he is unsure exactly how to go about it, unsure how his words will be received and whether his intended audience, whom at this point he has never even met, will comprehend or misconstrue them. He is, in short, saying something *new,* albeit based on declarations that all Messianists would have understood; and when a writer has something new to say, he must always be anxious about its reception. Here, as in so much of Paul, we are watching original theology in the making.

The "death to sin" that Paul speaks of is basically a relinquishing of power; it is to live a life that is the opposite of the lives of the Alexanders and the Caesars and all the "gods." Now, you may say, most of his hearers had little chance of imitating such exalted and august models. But Paul makes clear that the power plays of the Great Ones are imitated over and over again in the lives of little ones—through acts of petty cruelty. But those who have "died with Christ," who have allowed themselves—at least vicariously—to experience all the depth of human suffering, can never stoop to gaining advantage over another, even if the other is clearly in the wrong. "Sisters and brothers," Paul admonishes the Galatians, "even if someone is caught red-handed, you who have received the Spirit should restore such a one with all gentleness—and watch out that you don't end up in the same position yourself! Carry one another's burdens: this is the way to fulfill the 'Law' of Christ."

Just a little before this he had told the Galatians not to go "snapping at one another and tearing one another to pieces" (which some of them must have been doing). Even though "you were called to be free, do not use your freedom as an opportunity for self-indulgence, but be servants to one another in love, since the whole Law [of Moses] is summed up in a single commandment: *Love your neighbor as yourself.*" In Matthew's Gospel, Jesus, questioned by a Pharisee who wants to expose him, is asked: "Rabbi, which is the greatest commandment of the Law?" Jesus answers: *"'Love the Lord your God with all your heart and with all your soul* and with all your mind.' This is the first and greatest commandment. And the second is like it: 'Love your neighbor as yourself.'"* Paul appears to be alluding to this probably well-known Jesus anecdote in his admonition to the Galatians.* But he omits love of God! So, within a few decades, love of neighbor, now tagged as the "'Law' of Christ," became—within Pauline circles and no doubt far beyond—the ultimate and only guide for a believer's conduct.

Paul's repeated emphasis on free-

135

✡ A summary of the Mosaic Law similar to Jesus's is found in the Mishnah (the early rabbinic law code), which may have been circulating as early as Jesus's day and on which he may have based his teaching. Conversely, Jesus's teaching may have influenced the standard rabbinic formula. Note that Jesus quotes freely from the texts of the Jewish scriptures. *"Love the Lord your God . . ."* is the Sh'ma, Israel's holiest prayer, found in Deuteronomy 6:5. *"Love your neighbor . . ."* is Leviticus 19:18. Both quotations are from the Torah, and therefore especially sacred. But Jesus quotes the first freely (the original has not "mind" but "strength") and expands the meaning of the second (in Leviticus "neighbor" means fellow Israelite; in the gospels it means whoever falls across one's path, i.e., every human being). Jesus, as was pointed out in Chapter Two, felt so at home in his religious tradition that he could adapt its texts with a certain freedom—in what is still typical rabbinical style. Paul probably felt he had a similar latitude in adapting the oral "texts" of the emerging Jesus tradition.

dom—that we who are freed by Jesus's cross-and-resurrection are no longer slaves but sons—gets him into repeated trouble. He receives grim reports of his converts among the Galatians, a Celtic tribe settled in Asia Minor between the Mediterranean and the Black Sea and who like all Celts were extremists—and hardly experts in subtle distinctions. So Paul finds he must advise them that their new freedom doesn't really include attending "orgies and such things," which are only occasions for relinquishing one's newfound freedom and putting oneself under the power of heedless passions. Under the heading of "such things" Paul includes a laundry list of favorite Galatian pastimes, "whoring . . . idolatry and witchcraft . . . faction-fighting and malice, drunkenness." Sounds like the Celts, all right.

But if the Galatians sometimes get things skewed, the Corinthians never seem to get things right. Corinth, vindictively destroyed by the Romans in the second century B.C. but reestablished by Julius Caesar as an exile for undesirables, had become a boomtown, full of retired army grunts, resettled freedmen, and assorted misfits and refugees from more conventional lifestyles, a place where anything might happen. To his Corinthian converts, who were always giving him hives, Paul sent his most eloquent exposition of the life of a true believer, hoping that with such a detailed description they would finally get things straight. This is Paul's "Hymn to Love," a Himalayan peak of world literature:

> And now will I show you the best Way of all.
> If I speak all the tongues of men and angels, but speak without love, I am no more than booming gong or clanging cymbal. If I can prophesy and fathom all mysteries and knowledge, and if I have so

much faith that I can move mountains, but have not love, I am nothing. If I give all my possessions to the poor*—and even my body that I may boast—but have not love, I gain nothing.

Love is patient. Love is kind. It does not envy or boast or think highly of itself. It is not rude. It does not insist on its own way. It does not take offense, nor does it keep any record of wrongs. Love does not enjoy evil-doing but enjoys the truth. It bears all things, trusts all things, hopes all things, endures all things.

Love never ends. Prophecy will cease. Tongues will be stilled. Knowledge will fail. For we know in part and we prophesy in part, but when the Fulfillment comes, the partial will be done away with. When I was a child, I spoke as a child, I saw as a child, I thought as a child. When I became a man, I put away the things of a child. Now we see as in the distorted reflection of a glass, but then we shall see face to face. Now I know in part, but then I shall know as fully as I am known.

For now, faith, hope, and love abide, these three. But the greatest of all is love.

Could the Corinthians miss the point of this large and humble essay, in which Paul, admitting what he does not know, sets out so clearly that the life of the believer is to be— at least ideally—a series of acts of generosity toward others without regard to self-indulgence or self-seeking? Well, the Corinthians were a difficult bunch. They required additional visits and several let-

⚔ This giving away of all one's possessions is an allusion to Jesus's hyperbolic advice, which is rejected by the rich young man we met in Chapter Two.

ters (not all of which have come down to us). Even in this letter you can read between the lines Paul's anguish at how many
things they have bollixed up.

They have allowed themselves to be split into factions, one
of which encouraged a more "spiritual" form of belief in Jesus,
a belief that did not take serious account of his humanity and
suffering—a point of view that Paul, always the Jew, always
aware of the physical dimension, cannot stomach. These
"spirit" people think themselves superior to the others and
possessors of special wisdom. They may be forerunners of the
Gnostics who in the second century will deny that Jesus was
ever anything so base as a human being; he was rather a spiritual apparition who *seemed* to die. To the smug superiority of
the "spirit" people and their rarefied "wisdom," Paul opposes
the "folly" of the bloody cross:

> Do you not see that God has shown human wis-
> dom to be foolishness? Since, in the wisdom of God,
> the world was unable to recognize God through its
> "wisdom," God was pleased, through the foolishness
> of our preaching of the Gospel, to save those who be-
> lieved. For . . . we are preaching a crucified Christ
> [not a "spiritual" one], to the Jews a stumbling block
> they cannot get past, to the gentiles foolishness. . . .
> [But] God's foolishness is wiser than human wisdom,
> and God's weakness [that is, Jesus crucified] is
> stronger than human strength. Consider, sisters and
> brothers, how you were called: not many of you are
> wise by human standards, not many influential, not
> many of noble birth. No, God chose the fools to
> shame the wise, God chose the weak to shame the

strong, he chose the common and contemptible—indeed those who count for nothing—to reduce to nothing all those who count for something,* so that no one may boast before him.

These proto-Gnostics, whose influence on the impressionable Corinthians Paul is trying to quash, had dreamed up any number of kooky variants on his teaching. Since they had entered the time of fulfillment—since they were now perfect—they could look down their noses at the imperfect: those without *gnosis,* or secret knowledge, those who could not speak "in tongues," those trapped in marriage (of all things). Since they were now by their baptism free, they could do as they liked. While exalting the single life, they seem to have had no problem with incest and other sexual irregularities—on the supposition that the perfect do perfectly and the free do freely. (E. P. Sanders, one of America's most cherished biblical scholars, once characterized the Corinthian attitude as: "Christ has come—whoopie, bend over!") Nor were they adverse to taking one another to court, not exactly the best way to build community. "Your self-satisfaction," writes Paul with considerable understatement, "is ill-founded."

As he tries to sort out each of the Corinthians' bizarre innovations by turn, nothing sends Paul further up the wall than their celebration of the Lord's Supper, the reenactment of Jesus's last night with his disciples before his crucifixion, during which he asked them to memorialize him in future by consuming bread and wine as his body and blood. Paul, writing to the Corinthians from Ephesus, has had word of their liturgical variations from "the house of Chloe," probably a refer-

139

* The language is very reminiscent of Mary's Magnificat.

ence to visitors to Corinth from an Ephesian house-church under Chloe's direction.* It seems that Chloe and her people attended a Eucharist led by a flamboyant male transvestite and a strange woman who sported a butch haircut (never worn by women in the ancient world, except for humiliated prisoners of war). Chloe and her people were not edified. To come from Ephesus to Corinth in those days would have been a little like coming from Victorian Boston to Dodge City, where you would certainly see any number of things you had never seen before. Paul, himself the straightest of straight arrows, tries not to be too exasperated, but his impatience seeps through his instruction. Look, he writes, "I congratulate you for remembering me so consistently and for maintaining the traditions exactly as I handed them on to you"—that is, for living in freedom—but, God help us, a man should dress like a man and a woman like a woman. He is actually only reminding them of the conventions of the time (and that anything too boldly theatrical can give unnecessary scandal to more conventional palates), but he ends with the true democrat's ultimate stance: "The decision is yours. Does it really seem right to you that a woman should pray to God with her hair exposed

* Within each of the larger communities of the Jesus Movement, such as at Ephesus and Rome, there were several subcommunities. Since there were too many Ephesian and Roman Messianists for a single meeting, each subcommunity would meet separately in some designated home to celebrate the Lord's Supper. These clandestine meetings are the beginning of the "house-churches" of the Jesus Movement. Some of these houses will at length, after the legalization of Christianity in the early fourth century, be turned into public churches. Each house-church looked after its own affairs as best it could, and responsibilities (such as taking care of the poor and making arrangements for the celebration of the Lord's Supper) rotated among those who could best take them up. The owner of the house—often a woman, such as Chloe—would have been the person who normally presided at the Lord's Supper (or Eucharist, i.e., Thanksgiving). This was as close as the Messianists came to having a power structure.

[something never seen in any temple or shrine of the ancient world]? Doesn't nature itself teach you that a man with the elaborate hairdo of a woman is impossible to take seriously, whereas a woman with long hair is a glorious instance [of God's Creation]? Wasn't it God himself who gave her this covering [for her nakedness, as Eve in Paradise]? But if anyone wants to get into an argument over all this, then I say that we don't— nor do any of God's churches—have such a thing as 'custom.'"

But thus, paradoxically, can customs begin; and this passage from Paul, misinterpreted by centuries of earnest literalists, is the source of the convention about hats in church (always for women, never for men). The earnest misinterpreters have managed, however, to slide over the most important—and only ageless—point that Paul has to make in this whole business about dress: "In the end—and in the Lord [that is, from the Christian point of view]—woman is not otherwise than man, and man is not otherwise than woman; and though woman came from man [since Eve came from Adam's side], so does every man come from a woman—and everything comes from God." More radical feminists may take exception to the sexual complementarity that may seem hinted at in these words. But equality, not complementarity, is Paul's subject: what he is doing here is taking the Genesis account of the Creation, which was the aboriginal Jewish *locus classicus* on the inequality of women, and turning it on its head by subtly reminding his readers that even the Messiah needed a mother. Most of us should be cheered that here, plunk in the middle of this old-hat stuff about what to wear, we have the only clarion affirmation of sexual equality in the whole of the Bible— and the first one ever to be made in any of the many literatures of our planet.

If Paul insists (the first person in history to do so) on the essential equality of the sexes, he is downright rabid on the subject of economic equality. He is not so unrealistic as to expect that all members of the community should have the same income, but he will have no part in treating anyone *according to income.* "In the Lord"—that is, within the community of believers—everyone is to be treated equally. But the Corinthians have taken the *agape,* the "love-feast" that was held in the local house-church prior to the Eucharist, and turned it into a textbook demonstration of economic inequality. The *agape* was meant to serve as a Christian version of the Greek *symposion** (and its Roman equivalent, the *convivium*): a convivial common meal for sharing food and thoughts and strengthening the bonds of community. But the Corinthians, in their positive genius for getting things back-to-front, have made the house-church *agape* into an opera house of economic distinctions—from elegant box seats for the well-heeled to out-of-the-way railings for the standees. "I cannot congratulate you," says Paul between clenched teeth, "on the meetings you hold, which do more harm than good. . . . When you meet together, it is not the Lord's Supper that you eat, since each one of you brings his own supper first, and while one goes hungry, another is getting drunk. Don't you have homes of your own for this sort of thing? Or have you such contempt for God's church that you can parade shamelessly in front of those who have nothing? What do you expect me to say to you? 'Congratulations'? Not this time."

Despite his agitation, Paul, calming himself, attempts to make the Corinthians

* The *symposion* (or, in its English equivalent, symposium) was originally a wine-soaked banquet run on the assumption that much wine would elicit much truth from participants. See, for example, Plato, *The Symposium.*

see why their "Eucharist" is a mockery by recalling one of
Jesus's most sacred discourses, preserved with a hushed solemnity
equaled by few other aspects of the emerging Jesus tradition:

> For the tradition I received from the Lord and also
> handed on to you is that on the night he was be-
> trayed, the Lord Jesus took bread and, after he had
> given thanks, broke it and said, "This is my body,
> which is yours. Do this as my memorial." In the same
> way, he took the cup after supper, saying, "This cup is
> the New Covenant in my blood. Do this, whenever
> you drink it, as my memorial." So, whenever you eat
> this bread and drink this cup, you are proclaiming the
> Lord's death until he comes. Whoever, therefore, eats
> the bread or drinks the cup of the Lord unworthily
> will be answerable for the body and blood of the
> Lord. It is imperative that you examine your con-
> science before you eat the bread or drink the cup,
> because anyone who eats and drinks without recog-
> nizing the Body is eating and drinking his own con-
> demnation.

143

These are tough words, and who knows whether they sank
in. But Paul uses here a phrase that is not immediately explicable: what does it mean to *recognize the Body?* The elements of
the Eucharist—the bread and wine—are *somehow* Jesus's body
and blood; but the Corinthians already know this, and long before Paul gets to the inexplicable phrase he has made this
point. The Body of Christ, the Body that suffered, died, and
rose, is now the mysterious Eucharist—but it is also the
Church, the gathering of God's people. No one knew this bet-

ter than Paul, who had been given a privileged insight into this
metareality: "Saul, Saul, why do you persecute me?"—me
Jesus, me the Church. But it is one thing to have an insight,
another to express it. Over the course of his many epistolary
instructions Paul will attempt to communicate his insight
about "the Body" to his many and varied converts. He recog-
nizes the Body, and they must, too:

> For just as the human body is a unity with many
> parts—all the parts of the body, though many, still
> making up one body—so it is with Christ [that is, in
> the Christian reality]. We were all baptized into one
> body with one Spirit, Jews and Greeks, slaves and
> freedmen, and we were all given the same Spirit to
> drink.* And indeed the body is made up not of one
> member but of many. If the foot were to say, "I am not
> a hand, so I do not belong to the body," it does not be-
> long to the body any the less for that. Or if the ear
> were to say, "I am not an eye, so I do not belong to the
> body," that would not stop its belonging to the body.
> If the whole body were an eye, how would there be
> any hearing? If the whole body were hearing, how
> would there be any smelling?
>
> As it is, God has arranged all the
> separate parts into the body as he
> chose. If they were all the same part,
> how could it be a body? As it is, there
> are many parts but one body. The eye
> cannot say to the hand, "I don't need
> you," and nor can the head say to the
> feet, "I don't need you."

144

⊠ The Jews, more materi-
alistic (in their thought and
language, not in their lives)
than the Greeks, had no
ready equivalent of the
Greek "soul." If to eat the
bread is to eat the body of
Christ, to drink the wine is
to drink his blood and
therefore his Spirit—the
blood being seen as the life,
or spirit, of the body.

Rather, the very parts of the body that seem the most vulnerable are the indispensable ones, and the parts we think least dignified that we clothe with the greatest dignity; thus are our less presentable parts given greater presentability, which our presentable parts do not need. God has composed the body so that the greater dignity is given to the parts that lacked it, so that there may be no dissension within the body but each part be concerned equally for all the others. If one part is hurt, all the parts share the pain. And if one part is honored, every part shares the joy.

Now you are the Body of Christ, each of you with a part to play in the whole. And God has appointed in the Church first apostles, second prophets, third teachers, then miracle workers, then those with gifts of healing, those able to help others, administrators, those who speak in various tongues. Are all apostles? Are all prophets? Are all teachers? Do all work miracles? Do all have gifts of healing? Do all speak in tongues? Do all interpret? (By all means, set your mind on the higher gifts.)

In First Corinthians, the earlier of Paul's two surviving letters to the crazy Corinthian church, this passage on what has come to be called the "Mystical Body of Christ" is followed directly by the "Hymn to Love." In other words, those who recognize the Body—and therefore recognize that everyone they meet is part of Christ—are obliged above all else to charity, to the selfless love of everyone who falls across their path, for this alone follows as the necessary moral consequence of "recognizing the Body." Those who recognize this obligation fully are likely to be already a conscious part of the Church. But everyone, whether he knows it or not, whether she wishes it or not, is "of the Body." For whatever a human being's disposition, he "does not belong to the Body any the less for that." Individual believers in Jesus, gathered together in their weekly meeting, sharing the bread and wine of Christ, should be—consciously—his Body. But even the unconscious, even those who have never heard of Jesus, are part of the Body. The Jesus who suffered and died, now raised and exalted by the Father, has (as Jesus will say in John's Gospel) "draw[n] all people" to himself. He has, in Paul's vision, drawn all things *into* himself, which is why the inanimate realities of bread and wine can be his body and blood. But if all Creation is now identifiable with the glorified Body of Christ, how much more than inanimate matter are Jesus's sisters and brothers, the adopted children of the Father—the peak of Creation—to be identified with Christ. All humanity—"all flesh," in the ancient Jewish formulation—is subsumed into this cosmic Christ. For "the glory of the Lord will be revealed, and all flesh shall see it together: for the mouth of the Lord hath spoken it." This enigmatic prophecy, delivered so long ago to the exiles in Babylon by the Second Isaiah, has, like all the prophecies, come true.

Paul knew perfectly well that his striking analogy would invite scatological speculation ("Which part of the Body do you suppose Bibulus is?"). But he hoped that when the laughter subsided, his recipients would continue to ponder the reality that lies behind the words: that all humanity is caught up in a great cosmic drama in which each one, however humble or ridiculous, has a significant part to play—and that we cannot do without one another.

Paul's dramatis personae of the primitive Church is most

intriguing: apostles like Paul—the traveling envoys who are witnesses to the risen Christ—head the list, followed by somewhat lesser instructors, the prophets and teachers, who, like apostles, tended to be visiting rather than permanent figures in the life of the local church. These were all offices of inspiration, certainly not of administration. "Administrators" will rise considerably in the lists of the later Church, gradually assuming the office of ruler, an office unknown to the primitive Church. Here, however, they stand just one step ahead of "those who speak in tongues," the ecstatics, who could only have been another headache for Paul—which is why he tries to direct everyone's thoughts away from becoming one of them ("By all means, set your mind on the higher gifts"). Even an administrator would be a better choice.

147

But the cosmic Christ, whose glory knocked Paul from his horse on the road to Damascus, who sums up in himself the whole of the created universe, eventually leads Paul to thoughts that no one has ever had before—thoughts about the equality of all human beings before God. In this ancient world of masters and slaves, conquerors and conquered, a world that articulates at every turn, precisely and publicly, who's on top, who's on the bottom, Paul writes the unthinkable to his Galatians, who may just have been goofy enough to receive it: "There is no longer Jew or Greek, slave or free, *male and female,* for you are all one in Christ Jesus."

This list is meant to be suggestive, not exhaustive, and Paul repeats it elsewhere with variations. Had he been writing to the class-conscious and conspicuously consuming Corinthians, he would surely have included "rich or poor, well- or lowborn." He breaks the rhetorical parallelism of "Jew or Greek, slave or free" with *"male and female"* because he is alluding once more to the Genesis account of Creation—"Male and female created he them"—and directly contradicting the assumption of eons of interpreters that this sentence of the Torah announces not only *la différence* but the natural and necessary subordination of women to men. "In Christ Jesus"—in the ultimate cosmic reality—there can be no power relationships. The primitive Church was the world's first egalitarian society.

N O   O N E "in Christ" is permitted to lord it over anyone else. "There is one Body, one Spirit [animating this Body] . . . one Lord, one faith, one baptism, one God and Father of all, over all, through all, and in all," writes Paul (or, possibly, one of his companions) in the New Testament letter to the church at Ephesus. This great cosmic unity does not bind but frees the believer. "Christ set us free," writes Paul to the Galatians, "for the sake of freedom. Stand firm, then, and do not let yourselves be bound once more to slavery's yoke." The yoke is, of course, the yoke of sin, the *hamartia,* or tragic fault, that runs through all the sons and daughters of Adam and Eve. Like Moses leading the People out of Egyptian slavery, Christ the Redeemer has ransomed us all from the slavery of sin. We must go forward into freedom, not backward into chains.

In Paul's radical view, this freedom has to mean freedom from all human rules and conventions. If it was more sensible for a man to dress like a man and a woman like a woman, this was nothing more than a prudent social norm. It was of no consequence to the cosmic Christ: "We don't—nor do any of God's churches—have such a thing as 'custom.' " In nothing was Paul more radical than in separating accidentals from essentials. In part, this came from his experience with the semi-civilized gentile world where, as he saw for himself, it was all too easy for half-barbarians like the Galatians and nouveaux riches self-made men like the Corinthians—people who lacked a long and disciplined tradition capable of subtle religious distinctions—to get almost everything backward. The theology that underlay the story of Jesus, as we have sketched it, was complicated enough. The last thing Paul wanted was to add any unnecessary complications.

The overwhelming majority of Jesus's original followers—and all the witnesses to his resurrection—were Jews, as devout about their religion as Jesus had been. In their encounters with Paul's gentile "Jews," they often found themselves shocked at the new converts' blank ignorance of Jewish law and practice. How could these strange new people, admittedly believers in the risen Jesus, be admitted to the fold of Judaism? They were unclean and knew nothing of the need for ritual bathings and washings; they ate *anything;* they did not keep the Sabbath; their men were uncircumcised,* their sexual practices unspeakable. Most of those critical of Paul's methods of instruction had, of course, never tried to carry the Gospel beyond their own comfortable circles in Jerusalem and Antioch, the old capital of Alexandrine Asia. They knew and cared nothing for his trials and labors through mountains and deserts and on the high seas, nor could they appreciate how the man's unceasing work had flowered so dazzlingly in such places as Philippi and

149

✠ Jews could react just as negatively to the uncircumcised as Greeks and Romans to the circumcised. As late as 1987, Philip Roth would write to Mary McCarthy, "I am still hypnotized by uncircumcised men when I see them at my swimming pool locker room. The damn thing never goes unregistered. Most Jewish men I know have similar reactions, and when . . . I asked several of my equally secular Jewish male friends if they could have an uncircumcised son, . . . they all said no, sometimes without having to think about it and sometimes after the nice long pause that any rationalist takes before opting for the irrational."

Thessalonica—"the churches of Macedon," Paul's favorites—
"and how, in the course of continual ordeals and hardships,
their unfailing joy and their intense poverty have welled up in
such an overflow of generosity . . . beyond all their resources."

Delegations of Judaizers began to follow in Paul's footsteps,
visiting the gentile churches he had established and telling
them that, unless they learned and implemented all the laws of
the Jews, they would be lost. If they were not "justified" according to the Law, they would be omitted in the great
roundup of the saved when Jesus returned. You can imagine
how puzzled this would have left the Galatians, how non-
plussed would have been the worldly but infantile Corinthians,
how confused the devout and generous Macedonians. It left
Paul boiling with anger. How dare these busybodies interfere
with his apostolate!

To an Orthodox Jew of a later period it would be clear that
the observant Jews were right: one cannot be a Jew if one does
not keep the laws of Judaism, as laid out in the Torah and interpreted in rabbinical commentaries to our own day. To a
Christian of a later day it would be clear that what the observant Jews of Jerusalem and Antioch were trying to impose on
the Greek converts—halakha—made no sense, for this whole
system of "observance" lies outside authentic Christianity. In
Paul's day the issue was not nearly so clear to anyone. The word
church was only gradually beginning to take on the meaning it
has for Christians today, and no one had even thought of the
word *Christianity* yet. Everyone—from emperors to rabbis—
thought of the insignificant Jesus Movement, if they thought
of it at all, as a variant form of Judaism. The Judaisms of the
first century were myriad, a spectrum that ran from the completely apocalyptic obsessions of the Essenes and the strict ob-

servance of the Pharisees to the laxity of the Sadducees and the strictly political obsessions of the Zealots; and there was, in any case, nothing new about Messianism among the Jews, who had seen any number of announced "messiahs" come and go (and would continue to experience periodic waves of messianism right into our own time). The movements that would become normative Judaism and Christianity were, in this very period, in the process of being born. If these two children of ancient Judaism would soon enough come to view each other as implacable enemies, that time still lay in the future. And it remains for us—with the many advantages of modern scholarship and hindsight—to recognize the ineradicable bloodlines of these brothers, who have lost track of their relationship.

151

The issue of whether or not to impose the Law on gentile converts became the first great theological crisis for the fledgling Church, and it took many years to settle. The issue first came to a head at a meeting of apostles and elders in Jerusalem—sometimes referred to rather too grandly as the "First Council of Jerusalem"—at which, at least according to the consensus-favoring Luke's account, Paul's approach basically carried the day. But according to the less irenic Paul, Peter, who appears to have been moderator of the meeting, was a shilly-shallier. And even though Luke presents Peter as having had a vision in which God told him that all food is "clean" (and could, therefore, be eaten without sin), Paul tells us that when Peter visited Antioch, following the Jerusalem meeting which had decided in Paul's favor, Peter lacked the courage to stand up to the most insistent of the Judaizers:

> When Peter came to Antioch, I opposed him to his face, because he was clearly in the wrong. Before cer-

tain people from James [Jesus's brother and principal elder of the Jerusalem church] arrived, he used to eat with the gentiles; but as soon as these fellows arrived, he withdrew and kept himself apart out of fear of the faction of circumcisers. And the rest of the Jewish believers put on the same act he did, so that even [Paul's good friend] Barnabas was carried away by this hypocrisy! When I saw, though, that they were not being true to the Gospel, I said to Peter in front of everybody, "You, a Jew, live like a gentile and not like a Jew. So how is it that you compel the gentiles to live like Jews?"

This passage, penned in the heat of controversy, can easily make Paul look as if he is rejecting Judaism, but that would be to consider what is happening here through the lens of later categories, long after positions had calcified. Paul gloried in what he would have called his essential—and fulfilled—Judaism. Though he was as indulgent and patient with his absurd gentiles as his urgent temperament would allow, he never forgot whence he—and Jesus—sprang. In the most considered letter he ever wrote—to the church already established at Rome, not long before he made his first visit there—Paul, the great nonboaster, who "boasts only of [his] weaknesses," at last allows himself to boast a little of his background and to touch publicly on his abiding love for the People who gave him birth. By this time, it is becoming clear that that Judaism, as a whole, will never consider Jesus to be its fulfillment:

This truth I am speaking in Christ, without pretense, as my conscience confirms it in the Holy

Spirit. There is great sorrow and unending agony in my heart: I could wish that I myself might be cursed and cut off from Christ, if this could benefit the brothers who are my own flesh and blood. They are Israelites; it was they [not the gentiles] who were [first] adopted as children. To them belong the glory and the covenants; to them were given the Law and the worship [of the one, true God] and all the promises. To them belong the patriarchs, and of their race, according to the flesh, is the Christ. . . .

But God does not change his mind: his gifts and his call are irrevocable.

153

PAUL INSISTED THAT since the Law of Moses is fulfilled in Christ, all the laws of the Jews, instituted to bring a certain righteousness upon Israel, are now beside the point and can only confuse converts, especially simple gentile ones with a tradition of magical thinking, who may imagine that all will be well for them if only they keep all these rules—613 ha-lakhot, by the count of the medieval rabbis. No one is made righteous by keeping rules, thought Paul, who had spent half his life in their careful observance. It is God who makes us righteous through his grace (the bountiful strength of the Spirit), especially through the grace available to us because of the saving actions of his son, Jesus.

We are not asked to observe scads of minute (and some-times contradictory) rules. We are invited to have faith in Jesus. Martin Luther, the revolutionary Augustinian friar who initi-ated the Protestant Reformation in sixteenth-century Germany, was right to see the many duties, obligatory rituals, and automatic magic enjoined by the medieval church as only too reminiscent of the laws of Judaism that Jesus had bracketed and Paul had rejected altogether—rules that enabled their keepers to pretend to a righteousness that could never be attained by merely human effort. But when Luther claimed to be Pauline by asserting that "man is saved by *faith alone,*" he was misunderstanding Paul—as so many have done in so many different ways. Unfortunately, it has taken four centuries to sort out the confusion, which still reigns in the churches if not in the universities, where scholars have come to a broad consensus. Yes, man is saved by faith, if by that you mean faithful commitment to the cosmic Christ—that is, to the poor, to the afflicted, and to the healing of the world. But this "faith" of which Paul spoke with such feeling is not a single thread, hanging above the abyss, by which the believer is attached to God—some new-fangled form of automatic, if perilous, salvation—nor is it Kierkegaard's blind "leap of faith" over the abyss itself. For when you have sorted through the whole, long, tangled Judeo-Christian tradition, Paul would say, what remains is not one, *sola fides,* but three: "For in the end, faith, hope, and love abide, these three. But the greatest of all is love."

Poor Paul. In addition to being repeatedly misinterpreted, he has been convicted of everything: a traitor to Judaism, an oppressor of women, and, most recently, a self-hating closet queen. He was none of these, and I hope my presentation of his intimate, if anguished, relation to Judaism (which rests on the careful scholarship of many twentieth-century Jews and Christians) will erase the first charge from the minds of my readers. The charge of being a secret, self-hating homosexual comes from a recent book by a bishop of the American Episcopal church; I would pass over this in silence, except that it has been given so much publicity. So far as I can judge, the charge is without probative evidence of any kind and based on egregious misinterpretation and wild conjecture. The bishop, for instance, thinks that when Paul makes oblique mention in Second Corinthians to "a thorn in the flesh" he must be referring to this secret torment. Jerome Murphy-O'Connor, who may have spent as much time with the texts and terrain of Paul as any living interpreter, suggests with sly Irish wit that Paul is referring here to his Corinthian converts, a far more likely conjecture.

Though we know much of Paul's personality, we know no more of his sexual life than we do of Jesus's.* Murphy-O'Connor speculates, as others have done, that he was a widower whose wife had died in some tragedy, this because of pretty good circumstantial evidence, such as that rabbis had to marry by the time they reached the age of thirty (or so). But this undoubted rabbinical obligation cannot be firmly dated to the first half of the first century. We just don't know much of anything about what today would be called the man's "personal life."

Paul's supposedly oppressive judgments on women have been taken out of context (such as when he is asking the

❧ Of course, Jesus also has been at times viewed as homosexual because of his affection for various males (Lazarus whom "he loved"; the Beloved Disciple, who leaned against him at the Last Supper) or because of the presentation of Jesus as a sort of sexually ambivalent ghost in Gnostic literature. But, from the point of view of comparative cultural history, what is far more unusual about Jesus is his open affection for the unattached *women* of his retinue; and the interpretation of his affection for male friends as an indication of homosexuality almost always comes from northern European and North American sources, where open displays of physical affection by Mediterranean peoples are easily misunderstood. The sexual ambivalence of the Gnostic Christ points not to anything factual about the historical Jesus but to how far removed Gnosticism was from the authentic Palestinian roots of the Jesus Movement: it is impossible to imagine the ethereal "Christ"-figure invented by the Gnostics attracting crowds of down-to-earth followers in gritty first-century Palestine.

155

Corinthians to consider being just a tad more conventional) or are ironic statements misinterpreted by casual readers (what comes of having your letters, written for occasions long forgotten, circulate for two thousand years). The worst instances of Pauline "sexism"—such as the infamous remarks in First Timothy forbidding women to speak in church and telling them to stick to childbearing—belong to letters attributed to Paul but written forty years or more after his death.* Women were as free to speak, to evangelize, and to administer the Pauline churches as was any man. First Timothy belongs to the period of the patriarchalization of the Christian churches, when bishops began to emerge as the only legitimate leaders and, surveying the disorder (or, more simply, lack of uniformity) they saw before them, endeavored to put all the "excessive" enthusiasms of the Pauline churches back into the box. Paul is actually the New Testament's ultimate democrat; and it is a pathetic irony that the first person in history to exclude consciously all social grades, isms, and biases from his thinking, believing that nothing—not birth, nor ethnicity, nor religion, nor economic status, nor class, nor gender—makes anyone any better than anyone else, should so often be made to stand at the bar accused of the opposite of what he believed so passionately.

He was a man under pressure, a sometimes contentious overreacher,

---

✎ The letters unquestionably written by Paul are Romans, 1 and 2 Corinthians, Galatians, Philippians, 1 Thessalonians, and Philemon. Colossians and 2 Timothy are likely from Paul's pen or written by him in collaboration with others. Despite some irregularities (and one big surprise in Colossians 3:18–4:1, *q.v.* 231ff.), these are largely in the spirit of the unquestionable letters. Ephesians is probably from Paul's "workshop," written by one of his companions in ministry, perhaps a woman. 2 Thessalonians was also likely constructed by a follower/followers of Paul. Titus, 1 Timothy, and Hebrews were all written decades after Paul's death and, despite their use of his name in the hopes of assuming the mantle of his authority, contradict his theology, sometimes in an almost perverse manner.

who accomplished more in one lifetime than most of us would achieve in ten. If he had his continuing disagreements with the Rock, the lives of both men took in the end an unexpected turn that has kept their memories forever entwined. Both showed up in Rome in the 60s and were martyred there during Nero's anti-Christian persecution, the empire's first. It was not the fact that Rome was the center of the empire but this twin martyrdom—this double act of state barbarism—that gave the city its centrality in the newly emerging Christian world. Peter was crucified upside down (because he beseeched his executioners not to crucify him as his abandoned Lord had been). Paul of Tarsus, Roman citizen, could not be dealt this ultimate humiliation reserved for non-Romans. He was beheaded. Peter is thought to have been buried where he died on Vatican Hill and where the most magnificent of all Christian churches rises above his humble bones. Despite the monumental San Paolo fuori le Mura, the shrine raised to Paul beyond the city's ancient walls, we are less than certain where Paul's bones may lie, an appropriate uncertainty perhaps for the most itinerant of all apostles.

But one can well imagine the old *gymnasion* boy, the sweat-streaming long-distance runner and winner of many a laurel crown, now going to the block in his grizzled sixties and thinking, as he wrote (in Second Timothy): "As for me, I am now being poured out as if I were a libation, and the time has come for me to depart. I have fought the good fight. I have finished the race. I have kept the faith. All there is to come for me now is the crown of justice that the Lord, the just judge, will give me on that Day, and not only me but all those who in their hearts have longed for his return." "For of this I am certain," he wrote to the Romans. "Not death nor life, nor angels, nor princes, nor anything present, nor anything to come, nor any power, whether of highest heaven or deepest abyss, nor anything else in all of creation, shall ever separate us from the love of God that is in Christ Jesus our Lord."

Encountering Evil

Some years after the Neronic executions of Peter, Paul, and many other unfortunate members of the Jesus Movement, a believer named John, exiled for his beliefs to the distant Aegean isle of Patmos, was the recipient of a revelation. Like a great film, John's revelation, recorded in the Book of Revelation, the last book of the Bible, is full of potent, troubling images that are impossible to erase from the memory once they have played before your eyes. John finds himself addressed by "one *like a Son of Man,*" whose eyes burn like flame, out of whose mouth comes a two-edged sword, and who tells John: "I am Alpha and Omega [the first and last letters of the Greek alphabet], the Living One, who was dead—but, look, I live forever and ever, and hold the keys to death and Hades." This initial vision, obviously of Jesus, instructs John to write to the "seven churches of Asia" (among them Paul's Ephesus) and tell them what he will be shown. If the figure of the Son of Man is easy to identify, the symbolic visions that follow sometimes seem to defy interpretation.

John is vouchsafed a vision of heaven, where an immense number of angels are gathered around God's throne and where there hover *"four living creatures, all studded with eyes"* and twenty-four elders, all worshiping in song *"the One-seated-there,"* who is described not physically but in terms of light—

"like jasper and carnelian," encircled by a rainbow "like *an emerald*"; and before the throne is spread a "crystal sea." To the right of the One is a scroll "inscribed front and verso and sealed with seven seals." John weeps "disconsolately because no one has been found worthy to open the scroll and read it." One of the elders tells him, "Do not weep. Look, *the Lion* of the tribe of *Judah, the Root* of David, has triumphed, so he can open the scroll, breaking its seven seals."

The "Lion of Judah" who is worthy to read the scroll turns out to be a lamb that has been sacrificed. At this point, we are still able to interpret the symbolism with some confidence. The twenty-four elders may represent the Twelve Tribes of Israel and the Twelve Apostles who followed Jesus. The four living creatures are borrowed from the Book of Ezekiel, where they appear in a prophetic vision not unlike this one. They are, like the massed angels, part of the heavenly court, all participants in the ineffable heavenly liturgy. The scroll is perhaps the deep truth of things or a narration of future events (or a mixture of both). The Lion-lamb is Christ, the Lion King who allowed himself to be sacrificed as a lamb.

The seven seals are broken and seven trumpets blown, each occurrence precipitating a new symbolic event. The breaking of the first four seals, for instance, brings forth in succession four horsemen who, riding horses of different colors, ravage the world. The first horse is white, and its rider, who holds a bow, is Conquest; the second is red, and its rider, who carries a gigantic sword, is Slaughter; the third is black, and its rider, who holds a pair of scales, is Famine; the fourth has the gray pallor of death, and its rider is Plague, with Hades "hard at its heels." I leave to the reader the unsettling pleasure of reading the full Revelation (or Apocalypse, after its

Greek title, meaning a "laying bare" or "revelation of hidden things").

One after another, cosmic disasters are hurled upon the earth.* There appears but one respite: "I shall send my two witnesses to prophesy . . . the *two olive trees* and the two lamps *in attendance on the Lord of the World.*" These prophets, however, are not welcomed:

> When they have completed their witness, the Beast that comes up from the Abyss *will make war on them and conquer them* and kill them. Their corpses will lie in the main street of the great city whose spiritual names are Sodom and Egypt, where also their Lord was crucified. For three and a half days will people from every race, tribe, tongue, and nation stare at their corpses and refuse them burial, and the people of the world will gloat and celebrate and exchange gifts, because these two prophets had so tormented the people of the world.

160

There is a bitterness in these words that seems to spring from personal experience. Are the visions mixing past, present, and future? Could John have known these "prophets," and could he have been, like Peter following anonymously behind the arrested Jesus, mute witness to their mortal humiliation? Could the "prophets" be Peter and Paul, and could the "great city" be neither Jerusalem (where "their Lord was crucified") nor Rome, but the corporate culture of

---

✠ One of these cosmic disasters involves the falling to earth of a "huge star" named "Wormwood," which pollutes a third of the rivers and springs of the world. This "prophecy" gave quite a turn to many Russians, not especially known in this century for their reading of the Bible. The Russian word for "Wormwood" is *Chernobyl.*

Roman administration, the frame of mind that makes such executions possible? And, if so, who is the "Beast that comes up from the Abyss"?

The visions all at once leave the ground and take off in a more phantasmagoric direction: "Now a great sign appeared in heaven: a woman, clothed with the sun, standing on the moon, and crowned with twelve stars," who gives birth to a child, which a huge red dragon tries to devour. But the child is "taken up to heaven," where war breaks out between the forces of the Dragon and the angels led by Michael, whose name means "Who is like God?" At this point, we are told directly that the Dragon, who falls with "his angels" from heaven to earth, is "the primeval serpent, known as the devil or Satan, who has led the whole world astray." The Dragon pursues the woman, who has hidden herself "in the wilderness" and continues to escape him with the help of heaven and earth. The Dragon, frustrated and enraged, resolves to "make war on her other children, those who keep the Commandments of God [the Jews] and treasure the witness of Jesus [the Messianists]."

The Dragon, thus resolved, takes his stand at the edge of the sea, invoking fresh horrors:

161

> Then I saw a beast rise from the sea: it had ten horns and seven heads, a coronet on each of its ten horns, and on each head a blasphemous title. . . . The Dragon handed over to it his own power and his throne and his immense authority. One of its heads seemed to have sustained a death blow, but this mortal wound had healed so that the whole world had marveled and followed the Beast. They worshiped the Dragon because he had given the Beast his authority;

and they worshiped the Beast, saying: "Who is like the Beast? Who can stand up to him?" The Beast was given a mouth to boast and blaspheme and was allowed free range for forty-two months;* and it opened its mouth to blaspheme God, desecrating his Name, his home, and all who shelter there. It was allowed to make war against the saints and to conquer them, and was given sway over every race, people, tongue, and nation; and the people of the world will worship it, that is, everyone whose name has not been written from the foundation of the world in the book of life of the Lamb that was slain. . . . This is why the saints must persevere in faithfulness.

162

Then I saw a second Beast, rising from the earth, having two horns like a lamb but shrieking like a dragon. This one exercised all the power of the first Beast, on its behalf making the world and its people worship the first Beast, whose mortal wound had healed. And it worked great wonders, even calling down fire from heaven onto the earth while people watched. Through the wonders which it was allowed to do on behalf of the first Beast, it was able to lead astray the people of the world and persuade them to put up a statue in honor of the Beast that had been wounded by the sword and still lived. It was allowed to breathe life

✹ The forty-two months (like the three and a half days during which the corpses of the two prophets were left in the street) is an indirect reference, which all educated Jews would have appreciated, to the three and a half years (or forty-two months) that the Abomination of Desolation was allowed to desecrate the Altar of Sacrifice in the Jerusalem Temple. In John's context, these numbers are not intended to be predictive of any set time but to betoken that the reign of evil has its limits (even though the limits may be unknown to us). Thus, also, does John give evidence of his extensive familiarity with Maccabean history and literature.

JESUS AS THE GOOD SHEPHERD
AND ORPHEUS WITH THE ANIMALS

In the earliest depictions of Jesus—in the Roman catacombs—there is
no attempt to portray him as he may have looked in life. Rather, the
first Christians relied on long-established conventions and types borrowed from pagan art. In their depiction of Jesus as the Good Shepherd
(above), for instance, he is shown as the typical beardless youth of pagan
mythological art. In fact, the whole scene is simply a re-presentation of
the conventional portrayal of the Greek hero Orpheus *(below)*, who,
because he was known to have pacified wild beasts with his music, was
always shown surrounded by peaceful animals.

ORANS FIGURE

Many of the figures of early Christian art are Christians themselves, anonymous to us, shown in their customary attitude of prayer, palms raised in front of them (the same posture that Muslims adopt to this day). This orans (or praying) figure was found in the Catacomb of Santa Priscilla, named for the same Prisca (Priscilla being the affectionate diminutive) who befriended Paul.

PETER AND PAUL

From the earliest attempts to depict them, Peter and Paul are shown not as conventional types but as real men with specific physical characteristics, leading us to the conclusion that their visages were well known to many Christians, especially in Rome, where both apostles spent their last years. Peter *(above left, below right, and overleaf)* is normally the larger of the two and has a round, sympathetic face, surrounded by curly white hair of head and beard. Paul *(above right and below left)* is smaller and leaner, usually with a pointed beard and sharp features and always bald. When the artist is skillful enough, Paul is inevitably represented with lines of tension across his brow.

FUNERARY PORTRAIT

Depiction of recently deceased people, on coffin lids and grave memorials, was
a custom that originated in Egypt and was common throughout the ancient
world in the time of Jesus. These portraits were usually created by the encaustic (or hot wax) technique, because it gave the artist who employed it greater
facility in portraying the deceased with as much realistic detail as possible.
These portraits were normally made on wood.

ENCAUSTIC ICON OF JESUS

This portrait of Jesus, from Saint Catherine's Monastery in Sinai, is our oldest surviving icon, dating to the sixth century. We have no earlier icons because they were all destroyed during the iconoclast controversy (from which Saint Catherine's was spared because it was under Muslim protection). But we know that each generation of icon painters was expected to imitate faithfully the previous generation's work and that, therefore, this icon represents a long tradition which may go back as far as the first century and even be based on eyewitness accounts. Unlike the catacomb depictions of Jesus, the icon is clearly meant (like the primitive portraits of Peter and Paul) to be a portrait of a specific man. Indeed, it is obviously a genuine descendant of the encaustic funerary tradition, made with hot wax on curved wood (not unlike a coffee lid). No print of this portrait can approach the effect of seeing it in person. The artist has used the curved surface as if it were a three-dimensional face, so that the eyes seem to look straight at you—an effect that is much reduced in a two-dimensional print.

THE SHROUD OF TURIN

In negative *(above)*, the face on the Shroud is remarkably like the face in the Sinai icon—with long hair parted in the middle, long face and nose, similarly shaped brow, similar beard. The similarities are so many that if a transparency of the icon face is placed over the Shroud face, the two will be found to be largely congruent. This congruence would be explicable if the Shroud is genuine and the icon goes back to an eyewitness tradition. But the icon is also a somewhat Hellenized Christ, with the refined, slightly idealized face of a Greek man (a natural evolution if we imagine the icon as the result of a centuries-old cultural tradition), whereas the Shroud, in no sense an idealization, is of a dead man with clearly Semitic features.

The full length of the Shroud *(in positive at left)* shows the body of a man front and back. He appears to have had a tail of hair in back, longer than shoulder length, indicating someone who, before catastrophe befell him, took pleasure in his appearance.

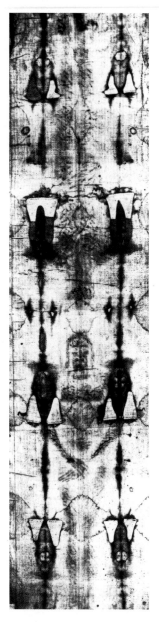

TRADITIONAL IMAGE OF JESUS

The icon tradition of realistic portraiture, rather than the idealized typological figures of the catacombs, came to dominate art to such an extent that all subsequent artists have given Jesus the same basic features, so that he is always recognizable, as in this portrait by Rembrandt.

into this statue, so that the statue of the Beast was able to speak, and to have anyone who refused to worship the statue of the Beast put to death. It compelled everyone—small and great, rich and poor, freedman and slave—to be marked on the right hand or on the forehead, so that no one could buy or sell without the mark of the Beast or the number of its name.

This calls for insight; but anyone with discernment may figure out the number of the Beast. It is the number of a man, the number Six Hundred Sixty-six.

In other words, despite the apparently esoteric nature of the narrative, the code behind it is meant to be easily cracked, as was the case with the symbolic stories and films created by Poles and Czechs during the Soviet oppression; and with this number we can work out the allegorical scheme as if it were a crossword puzzle. The writer, like all the ancients, knew nothing of Arabic numerals. In his world, letters were used as shorthand to represent numerical values, as is the case with the Roman numerals we are still familiar with. So we need only find a well-known historical figure (the writer implies clearly that this is "a man" known to everyone) whose name "adds up" to 666. The Hebrew alphabet contained no vowels. The name of the emperor under whom the Jesus Movement's two greatest "prophets" were executed was Nero Caesar, in Greek *Neron Kaisar,* in unvoweled Hebrew *nrwn qsr* or, giving these consonants their conventional numerical value, 50 + 200 + 6 + 50 + 100 + 60 + 200, which equal 666. The Beast is the Roman empire—more precisely, all the cruelties of Roman political domination—personified by

Nero Caesar. The Devil-Dragon, unable to devour the Messiah, who has been "taken up," and unsuccessful in his pursuit of the "mother," that is, Israel, which gave birth to the Messiah, calls forth the Beast, the political power, to harass this mother and, if possible, destroy her and "her other children."

Nero came to the imperial throne in 54 as a spoiled sixteen-year-old, a lyre player, athlete, and Hellenophile, who intended to raise Roman artistic and cultural standards. After some moves in the direction of justice, probably inspired by his tutor, the respected Stoic philosopher Seneca, the young emperor turned increasingly arbitrary and self-indulgent. Bristling under the influence of his advisers, he at length had his mother murdered and "invited" his old tutor to commit suicide. (The customary invitation to suicide was a short note from the emperor, *"Amicitia nostra dissoluta est"* ["Our friendship is dissolved"]. This was your cue to run the warm water and open the veins.)

During Nero's reign much of Rome was destroyed by fire, giving the emperor the opportunity to rebuild the city along the lines of his own quirky esthetic ideas, which included the never-completed Domus Aurea (or Golden House) for himself, which—with its artificial lake (where the Colosseum now stands)—occupied an enormous chunk of central Rome and displaced the unsightly dwellings of the poor. The grandeur of it all, coupled with the economic toll that it exacted, encouraged the rumor that Nero had set the fire himself. No, retorted the emperor, it was, um, the Christians, who as everyone knows hate humanity. Thus did the Neronic persecutions begin as a spectacular strategy to point the finger elsewhere. Tacitus, in a lighthearted vein, describes the scene, incidentally leaving us the first recorded instance in pagan literature of the term *Christian:*

> Nero . . . punished the notoriously depraved Christians (as they were popularly called) with every refinement. . . . Their deaths were made farcical. Dressed in the skins of wild animals, they were torn to pieces by dogs, or crucified, or [making the punishment fit their supposed crime] turned into torches to be ignited after dark as substitutes for daylight. Nero provided his Gardens for the spectacle, where he exhibited these displays in the [Vatican] Circus, during which he would mingle anonymously with the crowd or take his place in a chariot, disguised as a charioteer.

165

What fun. But Nero's increasingly arbitrary behavior began to erode his support; and when at length the Senate, believing that Nero had fled abroad, declared for Galba, Nero's short-lived successor, it also declared Nero a public enemy. Thus was Nero himself, Savior and Son of God, King of Kings and Lord of Lords—all the "blasphemous titles" of his station—forced to hide in the house of a former slave and there at the age of twenty-nine to commit suicide, dying with the fey exclamation "What an artist dies with me!"

Nero was the last emperor who could claim descent from Augustus; his death and its consequences precipitated a new round of civil wars, lasting two years. During this period a legend grew among the common people that Nero, whom they had rather liked for his *panem et circenses*—the "bread and circuses" by which he kept the plebeians distracted from more basic grievances—had not died but, like Czar Nicholas of a later day, was only wounded and would return. It is this legend that John's Apocalypse refers to when it says that "one of [the Beast's] heads seemed to have sustained a death blow, but this mortal wound had healed so that the whole world had marveled and followed the Beast." The wounded head is the Beast's fifth, and Nero was the fifth emperor in the line that began with Augustus. The Beast's name may be Nero, but the Beast is also Rome, for, as we are told later, "the seven heads are the seven hills; the seven heads are also seven emperors."

If the symbolism is elastic, so is the chronology. It ranges across the ages, borrowing allusions from the Jewish sacred books (especially Daniel) and treating readers to a veritable time machine of possibilities: sometimes we are in the past, sometimes the future, sometimes the present. Christ, the slaughtered lamb, is first seen in heaven, *after which* the Savior is given birth by Israel; the four horsemen, creatures of the diabolic powers, are introduced *before* the Dragon and the Beast—all subverting normal chronology and expectable sequence. The author employs the "logic" of dream and nightmare to allow the reader to see into the deeper reality of the human situation.

A cosmic battle is raging between heaven, the realm of God, and earth, which is under the power that Jesus called "the Prince of this world." He is Satan, the devil, evil personified. It is he who animates the earthly "powers"—all those who on this earth claim authority over others. The Beast is both Nero and the Roman empire, not because John is confused in his symbolism, but because he wants us to see that all exercise of power is bestial and all domination is of the devil. John's symbolic scheme is many-layered. If the Beast is the Dragon's deputy, the second Beast is a sort of cheering section for the first, his diplomatic corps, his publicity department—all the toadies and time-servers necessary to the vast and subtle mechanisms of domination. The talking statue is the image that the Beast presents to the world, an image that encourages mass adoration (long before television or fanzines were thought of). But behind the image, behind the publicity department's spin doctors and media consultants, behind the bureaucracy's many ministers and ambassadors, behind the great statesman, behind the distinguished bank president, behind the all-powerful CEO, stands the ultimate power—the insatiable Dragon, breathing his foul life into the whole complex edifice of human affairs and its structures of oppression. The Dragon, the enemy of God and therefore of all justice, has called forth the Beast, who calls forth the second Beast. They are a ghastly parody of the Trinity: the Dragon as the ultimate power; the Beast, the anti-Christ, being given the Dragon's power throughout the cosmos; and the second Beast, the anti-Spirit, "inspiring" humanity with its tricks. But, deprived of their distracting fireworks and the goodies bestowed selectively from their political pork barrels, they would be just repulsive beasts.

167

Does the New Testament conceive of evil only in terms of political and economic institutions? Jesus certainly saw evil as infecting social and religious institutions as well. His hair-raising excoriation in Matthew 23 of the scribes and Pharisees for their hypocrisy, vanity, and lack of sympathy for ordinary human beings must be understood as Jesus's indictment of the socioreligious establishment of his time (and should probably be read faithfully at the dawn of each new day by today's scribes and Pharisees, the members of the Christian clergy and religious orders). But evil also infects individuals physically (by way of disease and all the ills that the four horsemen bring) and morally. When Jesus tells Simon Peter at the Last Supper that "Satan will be allowed to sift you all like wheat," he is thinking of the disciples' coming cowardice and flight. These are, surely, not social or political but personal moral failures. But they are personal failures in a context of deadly political terror. How many people in any time, after all, will not break and run before the threat of torture and the pain of slow, excruciating execution? "But," Jesus assures his friend the fisherman, "I have prayed for you, Simon, that your faith not fail utterly; and, once you have recovered yourself, lend strength to your brothers"—once again, the social dimension of morality.

From the time of John the Visionary (who may have written shortly after Nero's death but is more likely to have written in the last decade of the first century) to the present day, the Book of Revelation has proved an insurmountable temptation to the twisted and the gullible. Religious leaders like Jerry Falwell are always finding hidden messages in this text and persuading their adherents of some "secret knowledge." But such interpretations are always misguided and often at direct variance with what John meant to convey. To take the many delicate strands of this skillfully woven tapestry and reduce them to some literalist fantasy about the present or future ("666 are the initials of the UN secretary general"; "the world will come to an end in three and a half years") is only to demonstrate once again the connection between fanaticism and simple-mindedness.

Unlike Paul, who wrote in the first flush of the Jesus Movement's success in gaining converts and spreading through Roman Eurasia, John lived to see in detail the brutal response of Nero and his successors to the movement. His Greek is the worst in the New Testament, often coming close to transliterated Hebrew/Aramaic. But if he lacks Paul's linguistic skills, his rich imagination astonishes us still. If, living in a more dangerous era, he betrays more of a siege mentality than Paul,* leading him to Maccabean visions of the eventual triumph of "the saints," his political analysis is surprisingly close to Paul's. Paul, too, speaks often of "princes" and "powers," meaning the spirit-crushing political-economic complex that dominates human affairs and is inspired by the cosmic forces of evil (the powers "of deepest abyss"). If these Satanic forces imitate the style of the forces of good, taking over their vocabulary and ritual, they are incapable of unleashing anything but death and destruction on the world. Their moment of greatest triumph, the crucifixion, was also the beginning of their downfall. But in their exultation at killing Christ they were blind to the implications of what they had done. Those who are mature in the faith, says Paul, are able to speak "of God's secret wisdom, hidden and destined for our glory before all time began [the wisdom contained in the heavenly scroll]. None of the powers of this age understood it, for if they had, they would not have crucified the Lord of glory."

169

People may be fooled by the dazzling displays of the "powers of this age"—which is also our age—into the fallacy of calling Caesar "Son of God." They may be seduced or terrorized into the demonic liturgies of the Beast, mistaking him for the Savior and singing in sacrilegious imitation of heavenly worship, "Who is like the Beast?" But, in the end,

✠ John sees not only the power of Rome but the opposition of anti-Messianist Jews ranged against him. He calls these Jews, whose persecution of Christians had increased significantly since the time of Paul, "the Synagogue of Satan." Though this term has sometimes been interpreted as an example of early Christian anti-Semitism, John is obviously himself a Jew who stands in solidarity with other Jews—except for those who have cut him off.

the saints will triumph, gathered into "the new Jerusalem" through which courses the healing River of Life. In John's vision, they will be "of a number so large as to be impossible for anyone to count, of every nation, race, tribe, and tongue"—finally separated out from all the demon-worshiping peoples with whom they were previously intermingled. Though they will have come through "the great tribulation," they will stand in joy before God's throne—the last remaining power—their "robes washed white in the blood of the Lamb." The Voice will call out from the Throne of True Power:

> "You see, here God lives with human beings. *He will make his home among them; they will be his people, and he will be their God, God-with-them. He will wipe* away every *tear from their eyes.* There will be no more death, and no more mourning or sadness or pain. The world of the past is gone. . . . Look how I am making all things new." . . .
>
> Then he said to me, "The End has already begun, for I am Alpha and Omega, the Beginning and the End. *To anyone who thirsts* I will give *the gift of water from the well of life.* Whoever overcomes will inherit all this; and *I will be his* God and *he will be my child."*

IV

The Gentile Messiah

Luke's Jesus

PAUL'S LETTERS, written over a decade and a half (from about the year 50 to the mid-60s), are the earliest writings of the New Testament. But the four gospels contain extensive passages, especially some of Jesus's teachings and the basic accounts of his trial and execution, that take us back to a time that clearly predates Paul's letters. For these are transcriptions of oral traditions that were current in the years following the crucifixion and may be fairly undiluted recountings of what people heard and saw during the lifetime of Jesus. Other passages, however, have been finessed to suit the view—or even the personality—of a particular evangelist or his need to frame his redaction in a certain way so as to communicate effectively with his intended audience. If Mark is the most primitive, often giving us what seem to be the very textures and odors of Palestine in the early 30s, and Matthew is the most Jewish, sometimes allowing his insistence on Rabbi Jesus's Torah-faithfulness to blot out all other considerations, Luke is obviously addressing himself to an audience more cosmopolitan than Mark's but with limited interest in the specifically Jewish questions that so concerned Matthew.

In Paul's letters, we see played out the conflict between Paul's disciples and the Judaizing Messianists, who insisted that new non-Jewish converts take on all the obligations of a Pharisaic interpretation of the Mosaic Law. Though the Judaizing party remained an element in Christianity into the second century, it was ultimately unsuccessful for several reasons, among these the inherent complexity of its own program, the strength of Paul's influence, and habits of mind and heart that made Greeks and Romans relatively unreceptive to the arguments of the Judaizers. In Luke's Gospel, we see how, as the Judaizers dwindled and the gentiles took their place, the Jesus Movement adapted the *kerygma*—and did not adapt it—to the needs of its new audience, the Greco-Roman gentiles who, largely thanks to Paul's exertions, began to fill its ranks.

In the cities of the Jewish diaspora (especially Alexandria, Antioch, Tarsus, Ephesus, and Rome), Jews were widely admired by their gentile neighbors. For one thing, they had a *real* religion, not a clutter of gods and goddesses and pro forma rituals that almost nobody took seriously anymore. They actually *believed* in their one God; and, imagine, they even set aside one day a week to pray to him and reflect on their lives. They possessed a dignified library of sacred books that they studied reverently as part of this weekly reflection and which, if more than a little odd in their Greek translation, seemed to point toward a consistent worldview. Besides their religious seriousness, Jews were unusual in a number of ways that caught the attention of gentiles. They were faithful spouses—no, really—who maintained strong families in which even grown children remained affectively attached and respectful to their parents. Despite Caesar Nero's shining example, matricide was virtually unknown among them. Despite their growing economic success, they tended to be more scrupulous in business than non-Jews. And they were downright finicky when it came to taking human life, seeming to value even a slave's or a plebeian's life as much as anyone else's. Perhaps in nothing did the gentiles find the Jews so admirable as in their acts of charity. Communities of urban Jews, in addition to opening synagogues, built welfare centers for aiding the poor, the miserable, the sick, the homebound, the imprisoned, and those, such as widows and orphans, who had no family to care for them.

For all these reasons, the diaspora cities of the first century saw a marked increase in gentile initiates to Judaism. Many of these were wellborn women who presided over substantial households and who had likely tried out some of the Eastern mystery cults before settling on Judaism. (Nero's wife Poppea was almost certainly one of these, and probably the person responsible for instructing Nero in the subtle difference between Christians and more traditional Jews, which he would otherwise scarcely have been aware of.) These gentiles did not, generally speaking, go all the way. Because they tended to draw the line at circumcision, they were not considered complete Jews. They were, rather, *noachides,* or God-fearers, gentiles who remained gentiles while keeping the Sabbath and many of the Jewish dietary restrictions and coming to put their trust in the one God of the Jews.

Pilgrimage to Jerusalem, however, could turn out to be a difficult test of the commitment of the *noachides.* For here in the heart of the Jewish world, they encountered Judaism *enragé,* a provincial religion concerned only with itself, and ages apart from the rational, tolerant Judaism of the diaspora. In the words of Paul Johnson:

> The Temple, now, in Herod's* version, rising triumphantly over Jerusalem, was an ocular reminder that Judaism was about Jews and

✹ This is Herod the Great, friend of Augustus, who was crowned "king of Judea" by the Romans and ruled from 37 to 4 B.C., just long enough to be the king who attempts to kill the infant Jesus by a wholesale slaughter of Bethlehem's male infants, as recounted in Matthew 2:16–18. His son, Herod Antipas, tetrarch of Galilee and Perea from 4 B.C. to A.D. 39 and stepfather of Salome, will execute John the Baptizer.

their history—not about anyone else. Other gods
flew across the deserts from the East without much
difficulty, jettisoning the inconvenient and embarrassing accretions from their past, changing, as it were,
their accents and manners as well as their names. But
the God of the Jews was still alive and roaring in his
Temple, demanding blood, making no attempt to
conceal his racial and primitive origins. Herod's fabric was elegant, modern, sophisticated—he had, indeed, added some Hellenic decorative effects much
resented by fundamentalist Jews who constantly
sought to destroy them—but nothing could hide the

essential business of the Temple, which was the ritual
slaughter, consumption, and combustion of sacrificial
cattle on a gigantic scale. The place was as vast as a
small city. There were literally thousands of priests,
attendants, temple-soldiers, and minions. To the un-
prepared visitor, the dignity and charity of Jewish dis-
apora life, the thoughtful comments and homilies of
the Alexandrian synagogue, was quite lost amid the
smoke of the pyres, the bellows of terrified beasts, the
sluices of blood, the abattoir stench, the unconcealed
and unconcealable machinery of tribal religion inflated by modern wealth to an industrial scale.
Sophisticated Romans who knew the Judaism of the
diaspora found it hard to understand the hostility to-
wards Jews shown by colonial officials who, behind a
heavily-armed escort, had witnessed Jerusalem at festival time. Diaspora Judaism, liberal and outward-
minded, contained the matrix of a universal religion,
but only if it could be cut off from its barbarous ori-

gins; and how could so thick and sinewy an umbili-
cal cord be severed?

This description of "Herod's" Temple (actually the Second
Temple, built in the sixth century B.C. and rebuilt by Herod)
is more than a bit overwrought. The God of the Jews did not
roar in his Temple: the insoluble problem was that, since the
destruction of the First Temple and, with it, the Ark of the
Covenant, God had ceased to be present in his Temple. Nor
would animal sacrifice have disgusted the gentiles, since
Greeks, Romans, and all ancient peoples offered such sacrifices
(though one cannot help wondering whether, had the Second
Temple not been destroyed, it would today be ringed from
morn to night by indignant animal-rights activists). But
Johnson is right to emphasize that Judaism, in its mother city,
could display a sweaty tribalism that gentiles would only find
unattractive. The partisan, argumentative ambience of first-
century Jerusalem, not unlike the atmosphere of the ultra-
Orthodox pockets of the contemporary city, could repel any
outsider, whether gentile or diaspora Jew.

Perhaps most important is Johnson's shrewd observation
that Judaism "contained the matrix of a universal religion." By
this time, the more percipient inhabitants of the Greco-
Roman world had come to the conclusion that polytheism,
whatever manifestation it might assume, was seriously flawed.
The Jews alone, by offering monotheism, offered a unitive vision, not the contradictory and flickering epiphanies of a fanciful pantheon of gods and goddesses. But could Judaism adapt
to gentile needs, could it lose its foreign accent and outlandish
manners? No one saw the opportunity more clearly than
Luke; his gospel and its sequel, the Acts of the Apostles, present

a Jesus and a Jesus Movement specifically tailored to gentile sensibility.

Careful contemporary scholars stop just short of accepting unequivocally the identity ascribed to Luke in antiquity and attached to his gospel—"a Syrian of Antioch, by profession a physician, the disciple of the apostles, and later a follower of Paul until his martyrdom"—but there is little reason not to assume that Luke was a Greek-speaking gentile, writing for gentiles, and that he is the "Luke" mentioned in the Letter to Philemon as Paul's "fellow worker" and as the "beloved physician" of the Letter to the Colossians. Luke may very well have come to Judaism as a *noachide,* spending many years in that position, since his knowledge of the Septuagint, the Hebrew Bible in its Greek version, is broad and deep—even if his knowledge of Palestinian geography is sometimes faulty, as well as his understanding of Jewish custom and ritual. He wrote after Mark (who wrote in the late 60s), probably in the 80s a little after Matthew. We do not know where he wrote or for whom, except that we are sure he did not write for Palestinians or for born Jews of any kind.

We are also sure that he did not know Jesus. As he tells us at the outset of his gospel, he is the recipient of extant traditions both oral ("just as the original eyewitnesses passed them on to us") and written ("since many have undertaken to compile an orderly account of the things that have come to fulfillment among us"). But these written accounts seem to be lacking something in Luke's eyes, moving him to create his own: "I too have decided, after investigating everything carefully from the beginning, to put [these events] systematically in writing." The earlier written accounts, though "orderly," lacked a refined system and were not careful enough in their research.

This would have been the typical reaction of a cultivated Greek writer to the stylistic infelicities and lacunae of a writer like Mark—and the tactful indirectness of Luke's criticism is further proof of his excellent Greek education. Luke opens his account with an elegant periodic sentence, which concludes with a characteristic Greek flourish of dedication: "for you, Theophilus, so that Your Excellency may realize what assurance you have for the instruction you have received." We know nothing of Theophilus—it is even possible that he is meant to be symbolic of all Luke's readers, for his name means "God-lover"—but the framing of a long narrative as if it were a letter is a common Greco-Roman literary device.

Mark, in giving Jesus his first utterance ("The Time has come . . . open your hearts"), sets forth the dominant theme of his gospel. Matthew does the same by giving us the Beatitudes at the beginning of Jesus's first sermon. No less does Luke lay before us his understanding of the core of Jesus's message by presenting us with a scene that he sets at the outset of Jesus's public ministry. After Jesus's baptism and his being tempted by Satan in the desert, he returns to Galilee "filled with the power of the Spirit":

> When he came to Nazareth, where he had been brought up, he went into the synagogue on the Sabbath as was his custom. He stood up to read the Scripture and was handed the scroll of the prophet Isaiah. Unrolling the scroll, he came to this passage [and read aloud]:
>
> *The Spirit of the Lord is upon me,*
> *for he has anointed me to bring the Good News to the poor:*

healing the broken-hearted,
proclaiming liberation to prisoners,
giving sight to the blind and freedom to the oppressed,
proclaiming the Time of the Lord's favor.

He then rolled up the scroll, gave it back to the at-
tendant, and sat down. And all eyes in the synagogue
were fixed on him as he began to speak to them:
"Today is this text fulfilled, even as you sit listening."

If Mark begins with his apocalyptic sense of "the Time"
that has come, and Matthew with his overwhelming Jewish
sense of the obligations of Justice incumbent on all those who
would live in God's blessedness, Luke sees Jesus himself as the
theme, Jesus the bearer of glad tidings to the poor (who are so
seldom the recipients of good news), Jesus the healer, Jesus the
liberator, Jesus who enlightens, Jesus who frees. We come to
the truth by watching Jesus intently ("all eyes . . . fixed on
him"), for his every movement (his standing up, his unrolling
of the scroll, his choice of text, his rolling of the scroll, his returning it to the synagogue official, his sitting among us) is
redolent with meaning. In Luke, the elegant writer from
whose polished pen the Greek flows effortlessly, Jesus moves
through his life with unhurried dignity—in almost stately pro-
gression—toward his appointed end. This is not to say that
Luke is inventing, just that he is capable of setting a scene to
dramatic effect with a facility unavailable to the earlier evangelists, who were probably translating in their heads from
Aramaic to Greek and just trying to keep their tenses straight.

But there are ways in which Luke not only dramatizes but
softens the material he has taken from Mark so as not to trou-

ble or unduly offend gentile sensibility. In Luke, though
Nazareth rejects Jesus (in prophetic foreshadowing of his rejection by the Jewish nation), Jesus's family never has any
doubts. Jesus never chastises Peter (as he does explicitly in
Mark and Matthew); and the stupidity of the disciples, who are
always misunderstanding Jesus in the earlier evangelists, is lessened and excused. By the 80s, the family of Jesus and his principal disciples, almost all of whom were now deceased, had
assumed heroic reputations in Christian circles; and Luke sees
no reason to emphasize their failings. But these alterations go
beyond tact. In Luke, we are looking at Jesus's story through a
gentile lens, which viewed the biographies of great men as ex-
emplars for others to emulate. So the great men and women   181
of the Christian tradition must not be shown as muddled, contentious, or craven; and the central figure, Jesus, must be allowed as much dignity and distance from criticism as possible.
Thus, in Luke's treatment of the call of Matthew Levi, the
Pharisees and their scribes direct their ire at Jesus's disciples,
not at Jesus himself (as they do in Mark), for eating and drinking with "tax collectors and prostitutes."

The Jews, in their emphasis on justice and its lack, were
familiar with guilt. They had no trouble portraying their
greatest king, David, as a murderer beset by lust, a man who
must come to feel the sharp, inner pangs of guilt for his
abysmally unjust actions. Greco-Roman literary and imaginative traditions enshrined no such scenes. For the Greeks
and Romans, sin—*hamartia*—was not personal, the result of
an evil choice, made against the Law of God written in their
hearts. Rather, it was an unavoidable flaw, such as Oedipus's
hamartia, his tragic mistake in murdering his father and mar-
rying his mother, while believing he had done everything to

avoid these very actions. For gentiles, what we may think of as a more "Oriental" orientation prevailed: rather than guilt, they were much more likely to feel shame, a far less socially constructive emotion.* The great figures of the Christian tradition must not, therefore, be shown by their admiring biographer in shameful, slovenly, or compromising situations.

Luke's alterations are occasional; and it is tempting to make more of them than is warranted by his text. In the controversy over Jesus's notorious dinner companions, for instance, Luke gives us the same answer as Mark, when Jesus, addressing the objections of the Pharisees and their scribes, says: "It is not the healthy who need a doctor but the sick. I have not come to call the upright but sinners"—Luke adding only *eis metanoian* ("to a change of heart"), which hardly constitutes a change of meaning. We discover in Luke's Gospel a subtle development of the *kerygma* for presentation to a gentile audience, but a development without substantial discontinuity.

If the pagan emphasis on outward show—the *bella figura* that still ices Italian social life—leads Luke to minor revisions of the Marcan tradition, other elements of gentile sensibility may have impelled the third evangelist to search for stories beyond those that Mark and Matthew had collected, stories that would enable his particular audience to connect with Jesus; and we find in Luke a series of encounters and anecdotes recounted nowhere else in the books of the New Testament. For example, in Luke's redaction of the dialogue in which Jesus articulates the two com-

* Of course, avoidance of shame is hardly confined to the Orient. Robert Graves was not far off the mark when, in *I, Claudius,* he gave the face-saving Roman imperial family all the elegant but empty manners of the English upper classes.

mandments that summarize the whole Law of Moses (love of God and neighbor), Jesus's interlocutor—a lawyer with a lawyerly turn of mind—poses a further question: "And just who is my neighbor?" Jesus replies:

> "A certain man was traveling down from Jerusalem to Jericho, when he fell into the hands of robbers. They stripped him, beat him, and left him for dead. Now it so happened that a priest was going down the same road, but when he saw the man [lying there], he crossed to the other side and continued on his way. In the same way, a levite* also came upon the scene, saw the man, crossed to the other side of the road, and continued on his way. But a traveling Samaritan came upon him; and when he saw him, he was moved to compassion. He went right over to him and bandaged his wounds, pouring olive oil and wine [costly salves] over them. He then lifted the man onto his own mount, brought him to an inn, and nursed him there. The following day, he produced two silver pieces, which he gave the innkeeper, saying, 'Take care of him, and on my return I shall reimburse you for any additional expenses you may incur.' Which of these three, would you say, was a neighbor to him who fell into the hands of robbers?" [The lawyer] replied, "The one who showed him kindness." Jesus said to him, "Go and do likewise."

183

It is fair to say that there is no teaching of Jesus with wider currency than this story of the Good Samaritan, who

---

Levites were lower clergy, who could assist at the Temple liturgy but could not offer sacrifice, which was reserved to the Aaronid priesthood.

makes his only appearance in Luke's Gospel. There is no cause to think that Luke made the story up and put it in Jesus's mouth. Its accurate Palestinian setting—the road from Jerusalem to Jericho, which was indeed perilous—all but forbids such a conclusion. More than this, the parable of the Good Samaritan is of a piece with the most basic substrate of Jesus's teachings: the obligation of kindness to everyone and anyone who falls across my path, especially someone in trouble.

But we may posit a reason why Mark and Matthew, evangelists closely associated with Jewish communities in Palestine and the diaspora, failed to include this story. The Jews despised the sectarian Samaritans, who possessed the Torah but not the Prophets and who worshiped not in the Jerusalem Temple but on Mount Gerizim to the north. There is no hatred so intense as *odium theologicum*—hatred for those nearby who are religiously similar to oneself but nonetheless different. Through the ages, Christians, for instance, have been far more hateful to Jews, to Muslims, and to one another than they have ever been to Buddhists and Hindus. The Samaritans were the neighboring heretics; and for them the Jews reserved a contempt they did not display even toward gentiles. Is it not possible that Mark and Matthew felt they could overlook this one example of Jesus's teaching on universal kindness (after all, they already had so many others), since a Samaritan as the model of Christlike behavior would rub so many Jewish Christians the wrong way?

But Luke's gentile Christians needed to be reassured that there was more than one way to be Christ-like, more than one path that could be taken if you would follow in the footsteps of the Master. You needn't be a born Jew, raised in the tradi-

tions of the ancestors. There was no background that was unthinkable: it was even possible to be something as freaky as a
Samaritan. As we stand now at the entrance to the third millennium since Jesus, we can look back over the horrors of
Christian history, never doubting for an instant that if
Christians had put kindness ahead of devotion to good order,
theological correctness, and our own justifications—if we had
followed in the humble footsteps of a heretical Samaritan who
was willing to wash someone else's wounds, rather than in the
self-regarding steps of the priest and the immaculate steps of
the levite—the world we inhabit would be a very different
one.

The parable of the Good Samaritan is followed immediately by a scene from Jesus's life that only Luke recounts. Jesus
enters a village where friends of his, Martha and Mary, have a
home. While Mary "sat at the Lord's feet and listened to what
he had to say," Martha "was distracted by her many household
tasks." At length, Martha, feeling sharply the inequity of the situation, upbraids Jesus: "Sir, don't you care that my sister has left
me to do all the work myself? Tell her to help me!" Jesus's
reply, though affectionate, is not what Martha was looking for:
"Martha, Martha, you fret and fuss over many things. But only
one is necessary. Mary has made the right choice, and it will
not be taken from her."

This encounter might seem intolerable if it concerned anyone other than Jesus. If we imagine Mary as the household
member who after dinner is far too absorbed in her guests' fascinating conversation to bother about clearing the table but
leaves all that sort of thing to her drudge of a sister, we may
find ourselves solidly on Martha's side of the argument.
Rather, we should read this anecdote in the context of Jesus's

(and presumably Mary's) understanding that his time is short, that his entire life is lived against the horizon of apocalypse. Mary is one of the wedding guests who rejoice while the bridegroom is among them, refusing to deprive themselves of the joy of his presence for the sake of some lesser goal. Whatever Martha is huffing and puffing about can be put off till Jesus moves on.

For Luke, Jesus has become the central reality, the yardstick against which all actions are to be measured. It is no coincidence that the story of Martha and Mary follows immediately on the parable of the Good Samaritan, whose actions are Christ-like. Only if we put Christ before all practical considerations—only if we clear a place for him in our hearts (rather than clear the table)—will we be able to behave as the Samaritan does. For us who (like Luke and his gentile readers) live in the time after Jesus, without the comfort of his physical presence, clearing a place for Jesus means praying. In Luke's Gospel, Jesus, despite the constant outpouring of his energy in preaching and healing, always finds time to "withdraw to some lonely place to pray." So, immediately after the story of Martha and Mary, Jesus teaches his disciples to pray:

OPPOSITE: ROMAN PALESTINE IN THE TIME OF JESUS

For the sake of effective administrative control, the Romans divided the ancient territory of the Jews in different ways at different times. At the time of Jesus's death, Judea-Samaria-Idumea was subject to Pontius Pilate, and Galilee to the north and Perea on the west bank of the Jordan were subject to Herod Antipas. The populations of these territories were quite mixed, Judea-Samaria-Idumea containing, as the names imply, Jews, Samaritans, and Idumeans, as well as Greeks, Romans, and other Eurasians. Rural Galilee was home to Samaritans as well as Jews. The Decapolis was largely composed of Roman settlers.

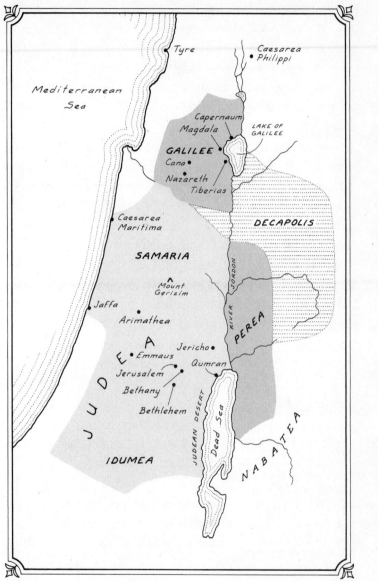

"When you pray, say:

Father, hallowed be your name.

Your kingdom come.

Give us each day our daily bread.

Forgive us our sins, for we forgive everyone who wrongs us.

And do not put us to the test."

Luke is not later than Mark and Matthew in every respect. Here he has recorded what is almost certainly the original form of the New Testament's most famous prayer. (Matthew's alterations and psalm-like parallelisms do little more than elaborate what is implicit in the original: "Our Father in heaven, hallowed be your name. Your kingdom come, your will be done on earth as it is in heaven. Give us this day our daily bread. Forgive us our debts, as we also have forgiven our debtors. And do not put us to the test, but deliver us from the Evil One.")*

✠ Matthew seems to have used a form of this prayer (traditionally called the "Our Father" or "Lord's Prayer") that was in current liturgical use, thus the "our." Being more apocalyptic (and more Jewish) than Luke, he substitutes for Luke's "each day" "this day," as if there may not be another. His version of the forgiveness clause is slightly more restricted than Luke's: instead of "sins," "debts," which are to be forgiven *insofar as* I have forgiven others; Luke assumes that the speaker has already forgiven everyone everything.

Luke is building up a purposeful sequence, which begins by answering the question "Who is my neighbor?" and goes on to remind the reader that unfailing kindness (even to strangers) is possible only if we keep Jesus in mind—that is, if we pattern our lives on his—and that such a resolve can be accomplished only if we pray as Jesus did, asking Jesus's loving Father (who is also our Father) to watch over us. What we say to the Father is not so important; and despite the fact that Jesus's sample prayer has become an unvarying

Christian incantation, he meant only to sketch one possibility, not to lock us into a formula.

In the last story of this Lucan sequence, Jesus gives us a midrash on his own prayer:

> "Suppose one of you has a friend, who comes [to your house] at midnight and calls out, 'My friend, lend me three loaves of bread, since a friend of mine on a journey has just arrived and I have nothing to offer him.' And suppose the man inside replies, 'Leave me alone! The door is already bolted, and my children are with me in bed. I cannot get up and give you anything now.' I tell you, even if he will not get up and give it to him out of friendship, shameless persistence will make him get up and give the other whatever he needs.

189

> "So I tell you: Ask, and it shall be given to you; seek, and you shall find; knock, and the door shall be opened to you. For everyone who asks, receives; everyone who searches, finds; and to everyone who knocks the door shall be opened. What father among you, if your son asked for a fish, would hand him a snake, or, if he asked for an egg, would hand him a scorpion? If, then, you who are evil know how to give your children what is good, how much more surely will the heavenly Father give the Holy Spirit to those who ask him."

There is a roughness to this parable—a man in a one-room house, closed up for the night, his whole family in the one bed; gruff fathers, showing their love for their children in acts of silent, seemingly begrudging, generosity—that easily convinces us of its Palestinian origin. Luke, the Greek biographer, has done his homework, however unpleasant it may have been, however persistent he had to be. But Jesus's understanding of the God we pray to is pellucid: if you are a good, though reluctant, neighbor, God is much more generous than you; if you are a good, though undemonstrative, father, God is a more loving father than you could even imagine being. Therefore, ask boldly and without fear.

⚑ The person in need can be oneself. Though the story of the householder is preserved only in Luke, Jesus's saying "Ask, and you shall receive . . ." also turns up in Matthew, both evangelists having derived it from Q. But in Matthew, who is likely to be closer to Q's words, the saying ends with Jesus's promise that "your Father in heaven will give good things to those who ask him." Luke's substitution of the courage-giving "Spirit" for "good things" almost certainly reflects his greater awareness of state persecution against Christians. If the hunches of some scholars are correct—that Matthew was based in Asian Antioch while Luke was active in the Pauline communities of Greek-speaking Europe (like Achaia and Macedon)—the difference in Roman policy toward Christian communities in these two regions could well account for the differing report of this saying in these two evangelists.

LUKE SEES CHRISTIAN LIFE as an alternation of two activities, prayer and kindness, each feeding the other. The plight of those in need sends me to prayer; prayer strengthens me to help those in need.* But for Luke there is one thing that can make a Christ-like life impossible. For Jewish Matthew, who was so sensitive to the haughty high-mindedness of the Pharisees, that one thing was religious hypocrisy. For Luke, at one remove from the conflicts of Jewish life and looking squarely at the far more insidious temptations of Greco-Roman society, the one thing that can make a Christ-like life impossible is wealth. Carefully pruning the many-branched tradition he has received, Luke presents us with teachings of Jesus that especially stress the evil obstacle of riches:

"Once there was a rich man whose lands produced abundant crops. The man thought to himself, 'What a delightful problem! My yield is now larger than my storage space. I know what I'll do: I'll tear down my barns and build even bigger ones. After that, I will gather all my grain into them and all my other goods, as well. Then will I say to my soul, Dear soul, you have so many good things stored up for years to come. Do take it easy now; eat, drink, and be merry.'

"But God said to him, 'Fool, this very night is your soul demanded of you. Then what will it matter who gets all this?' "

To this ominous parable, Luke adds his own ominous words: "This is how it will go with anyone who piles up treasure for himself but is not rich before God." And as if this parable were not enough, Luke gives us another that follows a similar rich man beyond the grave, where we find out what happens to those who die without being "rich before God":

"Once there was a rich man who dressed in *purple and fine linen* and feasted sumptuously every day. At his gate lay a beggar named Lazarus, covered with sores and longing to be fed if only with the scraps that dropped from the rich man's table. [He was so lowly that] even the dogs would come by and lick his sores.

"One day the beggar died and was carried by the angels to the bosom of Abraham. The rich man also died and was buried. But in Hades the rich man was tormented. Once he looked up and saw Abraham far off with Lazarus beside him. 'Father Abraham,' he cried, 'have mercy on me! Send Lazarus to dip the tip of his finger in water that he might cool my tongue, for I am in agony in these flames.'

"Abraham replied, 'Remember, my child, that you received only good things during your life, but Lazarus only evils. Now he is comforted here, and you are in agony. Besides, between us and you a great chasm has been fixed so that those who might want to cross over from this side to you cannot; nor can any come over from there to us.'

"Still did he plead, 'Then I beg you, Father, at least send him to my father's house, where I have five brothers, that he might warn them, lest they too end up in this place of torment.'

"Abraham replied, 'They have Moses and the prophets; let them listen to them.'

" 'No, Father Abraham,' said he, 'they will not listen. But if someone were to come back from the dead to them, they would open their hearts.' Abraham said to him, 'If they do not listen to Moses and the prophets, they will not be convinced even if someone should rise from the dead.' "

We cannot know if Jesus's original parable ended with this glancing reference to his own resurrection; but Luke certainly intends the Christian reader to catch it and therefore to reflect that even something as spectacularly singular as the revelation contained in the Torah and the Prophets or the resurrection of Jesus will not impress those who are determined to pursue only their own aggrandizement. And though Luke's many negative references to wealth make it clear that he saw personal riches as the preeminent blindfold to spiritual sight, he is not as far from Matthew's concerns as this might seem to imply. Both wealth and religious hypocrisy blind a man to his true responsibilities. The rich men of the Lucan parables can see only their wealth, which blinds them to the needs of others that they should be so able to minister to. The Pharisees of Matthew "shut up the Kingdom of Heaven in people's faces" and found their own justification on hairsplitting legalistic distinctions but "neglect the weightier matters of the Law—justice, mercy, good faith!" They "lay on people heavy [religious] burdens but will not lift a finger" to help them with those burdens. Their sanctimony in the service of their own self-aggrandizement is as blinding to them as the rich man's wealth is to him. So hoarded wealth and the arrogant complacency of churchmen—both of them forms of uncaring power—are just two of the traps that can keep human beings from seeing the true nature of their situation. For, says Jesus in Luke's Gospel, "The very things most valued by human beings are abominations in the eyes of God."

193

Wealth and religious hypocrisy may seem rather rarefied temptations, available only to the privileged few. But Jesus was aware that, for ordinary mortals, grinding worry could easily take the place of arrogance and greed. Jesus, always far more sympathetic to ordinary people than he ever is to the privileged, is far gentler in dealing with the stumbling block of worry, even though he sees it as an obstacle to a full life:

> "Do not worry about your life, what you will eat,
> nor your body, what you will wear. Life is more than
> food, and the body more than clothes. Consider the

ravens: they neither sow nor reap, they have neither storehouse nor barn; yet God feeds them. And how much more are you worth than birds! Which of you can by worrying add a single hour to his life? If you cannot do so small a thing, why worry about the rest?

"Consider how the lilies grow. They neither toil nor spin. Yet I tell you, not even Solomon in all his glory was arrayed like one of these. If that is how God clothes the grass of the field, which is here today, and tomorrow cast into the fire, how much more will he clothe you, O you of little faith? And do not set your heart on what you will eat or drink; don't even worry about it. For the pagans run after all these things, and your Father knows that you need them. Seek, rather, his Kingdom, and all these things will be added unto you.

This is Luke's redaction of the teaching, better known in its Matthean version. Both evangelists took it from Q—in whatever version of that surmised document each was using, which may account for the slight variations between them. Matthew's "birds of the air" become Luke's "ravens"; his "lilies of the field" become the more prosaic "lilies"; and his "Seek, rather, his Kingdom and God's Justice" loses its final phrase in Luke's version. But if the substantial similarity is proof of the care of both evangelists in an age in which research libraries and reference tools were virtually unknown, Luke's special material— all the parables (the Good Samaritan, the sleepy Palestinian householder, the stories of the rich men) and incidents (Jesus reading from the Isaiah scroll, Jesus with his friends Martha and Mary) that appear only in Luke—is proof of Luke's unremitting industriousness and his dogged resolve to compose a life of Jesus that, though as accurate as he could make it, was to be pitched specifically to gentiles.

There are in Luke's choices traces of the reticence that we find in the classical Greek dramatists, who kept violent and lascivious episodes off their stage. In relating the imprisonment and execution of John the Baptizer, which Luke has taken from Mark's earthy account, he carefully omits any mention of Salome dancing provocatively before her stepfather, Herod, reflecting, as Raymond Brown remarks, Luke's "distaste for the sensational." Similarly, when Jesus cleanses the Temple of those who, treating it as a bazaar, have set up businesses there, in Luke's version he merely "drives them out," whereas in Mark and Matthew he overturns tables and stalls and in John goes on to scatter coins and whip the vile shopkeepers into the street.

There is even in Luke a saying of Jesus that presents him very nearly as a typical pagan wise man, cautioning his followers on their manners at a banquet. Do not, advises Jesus, elbow your way to the best seat. "A more distinguished person than you may have been invited," and the host may have to ask you to move, much to your embarrassment. Better to take the most humble seat, "so that, when your host comes in, he may say, 'My friend, move up higher.' Then, everyone with you at the table will see you honored." Good advice, no doubt, for the upwardly mobile, but not much to do with the Gospel—and saved only by Jesus's final comment: "Everyone who exalts himself will be humbled, and whoever humbles himself will be exalted."

The "wisdom" of such a discourse would fit smoothly into any of the many ancient how-to books on good manners and laudable conduct, but its ring is not especially Jewish or Christian. In this passage, Luke, building perhaps on an authentic saying of Jesus about the last being first and the first last, may have added as illustration an exchange on table manners that does little more than exhibit his own social prejudices. These small indications of Luke's Greco-Roman predispositions have prompted some critics to the extreme assertion that Luke is a Stoic in Christian clothing or even that Luke's Jesus is a species of Stoic philosopher. Without championing such a notion, which would do violence to Luke's obvious overall intent, we may say that it would indeed be odd if Luke had no identity other than that of a God-fearer who had committed himself to the Jesus Movement. He had a family, an education, and a cultural background that would, whatever the strength of his adult commitment, leave some traces in his writings—and we should not be surprised to find such.

The Stoics were in favor of moderation and opposed to the indulgence of the Epicureans (the original "eat, drink, and be merry" crowd), but not one of them would have signed on to Luke's opinion of riches. Seneca, for instance, certainly the most prominent Stoic of his (and Luke's) time, was widely admired for being one of the wealthiest men in Rome. Luke's "holy poverty"—long before its Franciscan articulation—would only have appalled the Stoics, who would have found someone like John D. Rockefeller much more to their taste, a man famous for his temperance who also had the keenest appreciation of the holy importance of wealth. There was nothing otherworldly about the Stoics.

Luke's poverty of spirit went far indeed. He seems to have been, if anything, more radical than Jesus on this point. In Mark's Gospel, Jesus tells Peter and the other disciples, "In truth I tell you, there is no one who has left house, brothers, sisters, mother, father, children, or land for my sake and for the sake of the Gospel who will not receive a hundred times as much."When Luke recounts the same episode, his list of those to be left behind is telling: "house, wife, brothers, parents, or children.""Sisters" can be understood in the Greek "brothers," and "mother, father" has been collapsed into "parents.""Land" is gone, perhaps collapsed into "house"—or is it the sort of possession an urban evangelist would think too marginal to mention? "Children" in both quotations should be understood as referring only to adult children. But the startling Lucan addition is "wife." It is impossible to imagine Jesus, who made so much of equality and mutual faithfulness in marriage, asking his disciples to give up their wives—or their husbands, since there were certainly married female disciples. And in fact we know from an incidental remark of Paul in First Corinthians that "the other apostles, the brothers [and sisters?] of the Lord, and the Rock" himself all had spouses who accompanied them on their missionary journeys in the 50s and 60s.

In Luke's Gospel we are already a half century away from Jesus and decades away from the apostolic missions; and here we discover this gentile disciple, trying to hew as closely as possible to Jesus's intent but somewhat revising his teaching in an age of such difficulties for Christians that the combination of marriage and firm commitment to the Gospel, even to the point of martyrdom, may have seemed impossible. Beneath Luke's gentle surface is an uncompromising, all-or-nothing attitude, giving credibility to the second sentence of the identity ascribed to him in antiquity and attached to his gospel: "He served the Lord without distraction, without a wife, and without children."

I THINK WE MUST see Luke as an educated man of the first century whose critical assessment of the gross materialism of his own society and whose profound attraction to truth, first nourished perhaps by pagan philosophy, led him to the one God of the Jews and the compelling power of the Septuagint. Luke gives us an excellent imitation of the peculiar Greek of this translation of the Hebrew scriptures in the opening chapters of his gospel, in which the parents of John the Baptizer and of Jesus and the ancient devotees of the Temple cluster around the births of Jesus and his precursor, singing their exceedingly Jewish psalms and canticles. The Temple priest Zechariah in his vision, his wife Elizabeth in her insight, Mary in her Magnificat, Joseph in his obedience, Simeon in his ecstasy, and Anna in her prophecy are all meant, in the archaic Greek of their utterings, to remind us of Old Testament figures, the last figures of the old dispensation, singing in the Messiah.

The form of Judaism that Luke embraced involved, by the time he embraced it, a willingness to suffer and even die for this faith. The genuine perils he had experienced in his travels with Paul had paled before the insane cruelty of the rampant Beast, state persecution by Nero and his successors. Little wonder that Luke devalued material goods, which could so easily be expropriated by the state, and took every opportunity to remind his readers of how necessary it was to imitate Jesus in prayer if they were to resist not only the powers of this world but the gnawing fear in their own hearts. And little wonder that Luke comforted himself with the belief that his celibacy, like the exceptional celibacy of Jesus and (at least in his missionary years) Paul, was for the sake of the Kingdom.

Another indication of Luke's supposed "Stoicism" is how little emotion he allows Jesus to show. Once again, a comparison with other gospels, especially the primitive Mark, on which both Matthew and Luke depend for about one-third of their material, proves illuminating. Though Luke takes over many of Mark's episodes more or less whole, he consistently omits Mark's mention of Jesus "moved to pity" (Mark 1:41), Jesus "indignant" (10:14), Jesus "cursing" (11:21), Jesus in the dark about the future (13:32), Jesus overwhelmed by "terror and anguish" and "sorrowful unto death" (14:33–34), Jesus despairing and "forsaken" by God (15:34).

For Luke, Jesus remains the Jewish prophet and Messiah acknowledged by the first disciples. But to see Jesus only from this perspective would be to limit him to the Jewish religious context. Falling in step with his companion Paul, also Greek-educated if no gentile, Luke sees Jesus as a cosmic phenomenon, *the* cosmic phenomenon, the ultimate meaning not only of Judaism but of the universe. This, for both Paul and Luke, is to put Jesus in his proper philosophical-theological-global context. And to put Jesus in his proper social-political context, he is, as John the Visionary saw him, the very "Son of God" and "Savior" that the emperors have claimed (but failed miserably) to be. He must, therefore, be shown with a sublimely tranquil dignity even greater than the public portrayals of the imperial presence in statuary and literature.

199

The Jews, because of the commandment against graven images, had virtually no art, certainly nothing characteristic of them. If they had, it would not have looked much like the work of Phidias or Praxiteles, whose object was to exhibit to the world the supreme placidity and perfect balance of their gods and heroes—the ideal. The Jews had no such ideal. In Judaism, ideas were expressed in their most extreme form, and emotions ran from warm to hot, whether in great men and women or in God himself, who was, unlike human beings, "slow to anger but quick to forgive." We needn't go so far as to claim Luke for the Stoics in order to say that he ultimately sees Jesus not from a Jewish but from a gentile perspective.

If these small omissions of emotion, which represent a tiny fraction of Luke's Gospel, tell us more about Luke than about Jesus, it is still true that Luke, the painstaking researcher and skillful writer, is able to complete his portrait of Jesus with daring brushstrokes of brilliant color, impossible to his fellow evangelists. The scenes, unique to his gospel, that he (or, perhaps more accurately, Jesus) paints for us of penitence and forgiveness are as gripping as anything in world literature.

There is, for instance, the parable of the prodigal son, who insists on having his inheritance from his living father and goes off "to a distant country where he squandered his wealth in wild living." Famine comes upon the land and the prodigal is reduced to feeding pigs for a local farmer, who feeds his pigs better than his farmhands. This reminds the hungry man how well his father cared even for hired hands, and he resolves to return to his father and beg to be hired as a farmhand. " 'While he was still a long way off,' " recounts Jesus,

> "his father saw him and was filled with compassion for him. He ran to his son, threw his arms around him, and kissed him. The son said to him, 'Father, I have sinned against heaven and against you; I no longer deserve to be called your son.' But the father said to the servants, 'Quick! Bring the best robe and put it on him; give him a ring for his finger and sandals for his feet. Bring forth the fatted calf and kill it; let's have a feast and make merry, because this son of mine was dead and has come back to life, was lost and is found.' "

200

The prodigal's elder brother is puzzled when, returning from his toil in the fields, he hears—of all things—"music and dancing." This self-righteous son, in typical elder sibling fashion, seethes with anger when he learns what is going on. " 'Look here,' " he shouts at his father,

> " 'all these years I've been slaving for you and have never disregarded a single command. You never gave me so much as a goat to make merry with my friends. Now that son of yours has come back, the one who devoured your estate with prostitutes, and you have killed for him the fatted calf!'
>
> "But the father said to him, 'Son, you are always with me. All that I have is yours. But we had to make merry and celebrate. For your brother was dead and has come back to life, was lost and is found.' "

Luke does not always play down emotion. The pitiful, repeated refrain of the father ("was dead and has come back to life, was lost and is found") is so rich in human feeling that it can take a moment to realize that the father is God the Father and I the prodigal child, always welcome back whatever I may have done—as are all those whom I (in the role of elder sibling) may have felt safe to despise. Luke actually abounds in stories that are full of sentiment: a penitent tax collector whose sins God forgives; a "poor widow" who gives her "mite," the smallest coin of all, but everything she has; a Samaritan leper, one of ten lepers but the only one who remembers to return to thank Jesus for his cure.

Luke the celibate is in a league with Henry James when it

comes to portraying real women, like Martha and Mary. His most daring female character may be the prostitute who crashes the party at Simon the Pharisee's house, where Jesus is one of the guests. She has come only to encounter Jesus, which she goes about in a manner befitting her profession: falling to the floor at his feet, weeping over them and drying them with her lustrous long hair, then covering his feet with kisses, and at last massaging them with a precious ointment she has brought with her in an alabaster jar. The pious host, beside himself at the spectacle taking place in his home, thinks: "If this man were really a prophet, he would know who this woman is and what sort of creature is now touching him and just how bad a name she has [and he would, therefore, not suffer her attentions]."

202

Jesus, reading his thoughts, says:

> "Simon . . . I came into your house, and you poured no water over my feet, but she has cleaned my feet with her tears and dried them with her hair. You gave me no kiss, but she has been covering my feet with kisses ever since she came in. You did not anoint my head with oil, but she has anointed my feet with ointment. For this reason I tell you that her sins, however many they may be, have been forgiven her, because she has been so loving."

One can imagine the huffy reaction of Simon and his fellow Pharisees, in whose eyes the touch of a woman—any woman not one's wife—entailed ritual pollution. Jesus is playing dangerously on the word *love,* for a prostitute's "love" should mean paid erotic service. But this prostitute's excessive loving—her service to Jesus—has been the real thing. Though the weeping prostitute with the uncovered curls is often assumed to be Mary Magdalene (whence the words *magdalene* for "prostitute" and *maudlin* for "excessively weepy"), this is probably not so. Mary Magdalene is mentioned by Luke just after this scene in a list of women who "went with" Jesus on his preaching expeditions. Medieval interpretation further conflated the weeping prostitute, Mary Magdalene, and Martha's sister Mary into one person, whereas it appears to modern scholars that they were in actuality three different women. In this episode from Luke, however, is born *la traviata,* the fallen woman with the heart of gold, one of the most enduring archetypes in all of Western drama, fiction, opera, and painting.

203

The lesson that Jesus articulates to Simon—to us a fairly obvious one—would have cut through the proto-puritanical pieties of the Pharisees with all the shock of a sharp blade, encouraging renewed opposition to this renegade rabbi. But the unlikely encounter between a preacher and a prostitute may prompt the modern reader to a deeper consideration: why did the woman wish to approach Jesus in the first place? It is hard to believe that she could have expected to hear that her sins were forgiven and had engineered the encounter to this end. She appears, in Luke's telling, as a spontaneously expressive person, one who wears her heart on her sleeve. Filled with remorse, inexpressible in words if not in tears, she is drawn instinctively to Jesus because *she knows he will not reject her.*

The reason the scene is finally so shocking—whether in its original context or in ours—is that it is so difficult to imagine such an excessive woman, cheaply painted, her vulgar apparel chosen for the sake of a teasing display of her physical endowments, bawling her head off and crawling on her knees to the naked feet of a bishop or rabbi or imam—or whatever religious figure you might choose to imagine—while he not only allows her to proceed in full view of a dignified dinner party but shows himself to be entirely unembarrassed and even completely comfortable (not the sort of thing one can fake) with her prolonged and inordinate display. It takes quite some time, after all, to wash the dusty feet of a grown man with one's tears and then dry them adequately with one's hair. It may make the scene slightly easier to imagine if we bear in mind that Jesus was not in any sense an official religious figure (a priest or levite) but a layman—an anticlerical layman, given the scathing references in the parable of the Good Samaritan—whose disciples had bestowed on him the honorific title "Teacher."*

In Greek psychological theory, emotion was deemed a *daimon,* a spirit or demon that came to possess one. One goes from tranquility to emotion as the sea goes from undisturbed calm to roiling chaos when it is "possessed" by a storm. Thus one is "possessed" by eros or anger or pity or fear—all of them "gods" in some sense. This is probably the underlying reason that Luke has erased from his portrait of Jesus the catalogue of emotions attributed to him by Mark. Jesus, in Luke's view, cannot have been "moved to pity" or compassion. These minor gods cannot overcome his inner tranquility as they do ours. But this is not because Jesus is some sort of unfeeling Martian. He does not merely *feel* compassion, an emotion that can come and go and is dependent on outside forces; he *is* Compassion. Luke presents the prostitute as knowing this,

204

✠ We have come in modern times to think of rabbis as Jewish "clergy," but in the first century they were still an innovation and not considered officials (as were the Temple priests and levites).

thus crediting her with an instinctive understanding that a more conventional person might repress.

Despite the backdrop of Greek psychology, Luke found that he could not omit all reference to Jesus's emotions, especially as he shows the man approaching his last days on earth. "As the time drew near for him to be taken up [by crucifixion, resurrection, and enthronement in heaven at the Father's right hand], he resolutely turned his face toward Jerusalem," the Holy City of his terrible destiny; and "as Jerusalem came into view, he wept at the sight of it." Earlier he had lamented, "Jerusalem, Jerusalem . . . how often have I longed to gather your children together as a hen gathers her chicks under her wings, but you would not have it." Now, in tears, he predicts the destruction of the city.

205

Similar predictions occur in Mark and Matthew. The prediction in Mark, almost certainly written before A.D. 70, that is, before the city was actually leveled by the Romans, is vague. (After all, it hadn't happened yet.) The prediction as recounted by Matthew in the 70s or 80s, has an apocalyptic tinge that makes it seem more a prediction of the end of the world than of the city. The prediction in Luke, also written in the 80s, seems a reconstruction of the actual siege of Jerusalem, as it might have been reported to Luke by an eyewitness. Luke may wish to remind his readers that Jesus was capable of genuine prophecy, but, given his overall bias against depicting Jesus as "moved," even more important to his purpose here is his conviction that gentile Christians should in no way find the fulfillment of Jesus's prophecy a reason for rejoicing. Just as Jesus wept over the coming destruction, they must join their Jewish brothers in loving solidarity and mourning for the lost city.

Luke's version of the Last Supper, twice the length of Mark's and Matthew's, comes close to being a Jewish *symposion,* a convivial meal of ardent friendship, shared by Jesus and his disciples. "I cannot tell you how much I have longed to eat this Seder with you before I suffer," says Jesus to his friends. Only Luke gives voice to this passionate wish of Jesus, but it is likely to be an accurate remembrance of what Jesus said, since Luke appears here to be hewing as close to Semitic expression as he can. The painstakingly awkward Greek reads literally, "With desire have I so much desired this Passover to eat with you. . . ."

As Jesus is crucified, only Luke records him as praying, "Father, forgive them. They don't know what they're doing." While hanging in agony from his cross, a "criminal" crucified on either side of him, Jesus enters into a brief and final earthly dialogue. Besides enduring the horrible pain of crucifixion, the dying men are beset by the taunts of spectators and soldiers; and one of the criminals takes up the taunts of the crowd, screaming at Jesus: "Aren't you the Messiah? Then save yourself—and us, too!"

But, according to Luke, the other criminal rebukes him: "Have you no fear of God? We all got the same sentence, but you and I deserved it. We are paying for our crimes. But this man has done no wrong. Jesus, remember me when you come into your Kingdom."

And Jesus responds: "I tell you solemnly: today you will be with me in Paradise."

Could this dialogue, reported only by Luke, have taken place? Though it certainly accords with everything we know of the personality of Jesus, it seems almost too good to be true. But do we find it incredible because it is a relatively rational, sequential dialogue between two men dying hideously—or because the forgiveness offered seems too good to be true? It is certainly of a piece with the forgiveness offered elsewhere in this gospel, the forgiveness of the father to his prodigal son, the forgiveness of Jesus to the theatrical prostitute. The dialogue contains at least one additional clue to its possible authenticity: the crucified criminal calls Jesus by his first name alone, the single instance in any gospel where Jesus is not addressed by an honorific such as "Rabbi," "Master," or "Lord"—none of which a rough-hewn convict in his dying agony would have been likely to employ. Like the saying of Jesus about the Passover Seder, was Luke given this crucifixion dialogue on a trip with Paul to Jerusalem from someone who might actually have overheard it, perhaps one of the women who stood near the cross of Jesus or a Roman soldier converted by his exemplary death?

207

However that may be, Luke is preeminently the evangelist of God's mercy to sinners; and his gospel is the one that dramatizes most believably Paul's insistence to the Romans that "God's love for us is shown in that, *while we were still sinners, Christ died for us.*" Like the father of a prodigal child and like Jesus forgiving the executioners who drove the nails into his hands and feet, God does not wait for our repentance; he loves us *anyway.*

Luke is, in Dante's words, *"il scriba della gentilezza di Cristo,"* "the scribe of the kindness of Christ." Luke's portrait of Jesus is the one that has had the most effect on the West; it is, in fact, Luke's Christ that has made an indelible impression on the world's imagination. From *"Jesu dulcis,"* the "sweet Jesus" of Bernard of Clairvaux, to the "fairest Lord Jesus" of popular hymnody, from the merciful motets of Bach to the solemnly compassionate face sketched over and over by Rembrandt, the face that Jesus turns toward us is the face that Luke, with reverent devotion and superior craft, was able to show us, a face of mildness and love, a Jesus who almost seems to observe our follies with an affectionate twinkle in his eye.

It is this face that millions, even billions, of dying men and women have hoped to see at the last, as they have hoped to hear spoken to them the words recorded only by this "beloved physician" of souls: "I tell you solemnly: today you shall be with me in Paradise."

A Miracle for Me

We have already seen that, during the course of the history of New Testament interpretation, Mary Magdalene's identity was confused with both that of Mary the sister of Martha and that of the prostitute who wept over Jesus's feet. We know little of the historical Mary Magdalene, save that she hailed from the Judean town of Magdala, that she was one of Jesus's closest disciples and probably an "apostle," that (with other women) she followed Jesus to his cross, and that she was among the first to view the empty tomb. She may also have been the first recipient of an apparition of Jesus following his resurrection and the first to spread the news that "he is risen." This favor gave her in ancient Christian tradition the unique title of *Apostola Apostolorum,* "the Apostles' Apostle." She seems to have been a woman of substance and unconventional, for Luke tells us that she was one of "many women" who traveled with Jesus and his male disciples in an age and place where the mixing of the sexes was unheard of and that these unusual women "provided for [everyone] out of their own means"—that is, bankrolled the operation. Luke also provides us the baffling factoids that the women "had been cured of evil spirits and diseases" and that Mary, in particular, was one "from whom seven demons had been expelled," presumably thanks to an exorcism performed by Jesus.

With the miracles of Jesus the New Testament presents the modern reader with a conundrum so tangled that we may just about despair of making any sense of it. We admire Jesus's ideals (even if in a part of our mind we find them unrealistic) and his moral teachings (even if a part of our ego recoils from them). Having read our way through the dark works of the Eastern European fantasists from Kafka to Kundera, we are no longer so quick as we might once have been to dismiss the Book of Revelation as a grand expression of paranoia. Having lived through a time of state-sponsored terrors of unbelievable proportions, we no longer find Paul's antipolitics so peculiar. Living daily in a new economic order of Winner Take All, we may even begin to see the point of Luke's targeting the fundamental injustice of riches, of haves and have-nots. But stopping storms, curing blindness and leprosy, exorcising demons, raising the dead—come on. We either consign these marvels to the realm of fairy tales and the superstitions of prescientific peoples or take the more moderate view that there "may be something there"—a substrate of incidents that originally made perfectly good scientific sense but to which marvelous explanations were later appended. Couldn't Jesus's stopping of the storm on the Lake of Galilee have been just a coincidence: he said "cease" and, lucky for him, the storm just happened to end? Couldn't the feeding of the multitude of five thousand with five loaves and two fish be a simple case of inflation (of the numbers of people involved) and deflation (of the amount of food available) that occurred over time in the repeated telling of the story? Couldn't the supposed cures have been of hysterical, rather than real, illnesses? Could Jesus simply have been a clever magician who resorted to tricks, perhaps with the complicity of his closest disciples, in order to enlarge his gullible following?

The hypothesis of Jesus the Magician is actually pretty weak, since none of the miracles recounted in the gospels is explicable by this hypothesis alone. One needs to make additional assumptions—the disciples had heaps of food hidden in a nearby cave in preparation for the multiplication "miracle," the people raised weren't really dead, the "lepers" were wearing leper makeup from a Martin Scorsese film—that require either sleight of hand beyond the powers of even the most accomplished prestidigitator or a level of credulity that cannot be posited even of children. Beyond this, we must bear in mind that the witnesses *knew* the people whose ailments were cured, even knew those raised from the dead— which would make a pretended "cure" much more difficult to effect than would be the case nowadays in, say, the tent of a televangelist.

There is, in addition to the (very nearly) insurmountable difficulty of establishing the practical mechanics for such sham miracles, an invidious precondition to such a theory: Jesus himself must be shown to have been a sham, hoodwinking multitudes for his own questionable purposes. Though it is possible to imagine someone like Machiavelli descending to such trickery (or, more likely, advising someone else to try it), it is downright impossible to square such motivation with the man who is presented to us in the gospels. What is far more likely is that these stories accrued to

Jesus in the course of the development of the oral tradition and that by the time the evangelists came along there were already set "wonder stories," meant to prove that Jesus was the promised Messiah.

A careful analysis of the texts of the gospels, however, has convinced many scripture scholars that several, perhaps even a majority, of the basic miracle stories go back to the most primitive layer of the oral tradition—that is, to the testimony of the original eyewitnesses. One of these scholars is John Meier, whose multivolume study of the "historical Jesus," *A Marginal Jew,* still in progress, devotes more than five hundred pages to the miracles of Jesus—a more exhaustive analysis than, I think, has ever been attempted before. Meier is careful to distinguish between what is historically knowable and what is "metahistorical." The miracles—if they could have occurred—he classifies as "metahistorical" because they are, of their very nature, beyond anything that can be proved to have happened. Meier's modest conclusion is simply that "the statement that Jesus acted as and was viewed as an exorcist and healer during his public ministry has as much historical corroboration as almost any other statement we can make about the Jesus of history."

We seem to be faced here with a kind of irreducible historical mystery. We may grant that Mary Magdalene was not possessed, perhaps only the victim of a particularly vicious form of schizophrenia, symbolized by "seven devils," and that the "possessed boy" of Mark's Gospel was really an epileptic. We may grant that the "lepers" of the gospels had psoriasis or eczema or any of a variety of virulent skin diseases that ancient peoples had not the medical knowledge to distinguish from authentic leprosy. We can, according to Meier, claim that Jesus walking on the water never happened but is only a *theologoumenon*, a symbolic epiphany of Jesus who appears to us in the dark—that is, in our worst hour—to say: "It is I [or 'Here I am' or even the Hebrew God's 'I am'], so don't be afraid." But we cannot, it would appear, brush aside the miracles of healing as old wives' tales. The people who witnessed them believed they had occurred. At least some of the people, like Mary Magdalene, who experienced them found in this extraordinary attention reason to devote themselves permanently to Jesus's mission. To have been rendered sane or healthy or living once more must, after all, have struck the individual so cured as an overwhelming proof of God's personal care—a miracle for *me*.

These inexplicable phenomena were viewed by Jesus and his followers as proofs of the coming of God's Kingdom. They were, in their eyes, the fulfillment of the Isaian prophecies that the Anointed One would cast out all the evils that infect our world—disease and death, among them—and effect such a peace in nature that even "the lion shall lie down with the lamb." If the "mark of the Beast" signals hatred and destruction, the most salient mark of the Messiah is that he comforts and heals. When the followers of John the Baptizer come to Jesus on behalf of John, who has been imprisoned by Herod Antipas, they ask: "Are you the One-Who-Is-to-Come, or should we be looking for someone else?" Jesus replies, borrowing Isaiah's very words: "Go and let John know what you have seen and heard: *the blind coming to sight, cripples* walking, lepers cleansed, *the deaf hearing, the dead raised, and the Good News brought to the poor.* Happy indeed is anyone who is not alienated by what I do." This saying of Jesus, reported in identical passages of Matthew and Luke, clearly goes back to Q, the lost collection of Jesus's sayings that must have preceded these gospels by three or four decades.

In the final analysis, the modern problem with miracles is little different from what the ancient one would have been. If one believes in a God who heals, then healing in itself—whether of the quotidian kind or of an uncommon and spectacular sort—will hardly seem inconceivable or out of reach. If one cannot conceive of such a God—of an ultimate Goodness at the heart of the universe—miracles are, both intellectually and emotionally, off limits. In speaking of the medically inexplicable cures that have been occurring for a century and a half at the French shrine of Lourdes, John LaFarge, son of the American painter of the same name and a man who dedicated his life to peace and reconciliation, remarked cogently: "For those who believe in God, no explanation is necessary. For those who do not, no explanation is possible."

V

Drunk *in the* Morning Light

The People of the Way

✣

T HE PARTICULARS OF RESURRECTION, however one may interpret them, make for fascinating reading; and the encounters of the disciples with the risen Jesus, as the evangelists retell them, form a unique collection in the annals of the world. Their uniqueness lies not only in their singular subject but in the details inserted by the evangelists into the narratives, details which were, surely in some cases, divulged by the original participants. As I read the recountings of these explosively joyful experiences, I am always aware of the smells of spring breaking through the clotted earth and linen fresh from the laundry—the sweetness of life overcoming the molderings of death.

In Mark's narrative, as we have already seen, Mary Magdalene and two other women make their way to the tomb "very early on the first day of the week . . . as the sun was rising," this last, modestly inserted detail indicating that they will just miss the resurrection itself. Stunned to find the tomb open and, inside, a strange and talkative young man dressed in white, they drop their spices for the dead and run headlong from the tomb, frightened out of their wits, but on their way (according to Matthew) to "tell his [male] disciples," who are cowering elsewhere. The bright April sun must have made vivid the flowing robes and veils of the women, now wild and in full flight, and warmed their arms and faces till they could begin to suspect that something wonderful had happened.

In John's Gospel, Mary Magdalene is the first to behold the

risen Jesus. She is in a spring garden close by the tomb. Through copious tears, she sees a man coming toward her, whom she takes to be the gardener. "Woman," he asks her, "why are you weeping? Who do you want?"

"Sir," wails Mary, "if you have taken him away, tell me where you have put him, and I will go and remove him."

"Mary," says the "gardener"—and with that one word Mary knows who it is.

"Rabbuni!" she cries out, using the most august Aramaic for "rabbi," and clutches him to her.

Luke presents us with two dejected disciples leaving Jerusalem as the shadows are lengthening along the road in the sunny afternoon of this most unusual day. They are joined along the way to Emmaus by a third man, who listens politely to their talk of their rabbi, one "Jesus of Nazareth, who showed himself a prophet mighty in deed and word before God and the whole people." But he was "handed over" to be crucified with the complicity of "our chief priests and leaders." "Our own hope," admit the two travelers to the newcomer, "had been that he would be the one to set Israel free. And this is not all: it is three days [by Jewish reckoning, that is, from Friday to Sunday] since this happened; and some women from our group have astounded us: they went to the tomb early this morning, and when they could not find the body, they came back to tell us that they had had an angelic vision declaring him alive."

The third man, well versed in scripture, explains to them that "it was necessary that the Messiah should suffer before entering into his glory." Then, Luke tells us, "starting with Moses and going through all the prophets, he explained to them the passages throughout the scriptures" that concerned the Messiah. "As they drew near the village . . . he made as if to go on, but they pressed him to stay with them saying, 'It is almost evening, and the day is nearly done.'

"So he went into the village to stay with them. Now while he was with them at table, he took the bread and said the blessing, then broke it and gave it to them. And their eyes were opened," reports Luke, "and they recognized *him;* but he had vanished from their sight. Then they said to each other, 'Did not our hearts burn within us as he talked to us on the road and opened the scriptures to us?' "

The motifs of light and heat emphasize important themes. Time is precious; and just as the "day" of the prophets of Israel had to come to an end, the "day" of Jesus is "nearly done," to be succeeded by the Age of the Spirit that is about to break upon the disciples. The light of day—the limpid, physical presence of the Son of God in their midst, talking with them, breaking bread—will be transmuted into the fire in their hearts, the invisible presence of the Spirit to which they must respond from now on, even if their journey lies in darkness.

From now on. The Age of the Spirit is also the Age of the Church; and if such a phrase makes us shudder a little, bringing on historical memories of Grand Inquisitors and human bonfires, this was hardly the case for the disciples, whose insignificant "Church" was, to begin with, a collection of no more than a hundred-odd marginal men and women. They banded together, at first in fear that Jesus's fate might prove to be their own. But gradually they took courage, and finally they went public. The transition period—between the morning of resurrection and the first fearless, out-loud announcement that "he is risen"—took nearly seven weeks, stretching from the Sunday after the beginning of Passover to Shavuot, the Feast of Weeks, which Greek-speaking Jews called Pentecost.

At the beginning of this period, at least some disciples (and we don't know how many) were the recipients of appearances of Jesus, such as the appearances to Magdalene and the two travelers on the road to Emmaus. The huddled Twelve (now eleven since the betrayal and departure of Judas) became aware of Jesus in their midst on more than one occasion. These "appearances" were not like the appearance of an incorporeal ghost. Magdalene seems to have clung to a very material Jesus; he invited Thomas, the skeptical disciple who had been missing during an earlier appearance, to "feel" the wounds in his hands and side (where a soldier's lance had pierced him while he hung dead on the cross); and he even ate food.

It is impossible to say, after two thousand years and in a world whose categories and measurements are so different from those of the first century, what the nature of these appearances might have been. To set them down as a hoax would do a significant disservice to the teaching that surrounds them. As in the case of Jesus's miracles, we would have to imagine that the most sublime moral sentiments ever expressed had somehow been drafted in the service of a cheap fraud. To hypothesize that the disciples were the victims of mass hysteria would be almost as problematic: Jesus appeared to groups, certainly, but first of all to individuals (who cannot be accused of *mass* hysteria); and the disciples of Jesus, simple though many of them certainly were, were not notable so much for their fanciful imaginations as for their plodding literalness—hardly the ideal ground for hysteria of any sort. It seems wisest to say that the disciples *believed* that they had encountered the risen Jesus, that he was looking much better than when they had seen him last (to the extent that some of them didn't even recognize him at first), and that, despite the ease with which he appeared and disappeared, he was tangible.

How long this sequence of experiences lasted we cannot say. The evangelists seem to swing between asserting that everything happened in one day, after which Jesus withdrew from them permanently, and assuming a longer period of some forty days, after which Jesus took formal leave of his faithful disciples and ascended into the heavens. Either there was something about these experiences that left the minds of the recipients clouded as to time and circumstance or the experiences themselves were of such a timeless nature that it seemed afterward impossible to insert them into a normal, consecutive chronology.

The courage that the disciples would eventually display came to them, they believed, from "the Spirit," their reception of which was, like that of Jesus's resurrection, an experience unlike any other. In John's Gospel, the risen Jesus breathes on them and says: "Receive the holy Spirit." In Luke, he merely tells them in his final instruction to "remain in the city till you are clothed with power from on high." Then, in the Acts of the Apostles, written by Luke to extend the story of his gospel into that of the early Church, the Spirit is described as descending on the disciples ten days after Jesus's ascension, in a dramatic theophany replete with Old Testament wind and fire. "When the Day of Pentecost came," the Twelve, their number again complete by the appointment of Matthias to replace the lost Judas, were gathered together with Jesus's family and some unnamed male and female disciples (possibly one hundred twenty in all, probably fewer), in a house in Jerusalem,

> when suddenly there came from heaven a sound like
> the violent rushing of wind, which filled the whole

221

house where they were sitting. And they saw what
seemed to be tongues of fire, which divided and came
to rest on each of them. They were all filled with the
holy Spirit and began to speak in tongues other than
their own, as the Spirit enabled them.

They tumbled out into the street, where an immense
crowd of foreign pilgrims had collected, drawn by the strange
noises emanating from the house. According to Luke, the disciples, speaking in different languages, were able to make
themselves understood to the bystanders "each in his own
tongue." But not everyone was impressed. The disciples, wind-
blown, seized by the Spirit, and no doubt traumatized once
more, presented an excited and disheveled spectacle to the
nosy pilgrims. Some scoffed: "They've been slurping up the
May wine, that's all!"

Peter, he of the large shoulders and lungs, needed no mega-
phone but stepped forward and addressed the pilgrims in his
deep voice:

> Brother Jews and all you who live in Jerusalem, make
> no mistake about this but listen carefully to my
> words: these men are not drunk, as you suppose. It's
> only nine in the morning [and the grog shops are not
> yet open]! Rather, you are witnessing the fulfillment
> of Joel's prophecy:
>
> In the last days—the Lord declares—
> *I shall pour out my Spirit on all humanity.*
> *Your sons and daughters shall prophesy,*
> *your young people shall see visions,*

222

your old people dream dreams.
Even on the slaves, men and women,
shall I pour out my Spirit. . . .

Peter goes on to give a sermon latticed with very Jewish reasoning, declaring that Jesus, risen—"to which we are all witnesses"—and now "raised to the heights by God's right hand, has received from the Father the holy Spirit, who was promised, and what you see and hear is the outpouring of that Spirit."

Where did Peter, the cowering, semiliterate fisherman, get up the nerve to address this cosmopolitan crowd in such a confident fashion? Luke would have us understand that it is the outpouring of the Spirit on Peter that has made all the difference. Repeatedly in the text of Acts, the Spirit surges through assemblies and individuals, giving them the courage to do things that would ordinarily be impossible for them. Jesus, risen, has returned to his Father, as he told his disciples he must, but he has not left them orphans. He has sent them the Father's Spirit, which is also his Spirit. "Indeed," cries Peter, "the whole House of Israel can be certain that the Lord [of the Universe] and Messiah [promised through the prophets] whom God has made is this Jesus whom you crucified." Jesus, the obedient Adam (and, therefore, perfect human being), has been raised to "God's right hand," which means that God has given him permanent Lordship over the cosmos. In this way, mortal Time has been able to intersect with Eternity—so the Age of the Spirit, prophesied by Joel, is now under way.

It has always been a bit difficult to get a grasp on who or what this Spirit is. The Greek New Testament's word for spirit, *pneuma,* has precisely the same root meaning as the Hebrew

223

word, *ruach:* breath or wind. In the prophecy of Joel, as throughout the Hebrew Bible, *the* Spirit is God's Spirit, which, like a mother's breath on her newborn, "broods over the waters" at the Creation and, like wind, which cannot be controlled and is invisible except in its effects, "blows where it will." But the Feast of Weeks, which was called in this period the Feast of the Assembly because it called the diaspora Jews back to Jerusalem, was a celebration of the Covenant between God and the Jews; and Jesus's Twelve now confront the Twelve Tribes of Israel, symbolically assembled in the street, to announce the fulfillment of the Covenant in the very event of Jesus's exaltation and sending of *his* Spirit upon the new Assembly, the Church.

224

What are the effects of this Spirit? What did the disciples, imbued with new courage, actually succeed in doing?

According to Luke, their lively and convincing preaching of the risen Jesus brought many into their ranks. By the end of the day on which Peter preached his maiden sermon, "three thousand were added to their number." As with Jesus, it is not so much the words as the deeds of the disciples that draw fresh adherents. Peter and John, on their way into the Temple for evening sacrifice, pass a man in his forties, "crippled from birth," who has been begging at the gate for many years. The scene, as described by Luke, starts off with all the elements of the typical nonencounter between beggars and their prospective donors. The cripple puts out his hand in the usual automatic gesture, expecting Peter and John either to pass him by or, with carefully averted gaze, to drop a small coin into his hand. They do neither, but stop completely and insist that the man "look at" them, which he does, amazed and now hoping for a considerable gift.

"I have neither silver nor gold, but what I have I give you," says Peter, taking the man by the right hand and pulling him up. "In the name of Jesus-Messiah the Nazarene, walk." The man, wide-eyed, stands on his feet, stock still for a moment as he feels warm life surge into his feet and ankles, then tries out his legs, walking around in increasingly excited circles, then accompanies Peter and John into the Temple, walking between them, refusing to let go of their arms, praising God at the top of his lungs, and leaping into the air all at once. Definitely a cripple to be played by Roberto Benigni in the film version.

Reading this story of the beggar with newfound strength in his legs always makes me a little weak in the knees. It seems to knead all the meaning of the gospels into a new and unexpected loaf. Bumbling Peter, who once seemed permanently puzzled, has become the Good Samaritan: though Jesus is gone from their midst, the disciples now continue his work of healing and helping whoever falls across their paths, which they do in his supremely personal way, gazing forthrightly into the eyes of the other, speaking the truth, taking the other's hand. The strength they are able to communicate has nothing to do with worldly power, for they have "neither silver nor gold." But because these ex-fishermen have set aside their own egos and identities (and all worldly pretensions), they no longer present—as they once did—an obstacle to the Spirit, which can now flow through them to others as through an open channel. With the image of the jumping beggar before them, thousands more attach themselves to the apostles.

It is not long before Peter and John are hauled before the Sanhedrin for nothing more than "an act of kindness to a cripple," as Peter points out. The "rulers, elders, and scribes" of this high council, "astonished at the fearlessness shown by Peter and John, considering that they were uneducated laymen," let them go with a warning, but we can already see, looming on the horizon, the harassments, arrests, and even executions that await this fast-growing band of men and women, who call one another "brother" and "sister" and think of themselves collectively as the people of "the Way."

The first martyr is Stephen, one of seven "deacons" (or ministers) appointed by a democratic vote of the Church to distribute food to the poor. Luke tells us that Stephen was "full of faith and of the holy Spirit," a worker of miracles and a champion debater, who bests many of those who attempt to discredit the new faith. Brought before the Sanhedrin on charges of attacking Judaism, he gives a defense of himself that is actually an eloquent and orthodox summation of Jewish salvation history—till he ends with the shocking assertion that "I can see heaven thrown open and the Son of Man sitting at the right hand of God." Convicted of blasphemy and dragged outside the city walls, he is stoned to death, while uttering as his final, Christ-like words "Lord, do not hold this sin against them." Before his executioners begin the stoning, however, they strip off their cloaks for greater maneuverability, laying these at the feet of the apparent ringleader, "a young man named Saul." Within this scene, therefore, Luke sketches for us not only the theological tensions of Jerusalem in the 30s, but the as-yet-unknown force that will become the surprising mainspring of Christian expansion.

LUKE HAS BEEN DISMISSED for writing derivative Hellenistic "aretalogy," a conventional form of Greco-Roman biography in which the lives of good men of the past are inventively dramatized and held up as flawless and godlike models for men of the present. There can be no doubt that Luke is influenced by this format, as well as by his profound reverence for the memory of the apostles and other disciples, who had passed from the scene by the time he wrote his histories; and some of his dramatizations (such as the Pentecost "Spirit" experience) could well be imaginative Lucan reconstructions of plainer and less chronologically precise Palestinian recollections. But Luke, though he certainly sees the founders of the Jerusalem Church through the flattering filter of time, gives a basically factual, if polished, account of events he would surely much rather *not* report, such as the conflict between Paul and Peter over imposing the Law on the gentiles. Luke's recounting has a cordiality and even courtliness to it that is certainly absent from Paul's tirade against Peter and his inconsistencies. But it would be hard to stay angry for the forty years that elapsed from the time of these events to Luke's writing about them. Luke shows himself as revering Peter but siding with Paul, whose references to their arguments in his own letters are a confirmation of Luke's essential accuracy.

Luke is also sometimes accused of what might best be labeled "creeping Catholicism," a tendency to present the early Church as much more structured and hierarchical than the freewheeling, intuitive Church we read of in Paul's letters. This second objection is more easily met. Paul, even in the undoubtedly authentic letters, speaks of positions of defined responsibility within the Church, such as the apostles, prophets, and teachers of First Corinthians and the "bishops and deacons" whom he addresses at the outset of his Letter to the Philippians. We do not need to suppose that the Philippians already had "bishops" in our elaborate sense to recognize that

Paul is speaking of something more august than building superintendents. And Luke, in his account of the inchoate Church, leaves room for Pauline "freedom," in fact complements and expands on Paul's exhortations so that we may see more clearly how this freedom operated in practice.

Luke describes the growing Church as "remain[ing] faithful to the teaching of the apostles, to the brotherhood, to the breaking of the bread, and to the prayers," which he sees as the four constitutive elements of the new Assembly. In the 80s, when Luke wrote, the authentic teaching of Jesus was being compromised by people whom Luke would have viewed as false teachers, not only the Judaizers and proto-Gnostics with whom Paul had tangled but all the inventive revisionists who inevitably attach themselves to any movement. For Luke, the yardstick of orthodoxy was the "teaching of the apostles," the original envoys whom Jesus had commissioned to preach his message, and this is why he devotes so much of his narrative to the sermons of primitive Christianity's major figures. But since doctrinal orthodoxy would hardly have been at issue in the immediate aftermath of the Pentecost outpouring, we can gain a clearer picture of the Jerusalem Church by examining Luke's other three elements.

"The prayers" is a reference to the common prayer of the Jews in Temple and synagogue, which the Messianists attended as often as possible, many of them daily. The centerpiece of synagogue prayer was the reading from the sacred scrolls of scripture, which the Messianists heard as now-obvious prophecies of their Christ, so that this prayer branched out for them in two directions, confirming both their Jewish identity and their new insight into its previously hidden meaning. "The breaking of the bread," adumbrated in the common meal at

Emmaus, is Luke's formula for the rite of the Eucharist, which the Messianists celebrated in private homes. This "communion" was symbolic of the very thing they could not share with the mass of their fellow Jews in prayer: their incorporation into Christ and, thereby, their spiritual "brotherhood" with one another. When Christians were finally expelled from synagogue services in the 90s, they would appropriate the Jewish prayer service and make it into the prelude to the Eucharist, thus creating the Liturgy (or Mass or Lord's Supper) as we know it today.

"Brotherhood," the usual translation of the Greek *koinonia,* has unfortunate sexist overtones, which some attempt to alleviate by translating *koinonia* as "fellowship," marginally more serviceable perhaps but lacking the intimacy of "brotherhood." *Koinonia,* however, implies intimacy without sexism; it is the noun that stems from the adjective *koine,* meaning "common," and would best be translated into English as "common-ness," "community," or even "commonalty," did not those words have connotations that can take us even farther afield. "In-common-ness" or "sense of community" might serve, were these not too unwieldy to insert into most sentences. "Kinship" is close to being an English equivalent to *koinonia,* if we could erase its primary meaning of physical relatedness; and the slightly awkward "kindred-ness" probably comes closest.

229

These people, who called each other "brother" and "sister," cherished a lively sense of their mutual "kindred-ness"—which may sound as hollow as a press release, till one examines how they went about it. Because of the "signs and wonders" that the apostles and other disciples (like Stephen) were able to work through Jesus's name, "a feeling of awe" enveloped them all, Luke tells us; and this feeling prompted them to spend time in the enjoyment of one another's company and even to hold "all things in common: they would sell their property and their goods in order to give to anyone who was in need. They met together daily in the Temple courts, broke bread at home [that is, often dined together for the sake of fellowship], and ate with glad and generous hearts."

Tucked away in all this glad generosity is the awesome information that the first Christians, because they "held all things in common," were also the world's first communists. Theirs was not, of course, state communism, but it was an associative communism that they took most seriously. When two of their number, Ananias and his wife, Sapphira, make the grand gesture of "sell[ing] one of their properties" for the Church's benefit but hold back the lion's share for their own private benefit, they are both struck dead; and though it is difficult to tell whether their deaths are due to their own guilt or to the condemnation of the apostles, Peter makes clear that their wealth was always theirs "to do with as [they] liked": they were under no obligation to liquidate anything. Their sin was their pretense, their attempt to "lie to the holy Spirit," the animator of the Assembly.

So these first Christians were not obliged to dissolve their fortunes for the sake of the poor: the community of goods was purely voluntary. But what freedom—from want, from worry, from the endless burdens of management and accounting, from brinksmanship—it must have afforded those who participated "with glad and generous hearts," whether they were the once-poor or the once-rich. At the threshold to the third millennium, at the golden gate to a new age of untrammeled global capitalism and its consequent winners and losers, we can only wish that such a society existed still.

Despite this radical innovation, the brothers and sisters were very much people of their time and place, Jewish inhabitants of the Greco-Roman world. It seems, for instance, never to have crossed their minds to question outright the patriarchal household code of the dominant culture, in which wives were expected to obey their husbands, children their parents (especially their fathers), and slaves their masters. To do otherwise would be to overturn the natural order of things. Even Paul, whose democratic insight was more penetrating than any of the other apostles', wrote out a version of this conventional household code in his Letter to the Church at Colossae:

> Wives, be subject to your husbands, as you should in the Lord. Husbands, love your wives and do not be harsh with them. Children, obey your parents always, for this is what pleases the Lord. Fathers, do not carp at your children, lest they lose heart. Slaves, obey your earthly masters in everything, not only when their eye is on you, as if you had only to please human beings, but wholeheartedly, out of respect for the Master. Whatever you do, put your heart into it as done for the Lord and not for men, knowing that the Lord will repay you by making you his heirs. It is Christ the Lord you are serving. Anyone who does wrong will be repaid in kind. For there is no favoritism. Masters, make sure that your slaves are given what is right and fair, knowing that you too have a Master in heaven.

Quite a mouthful from the apostle of freedom and equality. Elizabeth Schüssler Fiorenza is one of a growing number of scholars who claim that this is so contradictory to Paul's central assertions that he could not have written it, that it was composed after his death by one of his disciples and should be dated to the last third of the first century. Murphy-O'Connor limits himself to commenting that "if [Paul] were true to himself, he should never have employed [this code]." Despite my admiration for the man, I tend to the opinion that Paul could have written this.

For one thing, no one's thinking is so well wrought as to be without its contradictions.* But Paul may also, as in his advice to the Corinthians about liturgical exhibitionism, have seen himself under an obligation to "keep the lid on" the Church, so that it would not draw more unwonted attention from the larger society than it was already drawing on account of its (absolutely necessary) theological and social positions.

Paul and his fellow Christians were already fighting a war on three cultural-political fronts: against Jews who accused them of the capital crime of blasphemy, against Greeks who found the Jewish notion of physical resurrection hilarious, and against Romans who were eager to round up "troublemakers," especially ones who prayed to a "god" that the Romans themselves had executed. In their monotheism, Christians were accused of atheism, in their Messianism, of heresy. In their communism, they appeared an obvious threat to the economics of class; in their joyous inner freedom and their comprehension of the essential equality of all human beings before God, they stood an outrageous challenge to the whole socio-

---

✂ The passage from Colossians accords well enough with another, First Corinthians 14:34–36, concerning the subordination of women "in the assembly"—though this is widely thought to be a later interpolation since it goes against an earlier passage in the same letter (11:5), which takes it as a given that women are free to "pray and prophesy" publicly.

political order of the Roman empire. How many more fronts could they fight on?

Sometimes we blind ourselves to the consequences of our own thinking because we cannot face those consequences. If, in addition to the wars they were already waging, Christians had followed their ideas to their logical conclusions and taken up cultural crusades against patriarchy and slavery, they would never have survived and we would never have heard of Christianity. If the passage above was Paul's way of exhorting his converts not to rock society's boat any more than they had to, it is also possible to read into the standard formulas that he trots out here a hint that his heart was not in his instruction. Josephus, the Roman-Jewish historian and general who was Paul's younger contemporary, defends Jewish family life against Roman suspicions by insisting that Jews are even more patriarchal than Romans: "The woman, says the [Mosaic] Law, is in all things inferior to the man. Let her accordingly be submissive, not for her humiliation, but that she may be directed, for the authority has been given by God to the man." Such apologias for Jewish mores, not infrequent in this period, imply Jewish defensiveness in the face of repeated Roman criticism; and against the unqualified enthusiasm of Jewish figures like Josephus and Philo, Paul's "approbation" of this code, balanced by instructions (missing from other contemporary articulations) on the corresponding obligations of the paterfamilias, looks downright tepid.

233

We can, moreover, still identify, in the subterranean depths of Paul's thought, repeated affirmations of his deepest convictions about freedom and equality. His famous dictum "It is better to marry than to burn" (so often misinterpreted as a reference to hellfire rather than to the unfulfilled sexual heat that Paul has in mind) is followed in First Corinthians by a long disquisition on the pluses and minuses of marriage and celibacy. It is an evenhanded presentation, divided into considerations of equal length for men and women, but at the tail end of the passage, Paul gives women an extra paragraph:

> A wife is tied down as long as her husband lives. But
> if her husband dies, she is free—to marry whomever,
> if she likes. . . . But she'd be happier to stay single, at
> least to my way of thinking (and I suspect the Spirit
> of God would agree).

Paul does not give patriarchal marriage and family life his unalloyed seal of approval. He is aware of its costs to a woman's spiritual freedom. There is no suggestion here of a woman's "inferiority," just that she's spiritually stuck with the dilemma of society's binding norms, unless she opts out of the marriage game altogether.

In like manner, Paul gives incidental evidence of his underlying repugnance toward slavery in his briefest letter of all: to Philemon, asking this Colossian paterfamilias to accept back his runaway slave, Onesimus, who had also stolen from him. When Paul writes, squeezing everything he has to say onto a single piece of papyrus, he is in prison, probably at Ephesus. This private letter (the only one of Paul's that we possess), intended for one family rather than for a regional church, is a masterpiece of person-to-person persuasiveness and a shining example of how the brothers and sisters dealt with one another in sticky situations:

> Paul, a prisoner of Christ Jesus, and Timothy our
> brother, send greetings to our dear friend and fellow

234

worker Philemon, to Apphia our sister [Philemon's wife], to Archippus our fellow soldier [probably their son], and to the church that meets in your home:

Grace to you and peace from God our Father and the Lord Jesus Christ.

I always thank my God when I remember you in my prayers, because I hear of your love and faith, which you hold in the Lord Jesus toward even *all* the saints.* I pray that the *koinonia* of your faith may enable you to understand every goodness that we have in Christ. I have indeed received much joy and encouragement from your love, because through you the hearts of the saints have been refreshed, brother.

235

For this reason, though I am confident enough in Christ to remind you of your duty, yet would I rather appeal to your love. So it is that I, Paul—an old man and now also a prisoner of Christ Jesus—I appeal to you for my child whom I begat in chains: Onesimus. In the past he was of no use to you, but now he can be of use to us both. [The Greek adjective *onesimos* means "useful."] Now in sending him back to you, I send my own heart. I wanted to keep him with me, for he could have stood in for you, helping me while I am in chains for the Gospel's sake. But I was determined to do nothing without your consent, for I put my hope not in forcing the issue but in your spontaneous kindness. Perhaps the reason he was separated from you for a while was so that you could have him back forever, no longer as a slave, but better than a

✠ *Hoi hagioi* ("the saints" or "the holy ones") was a common first-century term for one's fellow Christians, exactly parallel to the Hebrew *ha-hasidim* (regarding which, see note, page 41).

slave, as a beloved brother, especially to me, but how much more to you, both in the flesh and in the Lord. So if you grant me any *koinonia* [with yourself], welcome him as you would me. If he has wronged you in any way or owes you anything, charge it to me. I am writing this in my own hand: I, Paul, will repay you (not to mention that you owe me your very self).

Well, brother, I am counting on you in the Lord; refresh my heart in Christ. I am writing with complete confidence that you will comply, knowing that you will do even more than I ask.

One last thing: will you prepare a place for me to stay? I am hoping through your prayers to be restored to you.

Epaphras, a prisoner with me in Christ Jesus, sends you his greetings, as do Mark, Aristarchus, Demas, and Luke, my fellow workers.

May the grace of the Lord Jesus Christ be with your spirit.

"And also with you," would have been all Philemon could have whispered on finishing this. The Letter to Philemon reveals Paul's perceptiveness, even craftiness, in dealing with other human beings. Paul can win this one neither by fiat nor by a dazzling display of theological wit. Philemon is free to execute Onesimus for his flight or merely chop off his right hand for his theft. He is free, as he always has been, to do with him anything he likes. Slaves had no rights, and slave owners no legal restraints. So runaway slaves did not return willingly to their masters; and we may well imagine that Paul's more arduous challenge was not writing this letter but persuading

Onesimus, whom he had met in prison, that he should return to his owner rather than attempt the anxiety-ridden existence of a permanent fugitive. Having convinced Onesimus that he can turn the tide on his behalf, he takes up the invidious task of instructing the slave master in his Christian duty, while seeming not to do so.

It would be going well beyond the evidence to assume that Philemon was a villain. He may have been abstracted, aloof, and classist; after all, it is Paul who has "begotten" Onesimus in the faith that Philemon holds but had (apparently) never bothered to communicate to his slaves. He was undoubtedly a sincere man, or Paul could never have hoped to make headway with him on a decision that would only hold him up to scorn among his peers. But he was a Roman paterfamilias, master of life and death within the domain of his household, possessor of the largest male ego the world has ever known, whom no one but Caesar could gainsay. The normally forthright, aggressive, provocative, take-charge apostle has to pull in his horns and follow Jesus's ambivalent exhortation to his followers to be "wise as serpents and gentle as doves"—and he does so without a false step, waiting till his seventh sentence even to slip in Onesimus's name and never repeating it, never indeed offering Philemon any irritation more than necessary.

Scripture scholars have often questioned why this short letter about one individual, a letter supposedly lacking in general interest, was preserved when other letters of Paul were lost. To me, this magisterial entreaty says more about the people of the Way than do the exploding numbers of believers and the dazzling miracles of Acts. Paul, with thoughtful caring, puts all his talents into a "miracle" on behalf of a single lost soul. Like Peter's cure of the cripple, this is simply "an act of kindness":

"I have neither silver nor gold, but what I have I give you."
Philemon almost certainly freed Onesimus, sending him back
to Ephesus to work with Paul—how could he not? But like all
acts of kindness, this one seems to have yielded unexpected results. Onesimus is likely to have been in his late teens or early
twenties at the time of Paul's letter; and we know that at the
beginning of the second century the name of the bishop of
Ephesus, who is credited with making the first collection of
Paul's letters, was—Onesimus.

Ideas take a long time to ferment to dark fulfillment and
rich bouquet. Abraham's God wanted him to worship no
other, but it took the Jews a thousand years more to begin to
adhere to strict monotheism—and we're still trying to get it
right. Paul's encouragement of Christian widows to remain
free will blossom into the early monastic sisterhoods, then into
the autonomous convents of the Middle Ages, ruled by great
abbesses like Brigid of Kildare and Hildegard of Bingen. For
the first time, the world will experience the phenomenon of
women not ruled, sheltered, or protected by men: free women.
Each of these developments will serve as a stage in the gradual
blossoming of feminism. Paul's insistence to Philemon that
there are no slaves, only brothers, will prompt Patrick of
Ireland in the fifth century to condemn as immoral all trade in
human beings, then lead the Anabaptists in the late seventeenth
century to the conviction that slavery is against God's Word,
then induce the Abolitionists of the nineteenth century to
raise a universal agitation against the "peculiar institution," and
finally fire Martin Luther King in the twentieth century to de-
mand that Americans erase the residual effects of slavery. And
far beyond America's borders, everyone who fights to disman-
tle systems of class and economic oppression, who seeks to es-

238

tablish human rights and universal brotherhood, is, like Onesimus, a child begotten by Paul.

Not one of these developments, evolving over the ages, can be said to have reached its ultimate expression. But just as we can pinpoint Abraham's experience of the Voice as the beginning of monotheism—the sprouting seed—we can pinpoint the beginnings of feminism, abolitionism, and the movements for civil and human rights in the spiritual vision of Paul and his converts, who would no doubt be amazed at what we have made of insights that were for them so new, dynamic, and otherworldly.

Paul called his converts "the brothers and sisters loved by God," and Peter, in a vision, came to the conclusion that "God has no favorites." The Jesus Movement became a movement for the universalization of Judaism, making Jewish ideas and even the Jewish social context available and applicable to all humanity. We should not, however, see Jesus as the beginning of this development, any more than we see Moses, rather than Abraham, as the beginning of monotheism. Jesus, like Moses, took advantage of a living tradition that was astoundingly rich in possibilities. Long before Jesus, the classical prophets had already looked forward to the outpouring of God's "Spirit on all humanity," an incredible outpouring from which no one—not even the "women" and "slaves" of Peter's quotation from Joel—would be excluded. And we cannot be surprised that women and slaves, far more than any other categories of society, swelled the ranks of a movement that assured them that, however insignificant their places in society, in the eyes of God and his Assembly they were the equals of anyone.

FOR ALL THIS, the first Christians were not ivory-tower intellectuals but ordinary people confronted, as we all are, with the practical problems of daily life. A relatively small band to begin with, they knew one another and could rely on person-to-person interaction rather than edicts and memorandums. If they hadn't all known Jesus in life, they knew many who had—and this situation prevailed nearly to century's end, as the Jesus Movement grew into a Eurasian network of local churches, many with a resident elder or two who remembered his or her encounters with Jesus. We get a glimpse of how close-knit the leadership was when, at the close of Paul's Letter to Philemon, he sends greetings from Mark and Luke, who are with him at Ephesus. There is not much doubt that these are two of our evangelists, who, together with the author of the letter himself, may be responsible for nearly sixty percent of the pages of the New Testament.

Having, at least to begin with, "neither silver nor gold," the people of the Way relied on one another's hospitality. Peter is described in Acts as staying at Jaffa with Simon the Tanner in his house by the sea and "visiting one place after another," a project that presumes the hospitality of many. Lydia, an independent woman "in the purple-dye trade," insisted that Paul, who was chary of accepting favors, stay with her at Philippi and would "not take No for an answer." We have already seen the names of two who opened their homes to "house-churches," the regular assemblies of the people of the Way: the Ephesian woman Chloe of First Corinthians and Philemon (and his family) at Colossae. Nympha ran another house-church at Laodicea, not far from Colossae. Besides these, Acts mentions Mary, Mark's mother and aunt to Barnabas, another of Paul's many missionary companions. She was a middle-class woman who ran a Jerusalem house-church and kept an addled servant named Rhoda, who was so surprised to see Peter at the

240

peephole one day (he was supposed to be in prison but had escaped) that she neglected to open the door to him and left him standing in the street while she ran inside to give everybody the news. In his Letter to the Romans, Paul at Corinth sends greetings from "Gaius, my host and the host of all the church . . . and from Erastus, the city treasurer," who, like Magdalene and other women disciples of Jesus's day, must have helped bankroll operations.

Many, but scarcely all, of these hosts would have been people of means. On no one did Paul rely more than on the redoubtable Prisca and her husband Aquila, who like him were in the tent-making, pavilion-stitching trade. When Paul met them they were Jewish refugees from Rome, expelled in the early 40s by an edict of the emperor Claudius. According to the Roman historian Suetonius, the emperor had tired of Jews because of their "constant rioting at the instigation of Chrestus"; and behind Suetonius's careless reference, we can discern that the probable cause of Claudius's displeasure was the public conflict between establishment Jews and Messianists, which had already spilled into the diaspora. Paul first ran into Prisca and Aquila at Corinth, a magnet for all tentmakers because of the Isthmian games, second in importance only to the Olympic games and celebrated in a great swath of hucksters' booths and tourist tents encircling the sanctuary of Poseidon just outside the city.

But if it was business that brought Paul together with Prisca and Aquila, it was their common faith that kept them united. Though we don't know who evangelized them, these two were already part of the Jesus Movement when they encountered the apostle. They gave Paul shelter in their little house and allowed him to work with them and have a share of

241

their business. Though they opened their house to a "church," this cannot refer to a meeting of more than ten or twelve. The houses of tradespeople like Prisca and Aquila were woefully small affairs, usually of two rooms, the ground floor open for trade and the upper room reserved for living, the whole space measuring not more than fourteen feet wide by twenty-four deep, sometimes much less. Each story provided little more than enough height to stand upright.

When the church at Corinth grew beyond such confines, it had to move to Titus Justus's larger house (beside the synagogue), which probably boasted the cool inner court and frescoed dining room of the upscale urbanite. When Paul explained to Prisca and Aquila, however, that he needed their continuing help, the couple shut up shop at Corinth and went on to Ephesus to open a house-church there. For tradespeople like Prisca and Aquila, starting over for a second time cannot have been easy. But their trade, unlike most, did allow for such a possibility—and there was no part of the Near East that attracted more tourists than Ephesus of the Great Mother. Paul almost always mentions Prisca first, most unusual in a civilization where women, whether in the forum or in literature, invariably walk a step behind their husbands. It was Prisca who was the essential friend, probably more practical, almost certainly more devoted, than Aquila, however dear he may have been. We next spot the two tentmakers in Rome, after Claudius's death in 54, establishing yet a third house-church and continuing to give Paul their unfailing support, for, as he tells the Romans, "they risked their own necks to save my life." We glimpse these permanent pilgrims for the last time back at Ephesus, greeted by Paul in Second Timothy not long before his execution.

The pages of Acts and the Pauline letters overflow with such "fools for Christ," as Paul calls all those who persevere in the Way. They are engaging, affectionate, informal people, ready to roll up their sleeves and pitch in. They romp through this literature like clowns through a circus: the apostle Philip, cheerfully jumping into the chariot of an impatient Ethiopian eunuch in order to instruct him in how to read Isaiah; Dorcas, "who never tired of doing good and giving to those in need," weaving tunics for all the poor of Jaffa; Barnabas and Paul, abashed to be mistaken for Zeus and Hermes by the ecstatic Lycaonians; Agabus, the prophetic mime; Mark, pooping out at Pamphylia and angering Paul for his "desertion"; Paul's dream of the Macedonian—so like the Irishman who will appear four centuries later in Patrick's dream—who invites Paul to "come across [the sea] to Macedonia and help us," thus setting off the evangelization of Europe, as Patrick's Irishman will set off its re-evangelization. Here are Paul and his companions refusing to escape from prison after the doors have miraculously shot open and the prisoners' chains have come unlocked, so that their jailer, who blamed himself for the miracle, would not commit suicide ("Don't hurt yourself: we're all still here!"); Paul the Indefatigable preaching for five hours a day—right through the hallowed Mediterranean siesta—for two years in the lecture hall of Tyrannus at Ephesus; Paul preaching into the night in the upper room of a claustrophobic little house-church at Troas, till a boy named Eutychus, sitting in the window, nods off to sleep and falls out the window into the street below—a story that, after much commotion, ends happily.

If there is much commotion, solidarity, and camaraderie, there are also many kisses from afar, many last embraces, and many tears of farewell. "Timothy has returned from you and

243

has given us good news of your faith and your love, telling us that you always remember us with pleasure and long to see us, just as we long to see you," writes Paul to the Thessalonians. To Timothy, "dear son of mine" and Paul's most loyal missionary companion, the apostle writes in his last letter, "I remember you constantly in my prayers night and day. I remember your tears and long to see you again, so that I may be filled with joy." When he says his final farewell to the Ephesian elders, "they were all in tears," according to Acts. "They put their arms around Paul's neck and kissed him. What saddened them most was his saying that they would never see his face again."

244

These people, generous with their time, talents, and resources to the point of improvidence, actually liked one another. They make it possible to believe, as Paul encouraged the Corinthians to believe, that "Jesus Christ was never Yes-and-No; his nature is all Yes." They make it possible to hope, as Paul urged the Macedonians to hope, that human beings needn't "live in the dark, for we belong to the day." The people of the Way were not ideologues but believers. They did not organize protest marches or write op-ed pieces; and if they had, they would have been eliminated. They lived in a dangerous time under many strictures and disabilities—legal, social, economic, political—none of their own making. But it is hard to escape the impression that in their day they lived buoyantly.

Where Is Jesus?

Jesus, returned to the Father, had sent the Spirit. Was Jesus, therefore, finished with them? Did his ascent into the inaccessible heavens and the sending of the Spirit as his "replacement" mean that their contact with him was forever a thing of the past? Was he to be only a ghostly model to conjure in the mind but never to hold again in human arms? No; and this is not simply because Paul had taught them that Jesus was Lord of the Cosmos and they were his mystical Body. Such constructs are, in the last analysis, too cerebral to make a lasting difference in the ordinary lives of ordinary people like Prisca and Aquila.

The appearances that followed on the discovery of the empty tomb had given them a taste of Jesus risen and exalted. The disciples had, in effect, just caught him midway through his ascension from the realms of the dead—on his way to the Father's right hand. From time to time, long after Jesus's ascension, unusual individuals, like Paul on the road to Damascus, would be privileged recipients of such "out of time" appearances, as they may be even to our day.

But what of you and me, the less-than-privileged? What of folks like Prisca and Aquila, or tunic-making Dorcas and sleepy Eutychus, whom nobody would mistake for visionaries? Are we to be left only with faith?

The answer lies in Matthew's Gospel, which shows the public life of Jesus as getting under way with the Sermon on the Mount (and the articulation of the Beatitudes) and closes the narration of this trajectory with a scene no less memorable, Jesus's final sermon before his passion:

> "When the Son of Man comes in his glory, and all the angels with him, he will be seated on the throne of his glory. All the nations will be assembled before him and he will separate the people one from another as a shepherd separates the sheep from the goats. He will place the sheep on his right hand and the goats on his left.

"Then will the King say to those on his right, 'Come, you blessed of my Father, take your inheritance, the kingdom prepared for you from the foundation of the world. For I was hungry and you gave me to eat, I was thirsty and you gave me to drink, I was a stranger and you took me in, naked and you clothed me, sick and you took care of me, imprisoned and you visited me.'

"Then will the just reply to him, 'Lord, when did we see you hungry and give you to eat, or thirsty and give you to drink? When did we see you a stranger and take you in, naked and clothe you? When did we find you sick or imprisoned and go to visit you?'

"Then will the King answer, 'I tell you the truth: whatever you did for one of the least of these brothers and sisters of mine, you did for me.'

"Then will he say to those on his left, 'Depart from me, with your own curse upon your heads, to the eternal fire prepared for the devil and *his* angels. For I was hungry and you gave me nothing to eat, I was thirsty and you gave me nothing to drink. I was a stranger and you did not take me in, naked and you did not clothe me, sick and imprisoned and you took no care of me.'

"They will also reply, 'Lord, when did we see you hungry or thirsty, a stranger or naked, sick or imprisoned, and did not help you?'

"He will answer, 'I tell you the truth, whatever you did not do for one of the least of these, you did not do for me.'

"Then will they go away to eternal punishment,
but the just to eternal life."

To this heart-stopping lesson, Matthew adds the frightening comment: "Jesus had now finished all he wanted to say."

The Son of Man has become the Ward of all Mankind. Incarnated as the human Jesus of Nazareth, he is after his resurrection the principle of Jewish Justice itself, incarnated in the person of anyone and everyone who needs our help. It is ironic that some Christians make such a fuss about the elements of the Eucharist—bowing before them, kneeling in adoration, because Christ is present in them—but have never bothered to heed these solemn words about the presence of Christ in every individual who is in need. Jesus told us only once (at the Last Supper) that he would be present in the Bread and Wine, but he tells us repeatedly in the gospels that he is always present in the Poor and Afflicted—to whom we should all bow and kneel. It is perverse that some Christians make such a fuss about the bound text of God's Word, carrying it processionally, holding it with reverence, never allowing it to touch the ground, but have never considered seriously this text of Matthew 25, in the light of which we would always catch God's Needy before they hit the ground. It sometimes seems that it is to churchpeople in particular—to Christian Pharisees—that these words of Jesus are directed.

But the first-century churchpeople, the people of the Way, took this lesson with all solemnity. It gave them their constant focus—on the poor and needy. Though this focus will be abandoned soon enough as Christian interest turns in the second century to theological hatred, in the third century to institutional triumphalism, and in the fourth to the deadly game

247

of power politics, it has remained the focus of a few in every age. "Often, often often, goes the Christ in the stranger's guise" is the repeated refrain of a medieval Irish poem, "The Rune of Hospitality"; and the figure of Christ in the guise of clowns, beggars, and fools roams the literatures of Europe, the Americas, Africa, Oceania, and even Asia, from the earliest stories and plays of the Christian West to the novels of Shusaku Endo and the films of Federico Fellini. In every age, brothers and sisters of Jesus have come forward to heed the lesson, not least Dorothy Day, the twentieth-century saint of New York and founder of the Catholic Worker movement, who spent her life in service to the hungry and homeless, the displaced and dispossessed, who truly loved every Dostoyevskian idiot who crossed her path, and who once wrote:

> It is no use saying that we are born two thousand years too late to give room to Christ. Nor will those who live at the end of the world have been born too late. Christ is always with us, always asking for room in our hearts.
>
> But now it is with the voice of our contemporaries that He speaks, with the eyes of store clerks, factory workers, and children that He gazes; with the hands of office workers, slum dwellers, and suburban housewives that He gives. It is with the feet of soldiers and tramps that He walks, and with the heart of anyone in need that He longs for shelter. And giving shelter or food to anyone who asks for it, or needs it, is giving it to Christ. . . .
>
> If we hadn't got Christ's own words for it, it would seem raving lunacy to believe that if I offer a

bed and food and hospitality to some man or woman or child, I am replaying the part of . . . Martha or Mary, and that my guest is Christ. There is nothing to show it, perhaps. There are no halos already glowing round their heads—at least none that human eyes can see. It is not likely that I shall be vouchsafed the vision of Elizabeth of Hungary [thirteenth-century princess, later landgravine of Thuringia], who put the leper in her bed and later, going to tend him, saw no longer the leper's stricken face, but the face of Christ. The part of a Peter Claver [seventeenth-century Jesuit who nursed Africans caught in the slave trade], who gave a stricken Negro his bed and slept on the floor at his side, is more likely to be ours. For Peter Claver never saw anything with his bodily eyes except the exhausted black faces . . . ; he had only faith in Christ's own words that these people were Christ. And when on one occasion [those] he had induced to help him ran from the room, panic-stricken before the disgusting sight of some sickness, he was astonished. "You mustn't go," he said, and you can still hear his surprise that anyone could forget such a truth: "You mustn't leave him—it is Christ." . . .

To see how far one realizes this, it is a good thing to ask honestly what you would do, or have done, when a beggar asked at your house for food. Would you—or did you—give it on an old cracked plate, thinking that was good enough? Do you think that Martha and Mary thought that the old and chipped dish was good enough for their guest? . . .

For a total Christian, the goad of duty is not

needed—always prodding one to perform this or that good deed. It is not a duty to help Christ, it is a privilege. Is it likely that Martha and Mary sat back and considered that they had done all that was expected of them—is it likely that Peter's mother-in-law grudgingly served the chicken she had meant to keep till Sunday because she thought it was her "duty"? She did it gladly; she would have served ten chickens if she had had them.

If that is the way they gave hospitality to Christ, it is certain that that is the way it should still be given. Not for the sake of humanity. Not because it might be Christ who stays with us, comes to see us, takes up our time. Not because these people remind us of Christ . . . but because they *are* Christ.

We have reached a stage in our reflection where ordinary prose breaks down and only the words of scripture or of saints and poets will do. None of us will be lost in the abyss of nothingness and nonexistence; we will all be called forth at the Last Judgment. As Emily Dickinson wrote:

> *They dropped like Flakes—*
> *They dropped like Stars—*
> *Like Petals from a Rose—*
> *When suddenly across the June*
> *A Wind with fingers—goes—*
>
> *They perished in the Seamless Grass—*
> *No eye could find the place—*
> *But God can summon every face*
> *On his Repealless—List.*

But when we are called forth from the dust of death, the Just Judge will ask us if we lived by the Cosmic Code, the underlying principle that animates the universe, the code of justice and mercy, the code of caring for the neighbor who is in need. The Good Samaritans of this world, except in extraordinary cases, see only the man fallen among thieves, the person who needs help. They do not see Christ; they may never even have heard of him. But he is there, warming human encounters, softening the harshness of existence, lighting the darkness of faith, as Gerard Manley Hopkins wrote:

> . . . for Christ plays in ten thousand places,
> Lovely in limbs, and lovely in eyes not his
> To the Father through the features of men's faces.

VI

The Word
Made Flesh

*The Jesus the Beloved
Disciple Knew*

"WHO DO YOU SAY I AM?" asked Jesus of Peter. Peter's answer—that Jesus was "Messiah" and "Son of God"—pleased Jesus; and since he did not deny these titles, we may assume that he was not simply flattered: he thought Peter had got it right. But though "Messiah" can be rightly used of only one man (since the Jews do not seem to have been expecting more than one), "Son of God" is an oft-used phrase in earlier biblical literature: it is used both of angels and of prophets, indeed of anyone who could be considered God's mouthpiece. And we know that, like "Savior," it was in currency within the Roman world as a description of Caesar—whichever Caesar happened to be occupying the imperial throne. The Christian use of such phrases was meant to convey that Caesar was no messiah, just another inevitable disappointment; Jesus was the one Messiah. Thus, Christians found themselves relying on a Greek acronym to affirm their most basic belief:

ΙΧΘΥΣ

This acronym, *ICHTHUS* in Roman letters, is also the Greek word for "fish" but it stands for

Ιησους Χριστος Θεου Υιος Σωτηρ

in Roman letters *Iesous Christos THeou Uios Soter,* meaning "Jesus Christ, God's Son, Savior." The outline of a fish (⟨×), which we find scratched into the walls of catacombs among the earliest examples of Christian iconography, masqueraded as a seemingly harmless ornament, the radical political message of which would be overlooked by the uninitiated.

Did the first Christians mean by this that Jesus was "God's Only-Begotten Son" and humanity's only "Savior"? Apparently not. He was *Christos,* certainly (that is, God's Anointed, his Messiah); and, therefore, of necessity he was "God's Son" (that is, one who spoke God's message) and he surely came to "save" Israel or, as the disciples on the road to Emmaus put it, "to set Israel free." The Greek word *soter* means not only "savior" but "preserver" and "deliverer"—that is, the one who saves the polity from chaos, as Oedipus had saved Thebes from the terrorizing Sphinx. But to assert that Jesus was uniquely God's Son and mankind's savior seems to push beyond the articulations of the first Christians.

The earliest Christian preaching, like Peter's at Pentecost, emphasized that God's raising of Jesus from the dead was the ultimate confirmation of his life and message. He had been "anointed" to bring "the Good News to the poor," the afflicted, the lonely, the handicapped, the rejected—that is, to Israel—though, soon enough, the apostles come to believe that Christ's message is for all without distinction. But thanks to Paul's preaching, Christianity begins to deepen its understanding of Jesus's role as "savior"; and this is done through Paul's prayerful meditation on Christ's sufferings and cross. He is not only God's anointed healer and teacher. "Christ died for our sins," Paul tells the Corinthians, and thus set us free. This is how he has saved us; and this is the underlying "message of the Gospel."

But even for Paul, Jesus's "sonship" did not make him, in the words of the later creeds, "of the same substance as the

Father." He was a *human* son of God, made in God's image like all human beings, but the perfect image of God because he was the only child of Adam and Eve to act in perfect obedience to God—"even to death on a cross." None of the believers that we have encountered so far—neither Mark nor Matthew, neither Paul nor Luke, none of the apostles and none of the disciples who gathered around Jesus and then formed the early Church—considered Jesus to be God. This would have seemed blasphemy to them. Their belief in Christ was, after all, a form of Judaism; and Judaism was the world's only monotheism. God had raised the man Jesus and made him Lord. Even though his is now the Name by which we are saved, he did not raise himself—such an idea would have been unthinkable.

By the end of the first century, however, the Fourth Gospel, the one attributed to John, had reached its final form; and here we find, for the first time, Jesus acclaimed as God. This Gospel opens with a rewriting of Genesis, the first book of the Hebrew Bible, which begins with the words "In the beginning, God created heaven and earth" and goes on to describe how he went about it. John the Evangelist (whose relatively facile Greek precludes his identification with John the Visionary, author of Revelation) means to bring out the hidden meaning of God's original Creation, as described at the outset of Genesis, that Book of the Beginning of All Things. He begins:

> In the beginning was the Word;
> the Word was in God's presence,
> and the Word was God.
> He was present with God in the beginning.

Through him all things came into being,
and apart from him nothing came to be.
What has come into being in him is life,
life that is the light of human beings.
The light shines on in darkness,
for the darkness could not overpower it. . . .

He was in the world
that had come into being through him,
and the world did not recognize him.
To his own he came;
yet his own did not accept him.
But to the ones who did accept him
he gave power to become God's children. . . .

And the Word became flesh
and pitched his tent among us.
And we have seen his glory,
the glory as of a father's only son,
filled with enduring love. . . .

And of his fullness
we have all had a share—
love answering to love.

These are carved words; they have little in common with
Mark's roughness or Luke's cheerfulness. Before them,
Matthew's occasional attempts at an elevated style seem downright informal. They are intended to be chanted in clouds of
incense or incised in stone. Like a solemn organ prelude, they

sound notes that let us know that we are no longer seated in a comfortable circle chatting with Paul and Peter, Martha and Mary. We are meant to bow our heads.

We know nothing of the author of this Gospel apart from what we can glean from his text. The texture of its language, making it appear at times an alien body within the corpus of the New Testament, has sometimes driven scholars to fantastic theses about its composition. There have been those, for instance, who have maintained that this Gospel's philosophical complexity indicates that it belongs to the second half of the second century. Others have noted that its accurate use of detailed Palestinian Jewish information argues for a date in the 40s of the first century. The second-century hypothesis, based on an assumption of sophisticated Greek influence on the conceptual framework of the Fourth Gospel, lost ground when the Dead Sea Scrolls revealed that concepts once thought to have derived from Greek philosophical circles— such as "the Word" and the cosmic divisions between light and darkness—were current among the Essenes of the Judean desert even prior to Jesus's day. A growing scholarly consensus puts the composition of the gospel as we now have it in the last decade of the first century (or the first decade of the second century, at the latest). The Palestinian elements of this gospel, however, indicate that it was, to begin with, a work based on the testimony of an eyewitness to Jesus, but revised and expanded over the course of the first century by later hands. What we have today is a pastiche of early testimony and late theological reflection. The seams of the pastiche are almost invisible because this gospel has been given its present form by a refined and subtle editor. John's Gospel gives evidence, therefore, of being both our earliest and our latest gospel.*

The Jesus of Mark, Matthew, and Luke—the Synoptic Gospels, so called because they are so similar that their texts can be read in parallel columns—does not make himself central to his teaching. He is modest, even self-effacing, calling himself the "Son of Man"—a fellow human being—and only occasionally drawing attention to himself as having a special role, as when he prays so familiarly to God, his *Abba,* and when he tells his closest disciples that he is destined to suffer and die. In John's Gospel, however, Jesus makes the claim that "the Father and I are one." Whereas the Synoptic Jesus expects to be vindicated after his death, this hoped-for vindication may be little more than the hope of resurrection expressed by Jewish saints, such as the seven brothers tortured to death in Second Maccabees; and Jesus's "foresight" may be no more divinely prophetic than the foresight of any man who knows himself to have stirred up deadly political opposition. In John's Gospel, Jesus "the light" is in the dark about nothing and knows at all moments where his life is headed and that his cross will be the beginning of his being "lifted up," his cosmic exaltation. The theology of Jesus the New Adam (who initiates the New Creation, which is his Mystical Body, the Church) that Paul constructed

---

✠ There are several extant (and partially extant) writings, all dating to the second century or later, which are sometimes given the designation "gospel." These are works that were excluded from the New Testament (when its canon was closed in the fourth century) because they were not believed to have issued from apostolic auspices—and, therefore, were not seen as authentic witnesses to Jesus. These apocryphal "gospels" tend to be collections of sayings (therefore, not true gospels) or fictional fantasies about Jesus, usually influenced by Gnostic imaginings. A *few* reputable scholars (e.g., John Dominic Crossan, Helmut Koester) take one or another of these—such as the Gospel of Peter or, more defensibly, the Gospel of Thomas— seriously, but find I cannot. John Meier disposes conclusively of their arguments in *A Marginal Jew,* 1:112ff.

so carefully is elevated to new heights in John's thought. Jesus is now seen to be "the Word" of God—that is, God's meaning—present with God "in the beginning" and originally expressed in the Creation of the universe and then in the Incarnation, the taking-on-of-flesh of the human Jesus.

For the first time, Jesus is called, in this opening passage of John's Gospel, "God" and *"only* son"; and the sound and the stately movement of this gospel, replete with repetitive and nearly interminable speeches delivered by Jesus, is so different from the pithy, anecdotal Synoptics that it would be easy to exaggerate how odd John's Gospel is. But these references may be slightly more ambiguous than might at first appear. Certainly, the phrase "as of a father's only son," though clearly intended as an assertion of Jesus's unique sonship, is less bold than the later theological term "God's Only-Begotten Son" will be.

More than this, there is a continuity between the earlier theologies of Paul and the Synoptics, on the one hand, and the more developed reflections of John, on the other. Whether earlier or later, Jesus is seen to be human—made of flesh—and not the ghostly apparition of the Gnostics; he is raised from the dead and given supreme status over the universe; he is the culmination of all God's purposes, his definitive revelation. But if God can so reveal himself in flesh, Jesus must be God's *self*-revelation and, therefore, *of* God in a far more integral and essential sense than any previous (and *merely* human) prophet. It is this last thought that forms the bridge between the early theologies and the grand Christological assertions of the second century; it is John's Gospel more than any other document of the New Testament that gives us a picture of this bridge as it is being built, almost a snapshot of this novel theology in the process of construction. By the end of the second century, Ignatius of Antioch, one of the first of the great bishops, will speak without equivocation of "our God, Jesus Christ."

Are we observing, in this theological development, the dismantling of monotheism, Judaism's most precious possession? Certainly rabbinical Judaism in its articulated form would see it so. But, once again, we are throughout the course of the first century watching the two branches, rabbinical Judaism and Christianity, grow out of ancient Judaism—at first entwined, then gradually defining themselves against each other into separate entities. For Jews of the evolving rabbinical tradition, no modification of God's Oneness is tolerable. For Christians, God's Oneness is not denied but startlingly reaffirmed—and made more palpable—in Jesus, who can ultimately be understood only as *God incarnate:* "I am," proclaims John's Jesus, deliberately echoing the formula of God's own self-descriptions in the Hebrew scriptures. As he declares his eternal existence, prior to all Jewish history, to the scandalized worshipers within the precincts of the Temple itself: "Before Abraham was, *I am.*" As he reminds Martha and Mary: "*I am*—the Resurrection and the Life." As he teaches his disciples at the Last Supper:

> "*I am*—the Way, the Truth, and the Life.
> No one can come to the Father save through me.
> If you know me, you will also come to know my Father.
> Henceforth you do know him—
> for you have seen him."

Who sees him sees the Father; who hears him hears the Father; who touches him touches the Father. As the author of

John's Gospel will say elsewhere (in the first of the three Johannine letters): the ancient reality "that has existed from the beginning, that we have heard, that we have seen with our own eyes, that we have observed and touched with our own hands, the Word of Life—this is what we have to say." In other words, Jesus himself is the Gospel.

The church that gave this gospel to the world followed its own peculiar path, its evolution unique within the scattered first-century Christian communities of Roman Eurasia. Its principal elder seems to have been a minor follower of Jesus, one whom the gospel never names but calls the "Disciple Whom Jesus Loved." Despite the later attribution of this com-munity's gospel to the apostle John, the Beloved Disciple is someone who was "known to the high priest" and therefore a resident of Jerusalem, not a provincial Galilean fisherman like the John who was called by Jesus, along with his brother James, from his father Zebedee's fishing boats. The most reasonable way to look at the evolution of the Johannine corpus in the New Testament is to assume that John's Gospel went through three stages: first, as the oral testimony of the Beloved Disciple to his followers; then, as the work of a writer who set down this testimony, now colored by later controversies within the Johannine community (or church of the Beloved Disciple); and, lastly, in the form in which we now have it, given by an editor who added some final touches and smoothed away many of the wrinkles that this course of development had left within the text.

263

A similar development may be as-sumed for the three New Testament let-ters attributed to a John who calls himself *hos presbyteros,* "the Elder."* The

> ✠ The Medieval legend of Prester (or Presbyter) John derives from this self-description of the author of the three Johannine letters, as well as from the enig-matic statement of Jesus at

Greek *presbyteros,* or "presbyter," turns, after centuries of elided pronunciation, into the English "priest," meaning originally not a hierarch who offers sacrifice (like a pagan priest) but an older resident who dispenses wisdom to a community. Whether this John the Elder is to be identified with the Beloved Disciple or with the writer who subsequently set down the Beloved Disciple's testimony is still argued by scholars. But it seems most prudent to assume that both the gospel and the letters are substantially the work of the same writer, a man who was known in his day as John the Elder, who wrote at the turn of the century as the faithful disciple and successor of the now-dead Beloved Disciple and that this writer's work, at least in the case of his gospel, was then revised by a final editor.

264

Whoever the Beloved Disciple was—that is, the Johannine church's original eyewitness—he had a sharp eye and a keen ear, for he picked up on details ignored by the other evangelists. In many of Jesus's encounters, the dialogue has the quick, prickly humor of Greek theatrical comedy. After Philip is called by Jesus, he runs into Nathaniel (to be identified perhaps with the Bartholomew of the Synoptic tradition) and exclaims:

the end of John's Gospel that the Beloved Disciple, assumed in the Middle Ages to be John the Apostle, might "remain until I come"—that is, not die but live until the Second Coming of Jesus at the end of the world. Prester John was, therefore, imagined to be an undying king who ruled an ideal realm in deepest Asia (or Africa). As late as the sixteenth century, he figures in Ariosto's *Orlando Furioso* and is mentioned in Shakespeare's *Much Ado about Nothing.* Pope Alexander III in the twelfth century sent urgent letters to him by a special messenger, who never returned.

"We've found the One that Moses wrote about in the Torah and the prophets wrote about, too—he's Jesus bar-Joseph from Nazareth!"

"Nazareth! Please. What good ever came out of Nazareth?"

"Come and see."

As sneering Nathaniel ambles along with Philip in Jesus's direction, Jesus, observing his approach, remarks:

> "Well, well. A true Israelite, a man without guile."
>
> "Oh. How did you know me?"
>
> "I could see you under that fig tree, even before Philip called you."
>
> "Why, Rabbi, you're the Son of God, the King of Israel!"
>
> "You believe just because I tell you I could see you under the fig tree? You're going to see a lot more than that."

Not long after this encounter, John shows us Jesus sitting alone and exhausted under the noonday sun as it beats down on Jacob's Well, a source of water in Samaritan country ascribed by tradition to Jacob, also known as Israel, one of the primeval patriarchs of Genesis. A Samaritan woman approaches with a jar for drawing water. No pious Jewish male would acknowledge an unknown or unrelated woman, and no self-respecting Jew would address a Samaritan of either sex. But Jesus breaks through the conventions and shocks the woman by asking her:

> "Would you give me something to drink?"
>
> "You're a Jew. How come you ask me, a Samaritana, for a drink?"
>
> "If you only knew the gift that God holds out to you
> and who it is that asks you for a drink,
> you would have been the one to ask,

and he would have given you Living Water."

Pause.

"You have no bucket, sir, and the well is deep—
so how do you come by this 'Living Water'? I mean,
are you greater than our Father Jacob, who gave us
this well and drank from it himself with his sons [the
twelve progenitors of the Twelve Tribes of Israel] and
his cattle?"

"Whoever drinks this water

will thirst again.

But no one who drinks the Water I give him

will ever thirst again.

For the Water I give him

will become in him a fountain of water,

leaping up to everlasting life."

Pause.

"Give me that Water, sir, so that I may never thirst
or have to come back here again."

"Go call your husband and then come back to
me."

Pause.

"I don't have a husband."

"True enough. You've had five so far—and the
man you live with now is not your husband. You
spoke the truth there, all right."

Pause.

"Sir, I can see you are a prophet. Our fathers worshiped on this mountain [Mount Gerizim, site of
Samaritan worship and rival to the Jerusalem
Temple], though you [Jews] claim that Jerusalem is
the place of true worship."

"Believe me, Woman, the hour is coming
when you will worship the Father
neither on this mountain nor in Jerusalem.
You [Samaritans] worship what you do not un-
    derstand,
while we understand what it is we worship—
for salvation is from the Jews.
But the hour is coming—indeed it's already
    here—
when true worshipers will worship the Father in
    spirit and truth.
They are the worshipers the Father is looking for.
God is spirit,
and his worshipers must worship in spirit and
    truth."
Pause.
"I know that the Messiah is coming; and when he
comes he will explain everything."
    "*I am*—the very one speaking to you."

At this point, Jesus's disciples arrive from town with provisions and are unnerved to find Jesus in conversation with such a person, a person who has just been told more about the coming Time, free of conventional restrictions, than they have been able to comprehend. The Samaritan goes off to tell her neighbors about their extraordinary visitor, shouting, "Come and see a man who has just told me everything I've ever done! Could he be the Messiah?" John tells us: "Many Samaritans of that town believed in him on the strength of the woman's words. . . . So, when [they] approached him, they begged him to stay with them. He stayed for two days, and many more came to believe on the strength of his own words, and then they said to the woman, 'We no longer believe just because of what you told us. Having heard him ourselves, we know he is truly the savior of the world.' "

Did any of this really happen? There is probably a substrate of oral testimony here, a memory kept in the Johannine community of Jesus's unusual encounter with a woman at a well in Samaria, a woman who was neither sharp nor sainted but who found Jesus to be completely unusual and who somehow glommed onto things the disciples were still puzzling out. But the discussion about "Living Water" presumes an already elaborated theology of grace that is hard to credit as having emerged full-blown during Jesus's lifetime—or anytime before the last third of the century. More than this, the dialogue—I have inserted the pauses but believe they reflect the author's intention in depicting the Samaritan's confusion—is too polished to have been handed down from memory. So we can identify in this dialogue, as in many passages of John, two or three lightly concealed levels of theological and dramatic development that have gone into the construction of the finished product.

In this dialogue, as in the one with Nathaniel, Jesus possesses some of the ease and humor of the Synoptic Jesus surely, but he is now all-knowing, which he is never shown to be in Mark and Matthew, and of which there are but occasional flashes in Luke. But in addition to these marks of divinity, interjected no doubt by John the Elder, there runs throughout the narrative continuing evidence of Jesus's humanity, almost certainly the original contribution of the Beloved Disciple himself; and these details prevent Jesus from ever seeming an unfeeling, otherworldly phantom. Toward the end of his life, for instance, he weeps for the loss of his dead friend Lazarus, brother to Martha and Mary (and whom he eventually raises from the dead), while the bystanders exclaim, "See how much he loved him!"

After the raising of Lazarus, the brother and sisters hold a dinner of celebration at which Mary of Bethany anoints Jesus. This is a separate incident from the one that only Luke reports of the prostitute who anoints and weeps over Jesus's feet during the dinner at the home of Simon the Pharisee. The anointing described by John is also to be found in the gospels of Mark and Matthew, but what is especially intriguing is that John provides convincingly authentic details that are lacking in the work of the "earlier" evangelists. Only John mentions that "the whole house was filled with the fragrance" of the pure nard that Mary broke open for this anointing. And whereas Mark and Matthew mention that "some" of the diners complained about the extravagance of Mary's gesture, only John puts the objection on the lips of Judas, who says: "Why was this ointment not sold? It was worth three hundred pieces of silver and the money might have been given to the poor"—the predictably pinched complaint of the instinctively ungenerous Puritan who has his own agenda, an agenda that will lead him to sell out Jesus for only thirty pieces of silver. John then comments: "He said this not because he cared about the poor but because he was a thief." These two details—the fragrance that filled the house and the devious response of Judas—point to a perceptive eyewitness as the basis for this most concrete of the three evangelical accounts of this incident.

At the Last Supper, where the other evangelists place the institution of the Eucharist, John (who makes the institution

269

of the Eucharist part of the multiplication of loaves and fish) sets his own singular ceremony:

> Jesus, knowing that his hour had come to pass from this world to the Father, and having loved his own who were in this world, loved them to the last. . . . And so during supper, fully aware that the Father had handed over all things to him, and that he had come forth from God and was returning to God, Jesus rose from the table, shed his outer clothes, and wrapped a towel around himself. Then he poured water into a basin and began to wash the disciples' feet, drying them with the towel that was wrapped around him.

After he has taken his place at table once more, Jesus gives a long Johannine speech, the gist of which is "If I, the Lord and Teacher, have washed your feet, you must wash one another's feet." Even though the inflated rhetoric can only be the work of a later sensibility, the action itself, as well as its essential meaning, may well stem from an authentic memory.

Only John's Gospel offers a clear explanation of why the Jewish leaders had to resort to Pilate, the Roman procurator of Judea, to get a judgment on Jesus, for as they retort to Pilate: "We are not permitted to put a man to death." Only John explains why the reluctant Pilate, knowing Jesus to be innocent, renders the death sentence: "If you set him free," shout the Jews, "you are no 'Friend of Caesar.' Whoever makes himself king is the Emperor's rival." Only John mentions that Jesus's trial before Pilate took place outside Pilate's praetorium in a courtyard known as Lithostroton, or "Pavement of Stone." Outside the Antonia Fortress, probable site of Jerusalem's praetorium, there has been excavated a courtyard of some 2,300 square yards that was paved with massive stones more than a yard square and a foot thick. It is likely that upon this Lithostroton Jesus of Nazareth once stood and faced the Roman official who held life and death in his hands. Did the Beloved Disciple, pictured in John's Gospel as the only male disciple to follow Jesus all the way to crucifixion, loiter at the edges of the Lithostroton and overhear the frantic dialogue set down in John?

> Pilate had Jesus brought out, and seated himself on the Chair of Judgment at a place called Lithostroton, in Hebrew Gabbatha [High Place]. It was the Day of Preparation [when the Supper of the Pashcal Lamb was prepared], about noon [by which time all leavened bread and yeast had to be removed from Jewish homes, to be replaced by the unleavened bread of Passover]. "Here's your king," Pilate taunted the Jews; at which they shouted, "Away with him! Away with him! Crucify him!"
>
> "What?" exclaimed Pilate. "Shall I crucify your king?" The chief priests answered, "We have no king but Caesar!" At that, Pilate handed him over to be crucified.

271

The pleasures of John's Gospel tend to be more veiled than those of the other evangelists. In John, the delightful parables of the Synoptics are nowhere to be found, replaced by dignified but boring speeches that sometimes run to several pages. The author, determined not to let us forget who Jesus is, can overwhelm us with airless solemnity that leaves us begging for the sinewy, down-to-earth Jesus of the Synoptics. John's Jesus is always in control. In Mark and Matthew, Jesus dies on the cross in unspeakable pain, inarticulately, with "a loud cry," almost a terrifying shriek. In Luke, having forgiven everyone and promised Paradise to the Good Thief, he speaks his last, elegant words to his Father, quoting Psalm 31: "Father, *into your hands do I commit my spirit.*" Luke is already halfway toward the Johannine theology of the God-Messiah. But in John, Jesus at the point of death remains in control of everything. "All is fulfilled," says the Johannine Jesus. "And bowing his head," writes John, "he gave up his spirit"—which henceforth belongs to the whole world.

272

J O H N ' S   J E S U S   is the *gravitas*-encrusted Christ of the ancient creeds, of tasteless religious art, of German passion plays and Hollywood movies. He is the immobile icon loved by ecclesiasts and theologians. It is as if John's symbolic reverence has made an icon too awesome to be touched by the soiled and unconsecrated hands of ordinary humans—even though it is in John's Gospel that Thomas the Doubter is invited by Christ, crucified, lanced, and now risen, to "put your finger here and feel my hands. Give me your hand; put it into my side." The weight of the human and fleshly, the sweaty and smudged is finally overcome in John by the weightless illumination of the divine. This is the same process of iconization that will in later centuries lift Mary of Nazareth out of the Galilean hills and enthrone her amid the celestial constellations as *theotokos,* god-bearer, Mother of God, fresh incarnation of the Great Mother of Eurasia, replacement for the dethroned Diana of the Ephesians.

Like all religious innovations, John's theology grew out of

a culture and must be seen as part of a developing cultural process if it is to be understood. This culture was one of Hellenized, even Asiatic pomp and rhetorical exaggeration that began in Alexander's appreciation of Eastern ceremony. The cynical Roman senators, forever declaring one Caesar or another to be god, didn't take their own decrees literally; but they approved of the awe-inspiring marble statues and the overpowering clouds of incense, the shining vessels and the smartly togaed devotees, all bowing in unison: these were standard methods for creating political stability, based in part on popular gullibility. In the centuries following John's presentation of his high Christology, poetic and liturgical hyperbole will sometimes calcify into rigid dogma till everything the Church possesses—from consecrated priests to consecrated bread, from sacred books and vessels to Paschal candle, lauded in extravagant, ecstatic song on Easter night—will seem to glow in the light of its own divinization.

273

Many who are comfortable with the Synoptic tradition and even with Paul feel that here at the threshold of John's Gospel they must part company with the New Testament. They may be believers or half-believers, Jews, humanitarians, agnostics—all of whom may cheer the insights and advances of Paul and the Synoptic evangelists but find themselves abashed and compassless once they come into the field of John's unearthly glow. Nor is it only the exaggerated God-Man that renders them uneasy. For it is in John that we can locate not only the sure source of the exalted doctrines of later Christianity (not all of which even every Christian can assent to) but also a spirit of touchy exclusivity that will surface repeatedly and with increasingly devastating results throughout the course of Western history.

In John, "the Jews" are enemies, often (though not always) designated with contempt, the lost people who "have no king but Caesar." This attitude cannot have stemmed from the time of Jesus, when he and all his followers were Jewish. Nor can it be located in the mid-century controversies of the early Jesus Movement, when all the leaders—men like James, Peter, and Paul (that self-described "Jew of Jews")—were deeply aware of their Jewish roots and thought of themselves only as preachers of a fulfilled Judaism. The anti-Judaism of John is traceable rather to the last decades of the first century, when the tug-of-war between rabbis and Messianists had heated to the boiling point, and Messianists were being forcibly ejected from Eurasian synagogues and formally cursed in Jewish liturgies. The sense of loss that resulted from this hateful ostracism should not be minimized—though we cannot but be mindful of it, for it still throbs in the hurt feelings of the Fourth Gospel, retrojected into its account of the life of Jesus by a mixed community of Jews and gentiles of the 90s, probably now removed from Palestine to Ephesus but still smarting over the wounds of their final rejection. Unlike, for instance, Paul's gentile churches, the Johannine community had retained—through the presence of the Beloved Disciple and, after his death, through its reverence for his very Palestinian, very Jewish memories—a keen appreciation of its Jewish identity, so the final breakdown of *koinonia* between Jews and Christians may have been far more painful for the Johannine than for many other Christian churches.

But if it may be said that the rabbinical Jews won this first-century tug-of-war and continued to hold the upper hand for the next two centuries, the tide will turn in the early fourth century with the emperor Constantine's induction as a

Christian catechumen, after which Christians will spend the next sixteen and a half centuries rounding up Jews, hunting them down, depriving them of civil rights, torturing, massacring, and ridiculing to their heart's content. This centuries-long pogrom is the lasting shame of Christianity, even more of a blot than its centuries of crusades against the Muslim "infidels." If John, writing in the heat of controversy, can no more be blamed for the subsequent history of European anti-Semitism than can the *Birkat ha-minim,* the Jewish ritual curse on the heretical Christians, his gospel is still capable of leaving Jewish readers purple with rage and Christians red with embarrassment.

It may even be the rejection by Judaism that lit the furnace of the Johannine community's high Christology. As has so often been the case in religious history, the very thing that one is rejected for becomes the treasure one must never give up—a treasure that is emphasized, exaggerated, and made into one's badge of honor. It is just such a psychological process that creates obsessive positions that can bear no compromise—and that finally makes dialogue (between Jews and Christians, as well as among varieties of Christians) impossible.

B Y   T H E   T I M E the First Letter of John was written, however, in the first decade of the second century, the Jewish-Christian schism that has left its traces in John's Gospel was already fading into history, and the Johannine community had found new enemies. Gnostics were giving John's Gospel an interpretive spin that horrified more "orthodox" believers, for the Gnostics completely ignored Jesus's human dimension and reveled excessively in John's repeated emphasis on his divinity.

The Gnostics preferred to believe that Jesus had never been human anyway, just a spirit who appeared to be human (like a Greek god temporarily assuming a fleshly body). Though John's was much more to their taste than were the other gospels, John the Elder was appalled by their attachment.

His response to this theological challenge, however, was brittle, captious, and unforgiving: the Gnostics and other opponents are all "antichrists" and "children of the devil," and none of the good people are to have anything to do with them. C. H. Dodd, one of the greatest modern exegetes of the Johannine literature, once asked thoughtfully: "Does truth prevail more if we are not on speaking terms with those whose view of truth differs from ours?" It is a question that people like John the Elder seem never to consider.

276

The church of the Beloved Disciple had become like a species on an island that geological changes have cut off from the mainland. For many years, it developed separately—from Jews, from "heretics," even from other "orthodox" Christians. Without permanent offices of administration and authority, like the bishops and deacons of other Christian communities, it was wholly dependent on individual, prophetic inspiration—from "the Spirit"—and it rejected the notion that anyone but Jesus could be *pastor,* that is, their shepherd. Jesus was, as he had said, "the Good Shepherd," and we were all his sheep without distinction. Like John's Gospel itself, this church possessed intellectual and social treasures unknown in the other Christian communities, which were growing together slowly into the Great Church of succeeding centuries. For all its problems, the high Christology of the Johannine community gave its theology a profundity and piercing clarity that other churches lacked; and its Spirit-based social ambience encouraged equal participation by all, especially women, in its common enterprises of charity and prayer.

The Johannine church, indeed, sheltered unusual seedlings that would flower in succeeding centuries. If its individualist orientation and its insistence on personal encounter with the Lord remind us of the spirit of the modern Reformation churches, its unique reverence for the holiness of the physical (Jesus washing the disciples' feet, Jesus curing the blind man with a mixture of mud and his own spit) can only recall the later sacramentalism of the Orthodox and Catholic churches. But its insistence on there being but one way of thinking makes uneasy anyone who has ever had an unorthodox thought. It comes as no surprise that John is often the favorite evangelist of the uptight and unrelenting; and his rigidity can call to mind contemporary churchpeople of several unfortunate varieties. The difficulties of John's Gospel are extreme enough that to this day Christian churches use its passages sparingly in their lectionaries, whereas the other gospels are proclaimed in full.

For all this, the most characteristic passages of the Johannine literature bid fair to be the most beautiful of the New Testament:

"For God so loved the world
that he gave away his only Son."

"I give you a new commandment:
love one another."

"*I am*—the Vine,
you are the branches.

Whoever abides in me, and I in him,
bears fruit a-plenty. . . .
As the Father has loved me,
I have loved you.
Abide in my love."

God is love,
and he who abides in love
abides in God,
and God in him.

The first three quotations are words of Jesus from John's Gospel; the last are the words of John the Elder from his First Letter. Cut off from its Jewish roots, confronting theological controversy, and finally overwhelmed by disunity within its own ranks, the church of the Beloved Disciple, which placed such high value on love but could not resolve the arguments that continued to tear it apart, opted at last to reconnect itself to the mainland, to join in communion with the then-emerging Great Church. We know this from the coda that the final editor appended to John's Gospel after the death of John the Elder. In this epilogue, the risen Jesus appears on the shore of the Lake of Galilee, as if in a dream, and asks Peter three times: "Do you love me?" To each question Peter responds with an increasingly emotional affirmation; and to each answer of Peter's Jesus gives a pointed instruction: "Feed my lambs." "Care for my sheep." "Feed my sheep."

The church of the Beloved Disciple had finally admitted that it could no longer go it alone, defending itself from attack only by means of its own informal intuitions and pentecostal resources, but had to accept some mechanism of human authority. It needed more than the teaching of Jesus and the example of its Beloved Disciple. It needed the protection of the Great Church and its shepherds, the nurturing *pastores* of whom Peter was representative.

There was a trade-off here. The Johannine church, in accepting the protection of the Great Church, accepted its structures of authority and lost much of its freewheeling, Spirit-based pentecostalism. The Great Church, never so interested in theory as in practice, accepted the elaborate Christology and, after much debate, accepted alongside its own growing library of apostolic writings the peculiar literature of the church of the Beloved Disciple.

279

O F   T H E   M A N Y   E N I G M A S of John's Gospel nothing is more mysterious than the story that does not belong there. It interrupts the flow of John's tightly stitched scheme of narration, and though, like many Johannine episodes, it gives a starring role to a woman, its supple Greek has all the characteristics of Luke's pen:

> At daybreak, Jesus appeared again in the Temple
> precincts; and when all the people came to him, he
> sat down and began to teach them. Then did the
> scribes and Pharisees drag a woman forward who had
> been discovered in adultery and force her to stand
> there in the midst of everyone.
>
> "Teacher," said they to him, "this woman has been
> caught in the very act of adultery. Now, in the Torah
> Moses ordered us to stone such women. But you—
> what have you to say about it?" (They posed this

question to trap him, so that they might have something to use against him.)

But Jesus just bent down and started doodling in the dust with his finger. When they persisted in their questioning, he straightened up and said, "He among you who is sinless—let him cast the first stone at her." And he bent down again and continued sketching in the sand.

When they heard this, they went away one by one, starting with the oldest, until the last one was gone; and he was left alone with the woman, who still stood where they had made her stand. So Jesus straightened up and said, "Woman, where are they? Has no one condemned you?"

"No one, sir," answered she.

"Nor do I condemn you," said Jesus. "You are free to go. But from now on, avoid this sin."

This entire passage sounds like the Synoptics and could easily be slipped into Luke's Gospel at 21:38, where it would make a perfect fit. It was, in fact, excised from Luke, after which it floated around the Christian churches without a proper home, till some scribe squeezed it into a manuscript of John, where he thought it might best belong. But why was it excised in the first place? Because the early Church did not forgive adultery (and other major sins) and did not wish to propagate the contradictory impression that the Lord forgave what the Church refused to forgive. The Great Church quickly became far more interested in discipline and order than Jesus had ever shown himself to be. This excision is our first recorded instance of ecclesiastical censorship—only for the best reasons, of course (which is how censors always justify themselves). The anarchic Johannine church had had good reason for its reluctance to attach itself to the Great Church, which it knew would clip its wings; and for all we know, it was a Johannine scribe who crammed the story of the aborted stoning into a copy of John's Gospel, thus saving it for posterity.

The passage itself shows up the tyrannical mindlessness that tradition, custom, and authority can exercise within a society. The text of the Torah that the scribes and Pharisees cite to Jesus is Leviticus 20:10, which reads, "The man who commits adultery with his neighbor's wife will be put to death, he and the woman." Jesus, doodler in the dust and reader of hearts, knows the hard, unjust, and self-deceiving hearts he is dealing with. He does not bother to dispute the text with them, by which he could have asked the obvious question "How can you catch a woman *in the act* without managing to catch her male partner?" He goes straight to the heart of the matter: the bad conscience of each individual, the ultimate reason no one has the right to judge anyone else.

How marvelous that in the midst of John's sometimes oppressive solemnities, the wry and smiling Jesus of the Synoptic gospels, the Jesus the apostles knew, the holy fool, still plays his holy game, winning his laughing victory over the stunned and stupid forces of evil. This is the same Jesus who tells us that hell is filled with those who turned their backs on the poor and needy—the very people they were meant to help—but that, no matter what the Church may have taught in the many periods of its long, eventful history, no matter what a given society may deem "sexual transgression," hell is not filled with those who, for whatever reason, awoke in the wrong bed.

Nor does he condemn us.

The Bread of the Poor

As we look back over Christianity's first hundred years—from the birth of Jesus in the reign of Caesar Augustus to the final editing of John's Gospel (and the last of the New Testament letters) about the year 100—we see what seems an abnormally rapid-fire development. Jesus the Jewish prophet, who accepted the judgment of others that he was their Messiah (and may even have promoted this identification), was executed by the Romans in a manner so hideous that his followers could never forget it. Their subsequent claim that "he is risen" did not fall upon deaf ears but convinced many; and their small Palestinian sect grew into a movement that spread like scattered seeds through the Roman world, taking root especially in urban centers with substantial Jewish populations.

The religion of these adherents, who came to be called "Christians," appeared at first to be a somewhat kinky variety of Judaism but gradually grew away from orthodox Jewish tenets, not so much in its ethical concerns, which remained focused on characteristically Jewish values of justice, mercy, charity, and brotherhood, but in its innovative theology, which took Jesus to be not only Messiah but Lord of the Universe who sits at God's right hand. The closer the Christians came to deifying Jesus, the more they tended to alienate the Jews from whom they had sprung. The longer the Christians meditated on the events of Jesus's life and death and their subsequent experiences of his "resurrection," the higher he seemed to rise in the heavens, till they began to acclaim him not only "Savior of the World" but "God's Only Son," whose sufferings had redeemed us from sin and whose resurrection held out the promise of our own.

The writings these Christians began to collect—narrations

about Jesus and the first Christians, letters of exhortation and encouragement by early "apostolic" figures—gradually took on for them a sacred character, not unlike the character of the Jewish scriptures, the so-called Hebrew Bible—which the Christians continued to revere and read aloud at their meetings (and interpret from their own idiosyncratic theological perspective). The new writings would over the succeeding centuries be gathered into a definitive collection, called the "New Testament" and appended to the Greek translation of the Hebrew scriptures that they now called the "Old Testament." The first five books of this New Testament—the four gospels of Matthew, Mark, Luke, and John and Luke's Acts—became for Christians the new Torah, as the apostolic letters became the new Prophets, with Paul, the most important, at their head, just as Isaiah stood at the head of the Hebrew Prophets. The New Testament, at about one-third the length of the Old, contains no equivalent of the Writings, the third-ranking part of the Hebrew Bible, though the Book of Revelation, which closes the collection, is closely imitative of the apocalyptic Hebrew Prophecy of Daniel.

283

These books and letters of the New Testament are of varying quality and importance. Because they are the work of many hands, they exhibit some of the quirks and contradictions of the Old Testament, the story of whose composition spans more than a millennium and a half. But because they were written over a fifty-year period by two generations of authors, many of whom had some contact with one another, they also exhibit a marked consistency and even unity.

In nothing is their unity so evident as in their portrayal of Jesus. Though he is presented in various lights and shadows, depending on the concerns, personality, and skill of each author, he exudes even under this treatment a remarkable consistency, so that we feel on finishing his story, whether it is told well or badly, simply or extravagantly, that we know the man—and that in each telling he is identifiably the same man. This phenomenon of consistency beneath the differences makes Jesus a unique figure in world literature: never have so many writers managed to convey the same impression of the same human being over and over again. More than this, Jesus—what he says, what he does—is almost always comprehensible to the reader, who needs no introduction, no scholarly background, to penetrate the meaning of Jesus's words and actions. The Sermon on the Mount, the Good Samaritan, the Washing of the Feet, the Empty Tomb: all these and many more gestures, instructions, and symbols are immediately intelligible not only to the simplest reader but even to the unlettered and the immature.

There is no other body of literature approaching its two thousandth birthday of which the same may be said. The works of the Hellenistic historians, the Roman poets, and even the rabbinic commentators of the same period require learned introductions and a mass of accompanying footnotes to be penetrated by a reader of the twenty-first century. To appreciate how singular the gospels are, one should also attempt to comprehend a work like Virgil's *Aeneid,* written within a hundred years of the gospels but today requiring months of study of its cultural setting if one is to reach an elementary understanding of its meaning.

What especially makes the gospels—from a literary point of view—works like no others is that they are about a good human being. As every writer knows, such a creature is all but impossible to capture on the page, and there are exceedingly few figures in all literature who are both good and memorable. Yet the evangelists, who left no juvenilia behind them—no failed novels, rhythmless poems, or other early works by which we might judge their progress as writers—whose Greek was often odd or imprecise, and who were not practiced writers of any sort, these four succeeded where almost all others have failed. To a writer's eyes, this feat is a miracle just a little short of raising the dead.

In nothing do the evangelists succeed so unabashedly as in their depictions of Jesus's sufferings, their careful, step-by-step recountings of his arrest, interrogations, torture, humiliation before hostile crowds, condemnation, the public parade in which he is conscripted to carry the splintery instrument of his own death, his crucifixion with spikes, his slow dying, displayed to all in his death agony. If, as the Roman centurion admits after he is dead, "This man was truly God's son," then the Father chose for this son of his a time to be born in which one might die by the most painful means that human beings have ever devised.

So intense was the suffering of Jesus before and during his crucifixion that the early Christians could not bring themselves to depict it. We have, almost from the very beginning of Christianity, Christian art—pictures that form a distinctively Christian message: in grave slabs as early as the first century we see the Church depicted as the saving ark of Noah, the Holy Spirit depicted as the descending dove of Acts, and figures of early Christians, both men and women, praying with uplifted hands, as Muslims still do today. In the catacombs, we find a crumbling mosaic of Christ as the Unconquered Sun (an image borrowed from ancient mythologies), a quickly daubed Good Shepherd, many portrayals of the Last Supper, even a tender fresco of the Madonna and Child. But nowhere is there a crucifixion scene. The first one ever will be carved in wood as one of many scenes from Jesus's life—in a side door of the exquisite basilica of Santa Sabina, a Roman church of the fifth century that stands on the Aventine Hill. It will take the early Christians four centuries to bring themselves to portray the crucifixion of their Messiah. By the time they get around to it, Augustine of Hippo lies dying, the barbarian hordes are overrunning the empire, and Patrick is in Gaul making his fateful travel plans to evangelize the Irish. By the time they get around to it, in other words, they are no longer early Christians; they are already on the verge of the Middle Ages. And still they are careful not to let this abomination occupy a central place in their churches.

This central fact of Jesus's life, his grisly suffering and death, traumatized the first Christians; and even though it was the central reality they had to contend with, they could not look at it directly. Crucifixion was the ultimate form of Roman humiliation; and to understand it properly, we have to imagine a grove of huge poles set up in a central thoroughfare, where any day as we pass by we may see fellow citizens pinned to the poles with great iron nails, pierced through their joints, ripped open and left to be drained of blood as if they were animal carcasses. Every day freshly crucified victims appear on the poles as the old victims expire and are carted off for burial. The crucified men, twisted, bloody torsos stripped for all to see, anti-Adonises, writhe and grimace most horribly in their pain. Delicate citizens pass by quickly with averted eyes, while the more sportive and cruel among us taunt the nailed men, in the same way that people today stand outside prisons to scream at criminals on their way to the gas chamber, the electric chair, the lethal injection—the way people always gathered eagerly in ages past to witness public executions. We spit on the pierced men and tell them how happy their pain makes us, how richly they deserve it, that our only wish is to see their dying last as long as possible.

Not only their clothes but what John the Elder calls "the pride of life," the rightful pride that every man (especially a man as young as Jesus, in his early thirties) takes in his own body and bearing, has been stripped from these utterly naked men. The public, physical humiliation—beginning with the flogging of Jesus by Roman centurions, the mock crowning with thorns (which were pressed down into Jesus's scalp), and all that followed—this was a trauma not only to Jesus's followers but to Jesus, to his soul as well as his body. Lest he should miss out on even the worst psychological torment he could possibly experience, the Father himself—his *Abba,* whom Jesus always felt to be with him—withdrew his presence, forcing Jesus to cry out accusingly not long before his death in the words of Psalm 22, "My God, my God, why have you deserted me?" (The great American biblical scholar Raymond Brown used to remark that there is no human being who does not utter the words of this prayer sooner or later. But we, unlike Jesus, have good reason to expect God's absence.) What could anyone add by way of further suffering?

Were you there when they crucified my Lord?
Were you there when they crucified my Lord?
Oh, sometimes it causes me to tremble, tremble, tremble.
Were you there when they crucified my Lord?

We were there. Each of us can find ourselves somewhere in that brutal scene, as taunters, comforters, indifferent passersby. But, more profoundly, we were there because this entire action of Jesus, of submitting to this awful suffering, was done on our behalf, we the taunting, frightened, indifferent friends of Jesus. "Greater love than this no man has than that he lay down his life for his friends." That is Jesus's own explanation of his motivation. "God so loved the world that he gave away his only son. God sent this son of his into the world not to judge the world but that through him the world might be saved." That is the Fourth

Gospel's explanation of the Father's motivation. "Father, forgive them. They don't know what they're doing." That is Jesus's prayer to the Father, asking him to ignore our motivation.

The early Christians, the original friends of Jesus, so sympathized with Jesus's pain and had been so traumatized by it that they could not bring themselves to depict the stark reality of his suffering, except in words—that is, in the accounts of the four gospels, which are as clipped and precise as the four authors knew how to make them. Only in the fifth century, nearly a century after the Roman state had discontinued the practice of crucifixion and no one living had witnessed such a procedure, did Christians forget the shame and horror of the event sufficiently to begin to make pictures of it. By the time they began making such pictures, many of the gruesome details of actual crucifixion had been forgotten; and Jesus is depicted on the cross not as a man in agony but as the artist supposed he must have appeared at his resurrection. One detail, in particular, was completely forgotten. The gospels imply that Jesus was nailed to the cross through his hands and feet, fulfilling the description in Psalm 22 ("They pierced my hands and my feet"); and this serves well enough as a rough description. All artists from the fifth century on took this to mean that Jesus was nailed through the palms of his hands, and this is how we see him depicted down to the present day. But if a man were to be crucified through his palms, he would quickly slide off his cross, because the bones of the hands are insufficiently strong and stable to hold the weight of a body. Jesus was crucified through the bones of his wrists. We are now certain of this, because Israeli archeologists have dug up bodies from Jesus's time that were crucified in this Roman manner.

It may be that all during the centuries that Christians could not bring themselves to portray the crucified Christ they had a picture of Jesus's sufferings, a picture that they claimed was "not made by human hands." There is, at least, an ancient tradition that such an image existed as a treasure of the Eastern church and that, after many adventures, it came to rest at Constantinople. There are some indications that this picture may be what we now call the Shroud of Turin, which in the fourteenth century was brought back from the crusades by a plundering French nobleman and finally found its way to the cathedral of Turin in Italy. Ancient creases in the cloth give evidence that the Shroud was at one time displayed face out with the unsightly corpus of the crucified folded out of view. A few years ago carbon-14 dating done on the Shroud yielded a medieval, not a first-century, date. But since then other scientists have discovered that there is on the surface of the cloth a bioplastic coating—that is, a form of bacterium that reproduces itself and interferes with accurate carbon dating. Such a coating appears to cover many ancient objects made of fiber.

The Shroud is approximately fourteen feet long by three and a half feet wide and contains a faint, straw-colored image of a naked man, who would have stood about six feet tall. The corpse would first have been laid on its back on the lower half of the Shroud, which would then have been folded over the front of the body. The image on the Shroud is indeed of an entire body, back and front. There is no convincing evidence that the image was painted on the cloth. Rather, apart from the bloodstains, which were made by real human blood, the image appears to have been created by intense heat, but heat which did not scorch, a process no one can explain.

In 1898, Secondo Pia, a councilor of Turin, who owned a new invention called a camera, took photographs of the Shroud

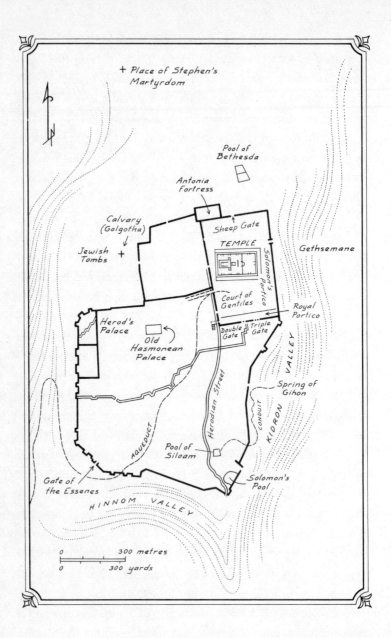

+ Place of Stephen's Martyrdom

Pool of Bethesda

Antonia Fortress

Calvary (Golgotha)

Sheep Gate

TEMPLE

Gethsemane

Jewish Tombs

Solomon's Portico

Court of Gentiles

Royal Portico

Herod's Palace

Old Hasmonean Palace

Double Gate

Triple Gate

Herodian Street

KIDRON VALLEY

Spring of Gihon

Conduit

Aqueduct

Pool of Siloam

Gate of the Essenes

Solomon's Pool

HINNOM VALLEY

0 — 300 metres
0 — 300 yards

during a rare exhibition. As he developed his negatives, something quite unexpected happened. Whereas Pia had looked forward to capturing, at best, the ghost of a ghostly image, the human face and body that began to show themselves on his negatives were far more definite and recognizable than the image on the Shroud itself. One sees a muscular, barrel-chested, well-proportioned man, pierced in wrists, feet, and side, the eyes of his haunting Semitic face closed in death. The Shroud image, however it was made, is a genuine negative (except for the bloodstains), which makes Secondo Pia's film "negative" a positive.

Though corpses laid to rest on cloth may leave smudged impressions which a forensic pathologist could discern, they cannot leave exactly proportioned images of themselves. We must look elsewhere for an explanation. But if we assume that the Shroud is a clever medieval forgery, we must assume that it was made by an artist whose grasp of the negative-positive properties of photography was five centuries in advance of his time and whose understanding of anatomy was far in advance of that of all his medieval contemporaries. Such a theory, however, falls apart after a careful look at Pia's negative. Every artist, especially one as facile as the Shroud artist would have to have been, is identifiable by his style, which is as characteristic of him as his signature or thumbprint. The negative image has no

OPPOSITE: JERUSALEM IN THE TIME OF JESUS

Golgotha, the site of Jesus's execution, was then outside the city walls. The Temple, which had become a focus of Jesus's criticism of the religious establishment of his day, towered over the Jerusalem skyline, as did Pilate's fortress. From the Garden of Gethsemane on the Mount of Olives, where Jesus spent his last night in prayer, he could look across the Kidron Valley and see looming above him the citadels of "church" and state that would convict him on the morrow.

style whatever; there is no hand in it. It seems obviously a photograph, that is, an image made by light.

A medieval forger would also need to have been the only human being between the time of the emperor Constantine and our own to have been completely conversant with the details of Roman crucifixion. Before his crucifixion, the man on the Shroud was stripped naked and scourged over his whole body, the scourge marks especially visible on chest and back. The scourging was performed by two men of unequal height, standing in front and in back of the prisoner, and was effected by whips, which the Romans called *flagri,* to the ends of which were affixed small metal dumbbells. He received a blow of great impact across his right cheek, which caused considerable swelling below the eye and some displacement of the nose. The puncture wounds all around his head suggest that he was made to wear a cap or helmet of sharp, spiky objects. He was also made to carry for some time something rough and heavy across his shoulders. He seems to have fallen, perhaps more than once, abrading knees and nose. The nails of crucifixion—actually spikes about a foot long—were driven through his wrists and feet. He died in agony, as do all victims hung in crucifixion, after hours of gradual suffocation and loss of blood. Soon after his death, his left side was pierced by an elliptical object, apparently aimed at his heart. From this wound, blood flowed copiously, collecting in pools at the small of the back and spreading across the cloth.

The hands, crossed over one another at the pubis, are almost too large for the body, reminding us that here is the body of someone accustomed to physical labor—"whose strong hands were skilled at the plane and the lathe," in the words of a Celtic hymn. But it is the face in Secondo Pia's negative that is the most arresting: humane, majestic, beyond conflict. Only a Rembrandt or an early icon artist could have come close to catching such an expression. This is the face of a dead man. Imagine, for a moment, what impact it would have if its eyes were to open.

Did those eyes open a moment later? Was this image impressed upon the cloth by the heat and light of new life? No laboratory will ever tell us, nor can any scientist give such questions a scientific answer. The questions are important, not because we can ever hope to answer them with human knowledge, but because they lead us to the ultimate question about Jesus: does his story make sense? For though we may admire his compassionate and uncompromising moral teaching, his healing care and prayerful life, his human story (like all others') ends in suffering and death, a death as overwhelming and incomprehensible as any of us shall ever undergo. What is there here to nourish us?

"The bread that I shall give is my flesh for the life of the world," said the Johannine Jesus. We do not have to adopt a theology of substitution—the theory that God required a spotless human victim to make up for human sin—to make sense of the crucifixion. Such a theory, it seems to me, is a remnant of prehistoric paganism and its beliefs in cruel divinities who demanded blood sacrifice. But Jesus's suffering body is surely his ultimate gift, for it is his final act of sympathy with us. From all ages, human suffering has been the stumbling block that no life can avoid and that no philosophy has been able to comprehend. In the Hebrew Bible's Book of Job, God refuses to explain why good people must suffer. In the New Testament, he still does not explain, but he gives us a new story that contains the first glimmer of encouragement, the only hint of an explanation, that heaven has ever deigned to offer earth: "I will suffer with you."

The flesh of Jesus is the bread of the poor, the sick, the miserable, the dispossessed—their nourishment. "For just as the suf-

ferings of Christ overflow into our lives, so does the encouragement we receive through Christ," Paul tells the Corinthians.
Whatever pain we suffer, he has suffered. However acute our
suffering, he too has borne the whips, the thorns, the nails, the
lance, the cross. "It makes me happy to be suffering for you now,
and in my body to complete all the hardships that still must be
undergone by Christ for the sake of his Body, the Church," Paul
tells the Colossians. Because Jesus meant to sympathize with the
pain of every man and woman, his sufferings continue in us and
ours in him. "To sympathize" means literally "to suffer with."
"Though he possessed divine estate," goes a primitive Christian
hymn, quoted by Paul to the Philippians,

294

> he was not jealous to retain
> equality with God.
>
> He cast off his inheritance,
> he took the nature of a slave,
> and walked as man among men.
>
> He emptied himself to the last
> and was obedient to death,
> to death upon a cross.

While huddled with others in a London air-raid shelter in
1940, Edith Sitwell listened through the night to the sounds
from the sky, both bombs and rain:

> *Still falls the Rain—*
> *Dark as the world of man, black as our loss—*
> *Blind as the nineteen hundred and forty nails*

> *Upon the Cross. . . .*
> *Still falls the Rain—*
>> *Still falls the Blood from the Starved Man's wounded*
>> *Side:*
>> *He bears in His Heart all wounds—those of the light*
>> *that died,*
>> *The last faint spark*
>> *In the self-murdered heart, the wounds of the sad*
>> *uncomprehending dark,*
>> *The wounds of the baited bear—*
>> *The blind and weeping bear whom the keepers beat*
>> *On his helpless flesh . . . the tears of the hunted hare.*

295

Despite the bombs, the rain, the mercy of Christ, is falling through the universe:

> *Still falls the Rain—*
>> *Then—O Ile leap up to my God: who pulles me doune—*
>> *See, see where Christ's blood streames in the firmament:*
>> *It flows from the Brow we nailed upon the tree*
>> *Deep to the dying, to the thirsting heart*
>> *That holds the fires of the world—dark-smirched with pain*
>> *As Caesar's laurel crown.*

> *Then sounds the voice of One who like the heart of man*
>> *Was once a child who among beasts has lain—*
>> *"Still do I love, still shed my innocent light, my Blood, for*
>> *thee."*

"I have come to believe," said Martin Luther King not long before he died in a pool of his own blood, "that unmerited suffering is redemptive." This can only be so if our sufferings are taken up into the redeeming sufferings of Christ. Like King, Oscar Romero, archbishop of San Salvador, was assassinated for his defense of the poor and mistreated. Having pronounced the words of offering over the bread and wine, he was gunned down at the altar by a Salvadoran death squad, his blood spattering over the Bread of Life and mixing with the Wine of Salvation.

The Church makes a bloody entrance into the world. In John's Passion account, the Roman soldiers smash the shinbones of the crucified victims to hasten their deaths. When they come to Jesus, he seems already dead, so they do not break the bones of this Paschal Lamb without flaw. Just to be sure, however, "one of the soldiers pierced his side with a lance, and at once blood and water flowed out"—witnessed, writes John, "by the one who saw it," the Beloved Disciple. This blood and water, the last drops of Jesus's wracked body, seem to have flowed copiously, if we accept the visual testimony of that strange Fifth Gospel, the Shroud, which may have been a treasure of the church of the Beloved Disciple, the same church that treasured the evolving Fourth Gospel.* In the early Christian centuries, the blood and water from the side of Jesus were taken as the principal sacraments of Eucharist and Baptism, symbolic of the Church's birth. The Church is born from the side of Christ as Eve was born from Adam. Humanity is redeemed by humanity—by the human suffering of Jesus

✠ The Fourth Gospel presents the Beloved Disciple as running with Peter to the empty tomb to check out Mary Magdalene's story. The Beloved Disciple, younger and swifter, reaches the tomb first but, out of deference, awaits Peter's arrival before entering. They both see the "the shroud lying flat" but only the Beloved Disciple, who alone among the male disciples had followed Jesus to the cross, "saw and believed" because of this sight. It is possible that the Beloved Disciple gathered up the Shroud, which was in later centuries associated with the Johannine church, especially its community in the city of Edessa in present-day Turkey.

issuing forth in even the last effusions of his human body. "The Church's one foundation," runs the grand old Methodist hymn,

> *Is Jesus Christ her Lord;*
> *She is his new creation*
> *By water and the word:*
> *From heaven he came and sought her*
> *To be his holy bride;*
> *With his own blood he bought her,*
> *And for her life he died.*

Jesus is the bridegroom. We are the bride.

297

VII

Yesterday, Today, and Forever

The World after Jesus

O N C A L V A R Y, in the pause between the lancing of Christ and the arrival of Nicodemus with his hundred pounds of myrrh and aloes, his lengths of linen, and his permission from Pilate to remove the body and place it in the new-hewn garden tomb—in the deepest silence of human grief, on that most terrible of the world's many terrible hills—John alone has the presence of mind to recall to us the dry-throated prophecy of Zechariah, rendered three centuries earlier: "And I will pour out upon the House of David and upon the inhabitants of Jerusalem the spirit of grace and of supplications: and they shall look on me whom they have pierced, and they shall mourn for him, as one mourneth for his only son, and shall be in bitterness for him, as one that is in bitterness for [the death of] his first-born."*

But in every age since Jesus's, the human race has done its best, as did the first Christians, *not* to look on him whom we have pierced. Not unnaturally, we prefer to this moment of abysmal bitterness the glory of the resurrection—which has surely led to the marked preference of the West for happy endings that come as a delightful surprise, wrested from most unlikely dra-

🖋 The second half of the Book of Zechariah, written soon after the conquests of Alexander, abounds in Messianic references that thrilled the first Christians: the entry of a humble Messiah, astride an ass, into Jerusalem (as Jesus would enter just before his Passion); the image of sheep deserting the shepherd, interpreted as a prophecy of the disciples abandoning Jesus; the "thirty pieces of silver, the sum at which the Precious One was priced," which would turn out to be the amount Judas would be paid for identifying Jesus to the soldiers who arrested him.

matic ingredients. Our most common reference to the horror
of the crucifixion is the sanitized cross, which, whether
Protestant-pure or festooned and entabled in the manner of
the Eastern churches, seems determined to keep our mind off
the "worm and no man" (of Psalm 22) who hung there, the
"man of sorrows" (of Isaiah), one "acquainted with grief," in
whom "no comeliness" remained "to attract us" and "from
whom, as it were, we averted our gaze." The crucified criminal, open-mouthed with pain and dripping with blood, is exiled to the cellars of Latin excess and the storerooms of
masochistic bad taste.

The poor and the miserable may know better. Whether
under a wayside Polish crucifix or a Baroque depiction of the
Ultimate Agony in a Mexican cathedral, the bowed people one
sees on their knees before this image seldom have the patina
of the well-heeled and self-satisfied. Nor is it only down-and-
out Christians who find their way to the man of sorrows.
Asher Lev, the Hasidic prodigy of Rabbi Chaim Potok's affecting novels, finds himself in the Duomo of Florence, his eyes
riveted on Michelangelo's final *Pietà:*

> I stared at the geometry of the stone and felt the
> stone luminous with strange suffering and power. I
> was an observant Jew, yet that block of stone moved
> through me like a cry, like the call of seagulls over
> morning surf, like—like the echoing blasts of the
> shofar sounded by the Rebbe. I do not mean to blas-
> pheme. My frames of reference have been formed by
> the life I have lived. I do not know how a devout
> Christian reacts to that *Pietà*. I was only able to relate
> it to elements in my own lived past. I stared at it. I

walked slowly around it. I do not remember how
long I was there that first time. When I came back out
into the brightness of the crowded square, I was astonished to discover that my eyes were wet.

Asher Lev remains, according to his own lights, "an observant Jew," but one who resolves to paint crucifixions, not because he is turning into a Christian but simply because "there
was no aesthetic mold in his own religious tradition into
which he could pour a painting of ultimate anguish and torment." This strikes me as just: however we avert our eyes from
his reality, the image of the crucified holds us and will not let
go. In the end, it has little to do with whether one believes
Jesus to have been Messiah or Son of God. One can believe, if
one prefers, that he never existed—or, at least, that he never in
life occupied the position of social or theological centrality
that the gospels assign to him. But the image does not let go.
Even if it explains nothing of heaven (or even of earth), it em-
bodies the depths of human pain.

"Traditions are born," says Asher Lev, "by the power of an
initial thrust that hurls acts and ideas across the centuries." In
the case of Christianity, these acts and ideas have often been
misidentified. This is because the radical society of friends, of
free and equal men and women, that came forth from the side
of the crucified was quickly overwhelmed by ancient patriarchy and has been overwhelmed in every era since by the social and political forms of the age. As we look back over the
ages of monarchical popes and princely bishops, engaged in
war games and power struggles with one another, these play-
ers of old shrink in size and begin to resemble figures on a
chessboard, retaining little of lasting relevance for us.

303

But the "ideas and acts" have been hurled across the centuries; and whenever an individual or gathering has had the courage to confront the Gospel anew, the society of its time has experienced transformation. When the apostles and martyrs were gone and Christianity had compromised itself by becoming part and parcel of the Roman state, some men and women remembered the desert of the Jews and sought it out as the natural place for a meeting with God. These hermits and anchorites became the first Christian monks and nuns, purifying a religion that would otherwise have devolved into mere political appendage and social decoration, not unlike its cultic pagan predecessors. But the desert people rediscovered the earth-shattering encounter with God that had occupied the lives of figures from Abraham to Paul; and they gave the West a consistent tradition of spirituality and mysticism. When the medieval papacy was growing into the most splendid irreligious despotism the world had ever known, a young man whose fun-loving friends called him "Francesco" stripped himself naked in the public square of Assisi in Umbria and dedicated his life to Christ's poor, definitively separating true religion from pomp of any kind and giving the Western world a conscience it can never quite get rid of. When in the late seventeenth century George Fox and his fellow Quakers began to read the gospels, Acts, and letters of Paul, it seemed to them as if no one had ever read them before, for they rediscovered there the blueprint for Christianity as the radical "society of friends" it had once been and the theological courage to oppose slavery, prisons, capital punishment, war, and even the unholy union of church and state.

Through the history of the West since the time of Jesus, there has remained just enough of the substance of the original Gospel, a residuum, for it to be passed, as it were, from hand to hand and used, like stock, to strengthen, flavor, and invigorate new movements that have succeeded again and again—if only for a time—in producing *alteri Christi,* men and women in danger of crucifixion. It has also produced, repeatedly and in the oddest circumstances, the loving-kindness of the first Christians. Malcolm Muggeridge, the supremely secular British curmudgeon, who cast a cold eye over so many contemporary efforts and enterprises, was brought up short while visiting an Indian leprosarium run by the Missionaries of Charity, the sisters founded by Mother Teresa of Calcutta. He had always imagined secular humanism to be the ideal worldview but realized, while strolling through this facility, built with love for those whom no one wanted, that no merely humanist vision can take account of lepers, let alone take care of them. To offer humane treatment to humanity's outcasts, to overcome their lifetime experience of petty human cruelties, requires more than mere humanity. Humanists, he realized with the force of sudden insight, do not run leprosariums.

But it is also true that the West could never have realized some of its most cherished values without the process of secularization. The separation of church and state was achieved in the teeth of virulent Christian opposition, as was free speech, universal suffrage, tolerance, and many other values we would not be without. That these values flow from the subterranean river of authentic Christian tradition points up, once more, the paradoxical validity of the distinctions Jesus made between the religious establishment and true religious spirit.

United Nations headquarters in New York bears on its facade the great antiwar quotation from the prophet Isaiah: "They shall beat their swords into plowshares, and their spears

into pruning hooks: nation shall not lift up sword against nation, neither shall they learn war any more." But this does not
mean that Jews, Christians, and Muslims—these Peoples of the
Book to whom the quotation should be most meaningful—
are the world's most committed proponents of peace. The
UN's magnificent milestone, the Universal Declaration of
Human Rights of 1948, grew out of the twentieth century's
European wars, to be sure, but also out of the subterranean
river of Western values—to such an extent that much of its
language and form are modeled on the American Declaration
of Independence. Mankind's most effective check on the
Alexanders and the Caesars, the Universal Declaration could
have issued only from Judeo-Christian sources (to which non-
Western tyrants everywhere give witness when they take exception to the declaration for espousing values not
"indigenous" to their cultures). Though it is only a weapon of
words, it is also a never-failing font for raising consciousness
worldwide, and it stands as an unassailable intellectual (and
even emotional) bulwark against political cruelty in all its
many forms. But the fact that it is obviously founded on
Gospel values does not mean that we should look to Christian
forces to uphold the declaration.

The Western values of individual destiny, hope for the future, and justice for all began in the world of the Jews, the in-
ventors of the West. These values were then elaborated into an
interpersonal tradition, which holds freedom and kindness in
tension and continues to evolve as the Spiritual Story of the
West. But the West has become the world; and this river of
Judeo-Christian values is now accessible to all, and everyone
can drink from its life-giving stream. If we find shining examples of true Christian spirit in the lives of people like George

Fox and Mother Teresa, we find equally compelling examples of the opposite in such contemporary "Christians" as the blood-soaked butchers of Rwanda and Serbia. Far more impressive than most Jewish or Christian lives are the examples of a Muslim economist like Mohammed Yunus, who has created the Grameen Bank in Bangladesh, which pioneered the financing of businesses run by women too poor to offer collateral, or a Buddhist like the Burmese opposition leader Aung San Suu Kyi, who has sacrificed a normal family life and puts her own life on the line daily for the sake of wresting freedom of speech and assembly from the fascist dictatorship of Myanmar. Kindness and care for one's fellow man, like the actions of the Good Samaritan, cannot be ascribed to one group of people more than another.

307

Does this then leave us with a spiritual tradition that has become so universalized that it may be claimed by anyone but can no longer boast any characteristic proponents?

WITH THE FRIGHTENED WOMEN of Jerusalem, we have stood on Calvary, where so many of the building blocks of our world were hewn—where even opposition to the death penalty began. With the children of Rome, we have wandered over the Janiculum and, in so doing, have reacquainted ourselves with our own ancient history—but in a freer, kinder world than the ancient Romans could ever have known. Let us now descend to the streets of Trastevere and ask once more the question Did the life and death of Jesus make any difference—to the world and to Trastevere?

The history of the West is too enormous, eclectic, and brutal for anyone to claim to discern a line of spiritual development running from Calvary to the present. To the Jews, who invented processive history, there is nothing inevitable about progress, for the future always depends upon the choices for good or ill made by individuals and communities in the present moment. We can sometimes, however, if we take into account large enough units of history, spot certain trends. The trends toward social justice, human rights, and political peace, though always being disrupted and pushed back, appear to have made undeniable advances. It is hard to imagine international organizations like the United Nations, the World Court, and Amnesty International existing in earlier times. And though war and injustice continue to rage, we have at last found words to describe and condemn these oppressions, rather than praise them as we might once have been tempted to do. Such trends, it seems to me, are well summed up in the words of the finely balanced classical historian Donald Kagan at the end of his monumental study of ancient and modern war, *On the Origins of War and the Preservation of Peace:*

308

> To understand the ancient Greeks and Romans we must be alert to the great gap that separates their views, and those of most people throughout history, from the opinions of our own time. They knew nothing of ideas such as would later be spoken in the Sermon on the Mount, and they would have regarded them as absurd if they had. They viewed the world as a place of intense competition in which victory and domination, which brought fame and glory, were the highest goals, while defeat and subordination brought ignominy and shame. . . .
>
> The Romans had even fewer hesitations about

the desirability of power and the naturalness of war than the Greeks. Theirs was a culture that venerated the military virtues, a world of farmers, accustomed to hard work, deprivation, and subordination to authority. It was a society that valued power, glory, and the responsibilities of leadership, even domination, without embarrassment. The effort needed to preserve these things could be taken for granted; it was in the nature of things and part of the human condition.

Modern states, especially those who have triumphed in the Cold War and have the greatest interest in preserving peace . . . are quite different. The martial values and the respect for power have not entirely disappeared, but they have been overlaid by other ideas and values, some of them unknown to the classical republics. The most important of these is the Judeo-Christian tradition, and especially the pacifist strain of Christianity that emphasizes the Sermon on the Mount rather than the more militant strain that played so large a role over the centuries. Even as the power and influence of formal, organized religion have waned in the last century, the influence among important segments of the population in the United States and other Western countries of the rejection of power, the evil of pursuing self-interest, the wickedness of war, whatever its cause or goal, have grown. There are now barriers of conscience in the way of acquiring and maintaining power and using it to preserve the peace that would have been incomprehensible to the Greeks and Romans.

It is this enormous shift in consciousness, the origin of which Kagan, a secular American Jew, rightly locates in the teachings of Jesus, that could save the children of the Janiculum and the Western world from the wars that wounded and killed the generations before them right through the hideous "world wars" of the twentieth century. The shift was long in coming, and has come, like many others—from abolition to labor relations, from suffrage to tolerance—only after centuries of struggle. Nor are any of these struggles won conclusively. There are still, for instance, pockets of slavery in the world; and even in the West, there remain abundant labor exploitation, the unjust incarceration of minorities, the demonization of immigrants, and the continuing sufferings of the poor. The Balkan peoples have awakened from their extended Soviet sleep as people of the nineteenth century, clutching their undying ethnic hatreds while living in the twenty-first. But everywhere the Christian value system makes demands unknown in earlier ages. Even in the extremities of the West—in Northern Ireland, for instance, and in Israel—the pressure to make peace is quite unlike anything the Greeks or Romans or even the Elizabethans could have imagined.

In none of these arenas would any but a madman be willing to abandon the gains the West has made and go backward even by a century or two into the past. Far beyond the West, we watch those who struggle for the freedoms we enjoy and wonder where they get their courage. But, says Yuan Zhiming, one of the Chinese intellectuals who supported the students of Tiananmen Square, "Democracy is not merely an institution nor simply a concept, but a profound structure of faith." We must consider that Christianity's "initial thrust" has hurled "acts and ideas" not only "across the centuries" but around the world.

So much for the world. What of Trastevere?

At the foot of the Janiculum there sits an unimportant square, embracing a small collection of buildings, once a clois-tered Renaissance convent, today the center of a worldwide movement, named after the old convent and called the Community of Sant'Egidio. Given the glories of Trastevere, you could easily pass it by, thinking it just another pedestrian church unmentioned in your travel guide. This is the heart of an ecumenical community of laypeople, founded in 1968 by a handful of Roman high school students, who decided during that year of student uprisings throughout Western Europe that they, too, wanted to do something revolutionary, something that would have permanent effect, not something that would vanish without trace. They wished to live in Rome as the early Christians had lived there.

They began to gather each night to pray together and read from the Bible, especially from the Gospel. They reflected on the Gospel and they did what the Gospel impelled them to do. That was thirty years ago. Today there are about ten thousand members of the community in Italy and a similar number be-yond its borders, representatives on every continent and in most of the countries of the world. They do not live together; they have normal jobs and normal lives. They have only one slogan that I am aware of: "The Gospel and Freedom." Though they gather to read the Gospel and pray together in small com-munities throughout the world, usually several nights each week, no member is obliged to attend anything. What has the Gospel impelled them to do? As I cannot describe the works

311

of each community, I will tell you about the works of the original community, which gathers each night for prayer in this ancient quarter of Trastevere, the same quarter where first-century Christianity gained its first Roman foothold.

Their church is filled to capacity, often to bursting. Though the founders are now in their late forties, the average age of the congregation seems about thirty, so the community continues to gather strength from fresh recruits. The prayer is the most beautiful I have ever heard, modeled on the sonorous chant of the Russian church and sung from the gut with reverence and feeling. Each night they choose a theme: on Monday night, for instance, there is "Prayer with the Poor," on Wednesday "Prayer with the Saints," on Friday "Prayer at the Foot of the Cross." On Friday night, they sing:

> *Non piangere, Madre di Dio,*
> *presso la croce del Signore,*
> *e gioisci perche Egli è risorto:*
> *nel suo corpo è nascosto*
> *tutto il riscatto e la salvezza di ogni uomo.*

> *Do not weep so, Mother of the Lord,*
> *standing in the shadow of the cross,*
> *and shout for joy because He is truly risen:*
> *in his body is hidden*
> *creation's redemption and the salvation of all mankind.*

They sing this three times with plangent conviction, as if to remind themselves of all those who have lost a child or a beloved or been themselves lost in the overwhelming tides of life and history. The darkness of the church is dramatically illuminated by icons, especially a riveting icon of Christ. There is a quiet but pervasive sense of community; and following the half-hour service, people linger in the piazza outside to renew friendship and go off in small groups to dine together. Friendship is a profound experience for these people: they are true friends to one another, and they wish to be friends to the world.

There are more than a hundred satellite communities in and around Rome, engaged in various works. Some are communities of old people, some of poor working people, some of students. Each community tends to have its own coloration. The Trastevere community, which is made up mostly of middle-class professionals, sends out tutors to students in the poor communities. Each night in Trastevere fifteen hundred homeless people are fed, not on soup lines but at sit-down dinners, served with style and graciousness. Once a week fifteen hundred substantial bags of groceries are prepared and distributed. The sorting of the food into bags takes an assembly line of a dozen volunteers all evening. An identification sheet is started for everyone who comes to Sant'Egidio for help, so that the community may offer continuity of assistance, not just a handout. This assistance takes many forms—from helping resident aliens cut through bureaucratic red tape to the publication each Christmas of a colorful, easy-to-read handbook, titled *Dove Mangiare, Dormire e Lavarsi a Roma* (Where to Eat, Sleep, and Wash in Rome), a gift especially prized by the homeless. On Christmas afternoon, the ancient basilica of Santa Maria in Trastevere opens its gates to a great feast for the poor, homeless, and elderly of Rome, hosted with true Italian generosity by the Community of Sant'Egidio. The Trastevere community runs three refuges for old people, two AIDS hospices, and a home for abused and abandoned children. Its members have founded throughout the poor perimeter of the city many after-school programs for small children called *scuole popolari,* or "people's schools," where the children are taught the things they are seldom taught in state schools—not only reading but kindness. There are free language programs for immigrants, outreach programs for gypsies, and biweekly visits to prisoners, all organized by Sant'Egidio.

Each October, the community organizes a torchlight March of Remembrance for the Roman Jews and all other Jews who perished under the Nazis. It starts at the portico of the basilica of Santa Maria (which contains the first-century Jewish and Christian grave slabs) and proceeds to Tiber Island (where the Jews of Rome were brought by the Nazis in 1943 prior to their deportation to Auschwitz) and ends at the steps of the synagogue beyond the river. Large black banners are held aloft, each with the name of one of the death camps printed in white letters. At the head of the march, which is silent (an unusual occurrence in Italy), the largest banner contains Santayana's famous sentence "Those who cannot remember the past are condemned to repeat it."

Several years ago, members of the community, believing they had a Gospel mandate to act as peacemakers, undertook a series of quiet, amateur efforts on their own and succeeded in arranging a peace in Mozambique between the guerrillas and the government (after sixteen years of war and one million casualties). The peace has held, as has a similar peace that the community has helped to achieve in Guatemala. They continue to attempt reconciliation in Algeria, the Balkans, and other hotspots, working intuitively and patiently, never abandoning hope, and true to their belief that "war is the greatest poverty of all." As I write, a million refugees are spilling out of Kosovo. At its muddy borders are the people of Sant'Egidio, constructing sanitation and housing, offering medicine, food, and schooling, and helping to coordinate the efforts of others. In this new mission of peace, the community has at its disposal only its own part-time volunteers (almost no one at Sant'Egidio is salaried) and what it calls "the weak strength of the Gospel."

But it also has a growing network of religious leaders of all kinds, committed to its vision that the religions of the world must take the lead in bringing peace to their regions. In this spirit, the community organized in 1986 the first Uomini e Religioni (People and Religions) conference in the Assisi of Saint Francis. Leaders of all the world's religions were invited—and they came, and they prayed and talked together for several days. Each year since then the community has organized a similar conference in a European city, in the course of which you may spy Arab sitting down with Israeli, Serb with Bosnian Muslim, Irish Protestant with Irish Catholic. Over time, this mingling in friendship could spell the difference between war and peace in many regions—and the difference between death and life for many individuals.

If there is no magic in the people of Sant'Egidio, there is much goodness. It is a goodness cultivated as any quality must be cultivated—with practice and attention—and, no doubt, in their case, with grace from above; and it has transformed the lives of countless human beings in Trastevere, in Rome, in Italy, and far beyond. But the only mystery here is the mystery of human will. Anyone on earth could do what they have done.

Cynics often say that "nothing can be done," meaning that nothing can really be accomplished to improve the lot of those who suffer. Defensive Christians are often heard to say of Christianity that "it has never been tried." But people like Mother Teresa and the Community of Sant'Egidio give the lie to all cynicism and defensiveness. This earth now holds six billion souls. How many Mother Teresas would it take to succor the abandoned and dying? How many Sant'Egidios would it take to transform the social fabric not just of Trastevere but of the earth itself?

As a percentage of global population, not all that many. It requires only that each of us take the first step—"open [our] hearts" and hold out our hands. When asked once by an incredulous interviewer, "But, Mother, how do you *do* it?" the shrunken and smiling Albanian nun replied, "One by one."

Tomorrow

There is an old French saying, "Hell is paved with the skulls of priests." I wouldn't know, nor does anyone. But I am pretty sure, harking back to Jesus's description of the Last Judgment, which is preceded by his excoriation of the religious establishment of his day, that many people, both high and low, are in for a surprise. When dealing with hallowed religious material, we must always be on our guard against a knee-jerk piety that obscures rather than assists insight and that prefers to judge, punish, and exclude rather than welcome. Christians, therefore, reading their own sacred texts and revering their own sacred objects, should welcome especially the insights of outsiders—like Chaim Potok's Asher Lev, Yale's Donald Kagan, and China's Yuan Zhiming—who can bring new depth to their experience.

Modern scripture scholarship, rising in nonsectarian, ag-
nostic circles, has brought believers new riches, allowing us to
see anew the life of Jesus and the story of the early Church—
to view these ancient treasures from venues never available before. Now we can appreciate the personalities, the strengths
and limitations, of each evangelist, even finding useful scripture
scholarship's "criterion of embarrassment"—the idea that certain elements of the text were so embarrassing to the sponsor-
ing community that the writer could have included these
things only because he did not feel free to leave them out.
Such a criterion gives us confidence that Peter (later a great
figure) was indeed the bumbler he is portrayed to be, that
women (later told to keep their mouths shut) like Magdalene
were leaders of the early church, that Jesus casually forgave
sexual transgressions, and that his crucifixion rattled his followers to their bones. Modern scholarship has also given us a
better sense of the continuities (and discontinuities) between
the teaching of Jesus and his first followers and among the various factions of the developing Jesus Movement, as it grew into
the Church of later centuries. All these are new insights that
give new strength.

If we take from the most modern, we also borrow from the
most ancient, for the worldview of the Jews is the rock-solid
promontory that supports Christian faith. Without the Jewish
sense of destiny, both corporate and individual, without the
Jewish sense of history and the meaning given to suffering, no
part of the story that Christians tell themselves would make
any sense whatever. It is from the Jews that we received the
idea of chosenness by God—"You have not chosen me; I have
chosen you"—and from the Jews that we learned that chosenness implies both suffering and redemption. Indeed, to ap-

proach the idea of chosenness with humility and imagination is to find oneself on the point of retching—because it brings one in fresh proximity with one's own suffering (past, present, and to come) and with the pain of others, of all others—the great moaning and shuddering that runs through the whole of human history.

But because it still requires a great artist or a great saint to "look on" Jesus in his suffering, all our approaches—scientific, Jewish, orthodox, pious—to authentic Christianity are likely to prove inadequate; and I wonder how far we have come—as a civilization—from his own mother's peasant judgment that what this guy is saying doesn't really add up. Jesus insists on forgiveness, turning the other cheek, peace, and compassion, *always* compassion—and which of us wants to hear *that?* The leaders of the Jewish religious establishment rejected Jesus in his own lifetime, not principally because he rejected the Torah of Moses or because he claimed to be God, but because of his midrash, his interpretation of God's word. He insisted that all of Jewish sacred scripture—the Torah and the Prophets—was asking them to live in a way that they considered unrealistic. Any Christian who imagines himself morally superior to those who turned away has only to glance at the subsequent history of Christian persecution of Jews to realize that Christians have been far more successful at rejecting Jesus than any Jew has ever been.

Despite this catastrophic bimillennial failure, the image of Jesus haunts our civilization in exceedingly persistent ways. Everyone knows who he is; everyone knows what he looked like; everyone knows what he expects of us. This consistency, this transultimate *reliability* is found in the four original gospel portraits and has persisted through the ages. As the ancient liturgy of Easter says of him: "Christ yesterday and today, the beginning and the end, Alpha and Omega—his are the seasons and the ages." Or, far less triumphally, as a Jewish woman confided to me recently: "I love Jesus. Don't get me wrong: I have no interest *whatsoever* in Christianity. But I love Jesus; I feel he belongs to me."

At the turn of the new millennium, it may be time for everyone to reassess Jesus. I hope that the process of Jewish-Christian reconciliation will soon have progressed far enough that Jews may reexamine their automatic (and completely understandable) fear of all things Christian and acknowledge Jesus as one of their own, not as the Messiah, but as a brother who called God *Abba*. For Christians, it may be time to acknowledge that we have misunderstood Jesus in virtually every way that matters. As Raymond Brown was fond of remarking, if Jesus were to return to earth, the first thing we would do is crucify him again.

319

But whether we are Jew or Christian, believer or atheist, the figure of Jesus—as final Jewish prophet, as innocent and redeeming victim, as ideal human being—is threaded through our society and folded into our imagination in such a way that it cannot be excised. He is the mysterious ingredient that laces everything we taste, the standard by which all moral actions are finally judged. As one poet, W. H. Auden, echoing centuries of others, says affectionately and without regard to dogma or creed:

> He is the Way.
> Follow Him through the Land of Unlikeness;
> You will see rare beasts, and have unique adventures.

> He is the Truth.
> Seek Him in the Kingdom of Anxiety;

You will come to a great city that has expected your return for
years.

He is the Life.
Love Him in the World of the Flesh;
And at your marriage all its occasions shall dance for joy.

Notes *and* Sources

I MEAN TO GIVE HERE not an exhaustive bibliography of everything I consulted (which, given the enormous accumulation of biblical and New Testament studies over the past half century, would dangerously increase the size of this book) but a sense of what I found most valuable. As I did in Volume Two of this series, I again recommend the six volumes of *The Anchor Bible Dictionary* (New York, 1992), now helpfully available on CD-ROM, as the best of all initial research tools. For those who prefer a more compact instrument, both *The Oxford Companion to the Bible* (New York, 1993) and *The New Jerome Biblical Commentary* (Englewood Cliffs, NJ, 1990), the latter containing particularly well focused overviews, are also highly recommended. Other excellent sources of information for the non-specialist are the back issues of *Bible Review* and *Biblical Archaeology Review*, in both of which well-regarded scholars are invited to write for the common reader about current breakthroughs and controversies.

INTRODUCTION

In confirming my presentation of the outlook from the Janiculum, I found helpful Christopher Hibbert's *Rome: The Biography of a City* (London and New York, 1985); *The Blue Guide to Rome* (London and New York, 1994); the Lazio volume (Venice, 1997) of the *Jewish Itinerary* series; and Ruth Liliana Geller's *Roma Ebraica* (Rome, 1984). Giacomo Debenedetti's small but unforgettable book about the Nazi roundup of the Jews of Rome, *16 ottobre 1943* (Palermo, 1993), is not available in an English translation, so far as I know. Livy's history of ancient Rome, *Ab Urbe Condita Libri*—from which I took the description of the Celtic invaders—is available in many editions.

The title of this book is a phrase from the beautiful blessing of Jacob on his son Joseph, found in Genesis 49:26. The phrase is translated in different ways—from "the utmost bounds of the eternal hills" (Jewish Publications Society) to "the delights of the everlasting hills" (E. A. Speiser). My translation is taken from the Latin of Jerome's Vulgate, which served for more than a thousand years in the West the same purpose that the Greek Septuagint served first in the Jewish diaspora, then in the Eastern church—as universal Bible. Jerome did not have at his disposal the Masoretic Hebrew text that has since become standard, but different versions of the Hebrew and Septuagint, which he used for comparison and correction. He translated the phrase: "*desiderium collium eternorum.*" Correct or incorrect, it is for me an image of the desire beyond articulation, the desire deeper than all (conscious) desiring.

I: GREEKS, JEWS, AND ROMANS

The "Axial Age," or *Achsenzeit*, is a term invented by the postwar German historian Karl Jaspers in his *Vom Ursprung und Zeit der Geschichte* (1949), in which he proposes his theory, since then widely accepted, of an age of extraordinary worldwide creativity with the fifth century B.C. as its white-hot center.

There is no one to whom I owe more in this chapter than the great Italian Jewish scholar Arnaldo Momigliano, who knew more than anyone about just about everything—certainly about everything in antiquity. Two of his books proved especially enlightening: *Alien Wisdom: The Limits of Hellenization* (Cambridge, 1971) and *Pagine ebraiche* (Torino, 1987), published in English translation as *Essays on Ancient and Modern Judaism* (Chicago, 1994).

For the Greek and Roman figures, I relied principally on Plutarch's *Parallel Lives* for Alexander, Pompey, and Caesar and on Tacitus's *Annals* and Suetonius's *Lives of the Twelve Caesars* for Augustus. These are available in many editions. Also helpful was a fine comprehensive study on "currents of culture and belief" by James D. Newsome, *Greeks, Romans, Jews* (Philadelphia, 1992).

The outstanding contemporary interpreter of Jewish apocalyptic literature is John J. Collins. I consulted his *Between Athens and Jerusalem* (New York, 1983), *The Apocalyptic Imagination* (New York, 1984), and especially *The Scepter and the Star: The Messiahs of the Dead Sea Scrolls and Other Ancient Literature* (New York, 1995).

The translation of the Sibylline Oracles is by Collins. The quotations from Isaiah are taken from the King James Version (KJV): these prophecies would have sounded ancient and venerable to the ears of Jesus's contemporaries, just as the KJV sounds to us. The quotations from First and Second Maccabees are taken from the New Jerusalem Bible (NJB), as is the long quotation from the Book of Wisdom (though revised by me). The translation from the Latin of Virgil's "Fourth Eclogue" is mine.

A caution is in order concerning my choice of biblical texts to illustrate the convictions of the Jews of Jesus's time in regard to both the possibility of an afterlife and the expectation of a messiah. My quotation from Job (taken from the Jerusalem Bible, *not* its successor, the NJB) may be criticized as being heavily colored by subsequent Christian interpretation. The Hebrew original would be more conservatively (and properly) translated simply to bring out Job's belief that his case is a just one, which he hopes can be established while he is still alive, and that it is actually God who is Job's adversary. But the translation I used was chosen not to make inferences unjustified by the original but to see this passage from Job as it was already being interpreted by Jews of the intertestamental period. Christians, to begin with, did not so much invent these adumbrations as borrow them from strains of then-current Jewish interpretation. In other words, though the body/soul dualism of the Greeks is completely absent from the text of Job, its author had—in his own time—no notion of a resurrection of the dead. But this notion was read into the text by subsequent commentators well before Christians appeared on the scene and, therefore, helped form the context of expectation into which Jesus was born. (By the fifth or sixth century A.D., rabbinical commentators, like their Christian counterparts, would come to assume as almost obvious that the soul is eternal, thus going a long way toward adopting the Greek view, but this is hardly the problematic of physical resurrection that we find the author of First Maccabees struggling with.)

Similarly, the last three lines of the first set of passages from Isaiah (these three lines taken not from the KJV but from a translation of the Vulgate, which is in its turn more dependent on the Greek Septuagint than on the best Hebrew texts) is invoked not to make Christian points but to point up the atmosphere of expectation in which the prophecies of Isaiah had come to be read—especially, perhaps, by diaspora Jews who read versions of the Septuagint rather than versions of the Hebrew—by the time of Jesus. The actual Hebrew, however, gives us an expectation that is abstract rather than personal: "Justice" rather than "the Just One"; "Salvation" rather than "the Savior."

If in dealing with the Book of Isaiah I fail to mention that there is a third voice—a Trito-Isaiah—to be found in chapters 56–66, this is because this particular deconstruction has no bearing on the point I am making. I should also mention that there is a raging scholarly controversy as to whether the Dead Sea Scrolls (DSS) were a library of the Essenes or of some other Jewish group, and another controversy as to what the relationship of John the Baptizer and/or Jesus may (or may not) have been to the Essene community. It seems plain to me that John was more extreme in his apocalyptic than Jesus, and what he has to say certainly sounds an awful lot like much of the material original to the DSS. If the DSS were not an Essene library, they were certainly the library of an apocalyptic sect of John/Jesus's period. Though most indications surely point in the direction of the assumptions I have made in the main text, nothing of my essential argument there would be disturbed by new findings about the provenance of John or of the DSS.

Finally, I am happy to admit that a case can be made against my claim that the Jews had "abandoned their ancestral language" by the time of Jesus's birth. I am aware that many educated Jews were trilingual, able to read and (to some extent) speak Hebrew, Greek, and Aramaic (as witness the Bar Kochba letters and the DSS themselves). But I very much doubt that such an accomplishment can be posited of the population as a whole, especially of the majority of the Galilean women and men who were Jesus's main audience.

II: The Last of the Prophets

In this chapter and throughout the remainder of the book, all translations from the Greek of the New Testament (except as otherwise indicated) are mine—but with an eye to other translations, especially two at opposite ends of the translation spectrum: the New International Version (NIV), which is moderately literal, and the NJB, which in its assiduously idiomatic English sometimes approaches paraphrase.

The now-classic work on the Judaism of Jesus is E. P. Sanders's *Jesus and Judaism* (Philadelphia, 1985), which sets out in an English prose that any writer might envy all the major scholarly considerations, few of which I am able to treat in any detail. Sometimes more helpful to my purposes was John P. Meier's *A Marginal Jew* (New York, 1991–1994), the exhaustive multivolume study of the historical Jesus, still in progress, and a model of clarity. Raymond E. Brown's *An Introduction to the New Testament* (New York, 1997) is virtually indispensable to anyone who wishes to appreciate the New Testament, but it is especially good on the gospels, on which Brown expended so much of his life. He was, till his death in 1998, the greatest American scholar of the New Testament, probably the greatest in the world, and a man of such kindness and generosity that no one who knew him can ever forget him. Also useful (in the excursus on Mary) was an earlier work of his, *The Birth of the Messiah* (2nd edition, New York, 1993), as well as the anthology *Mary in the New Testament* (Philadelphia and Mahwah, NJ, 1978) edited by Brown et al. The remark about comforting the afflicted and afflicting the comfortable was first said (so far as I can determine) not of the Gospel but of Dorothy Day—by Theodore Hesburgh when he presented her with the Laetare Medal at Notre Dame.

325

There are subjects customary in biblical studies that, as some may be surprised to observe, I fail to take up in this chapter. These include, for instance, the Temple fetish of the priests and Sadducees, which, whatever their relationship to the Mosaic Law, sets them far apart from Jesus, who attacked their clerical fixations; and the controversy over what (if anything) in the infancy narratives of Matthew and Luke can be taken as historical. But I ask the reader to bear in mind that my purpose is not to write an introduction to the New Testament but to answer these questions: Who was Jesus? What was his effect and that of his followers on their own world? What was their impact on subsequent history? Whether or not his mother was a virgin is far less important here than what kind of mothering she gave her son. Important and even controversial subjects that do not shed light on such questions have been militantly relegated to the margins of this study or, in some cases, left unmentioned altogether.

Whether Mary's pregnancy—following betrothal but prior to the actual wedding—would have caused a scandal is something of an open question. Joseph was certainly scandalized (since he and Mary had not yet had sex) and, according to Matthew, had to be persuaded by an angel that his betrothed was chaste. Judean Jews, who were more sophisticated than

Galilean Jews, permitted sex between betrothal and marriage; Galileans did not. Since Bethlehem is inside Judea proper, Joseph's relatives may have taken Mary's condition in their stride, even if her Nazareth neighbors would not have done so. We just don't know for sure. My point in this excursus is that the Christmas Story was full not so much of angel song as of ordinary human discomforts.

III: THE COSMIC CHRIST

Confirmation that Jesus, naked on the cross, was taunted sexually by a brutal crowd is not to be found in the reticent evangelists, but it is virtually impossible to imagine its not happening. The final passage from Mark's Gospel is taken from the translation by Reynolds Price, contained in his *Three Gospels* (New York, 1996).

326

Any work by E. P. Sanders can always be recommended with high enthusiasm, in this case his most illuminating *Paul and Palestinian Judaism* (Philadelphia, 1977) and *Paul, the Law, and the Jewish People* (Philadelphia, 1983). For my treatment of Paul, I am particularly indebted to Jerome Murphy-O'Connor, whose *Paul: A Critical Life* (Oxford, 1996) is full of both responsible scholarship and sensible speculation. I have presented his speculations about what may have been going on at the Corinthian liturgies less conditionally than he does. I am well aware that his is but one possible interpretation, but I find that it answers more questions than any other. Also helpful to me in various ways were many other books and articles by Murphy-O'Connor (all listed in the bibliography to his *Paul*); I would single out especially *St. Paul's Corinth* (Collegeville, MN, 1992) and *The Holy Land: An Archaeological Guide from Earliest Times to 1700* (3rd edition, Oxford, 1992). In addition to Murphy-O'Connor, mention must be made of Alan F. Segal, whose *Paul the Convert* (New Haven, 1990) is a milestone in interfaith studies, a balanced reexamination of Paul from the perspective of a Jewish scholar, and a treasure-house of riches for the careful reader.

A wonderfully eye-opening collection that came to my attention, *Paul and Empire: Religion and Power in Roman Imperial Society* (Harrisburg, PA, 1997), edited by Richard A. Horsley, was useful not only in my presentation of the political aspect of Paul but in suggesting a saner-than-usual approach to the Book of Revelation. In particular, I would recommend the two essays by Neil Elliott, "The Anti-Imperial Message of the Cross" and "Romans 13:1–7 in the Context of Imperial Propaganda," as well as Horsley's concluding essay, "1 Corinthians: A Case Study of Paul's Assembly as an Alternative Society." The essays by Elliott may also be found, with additional helpful material, in his splendid overview, *Liberating Paul: The Justice of God and the Politics of the Apostle* (Maryknoll, 1994). At the other end of the spectrum of reinterpretation lies the work of John Shelby Spong—for example, *Rescuing the Bible from Fundamentalism: A Bishop Rethinks the Meaning of Scripture* (San Francisco, 1991). In my opinion, Spong, the Episcopal bishop referred to in the main text, lacks the subtlety required to engage in the necessary task of "rethinking" that he sets himself. He certainly knows how to be "outspoken and controversial," as his dust jacket proclaims, but he is tone-deaf to the deep meaning of many of the passages that he tackles so "boldly."

I take some liberties in my portraits of Paul and Peter. There is no horse mentioned in Luke's account of Paul's experience on the road to Damascus, even though it is a constant in the iconographic tradition. Likewise, the physical descriptions of Paul and Peter are based on the constant traditions of very early paleo-Christian art, which I think we can trust as deriving originally from eyewitnesses. Some might quibble with my sketch of Paul's father, but I feel we can almost see and hear this ambitious man in his son's words.

As in the previous chapter, my overriding purpose—of tracing cultural impact—impels me to omit certain customary subjects, such as the meaning of the collection for the Jerusalem poor that occupied so much of Paul's attention and the even more important subject of the mode (and development) of his apocalypticism. Some may take exception to my portrayal of the Pharisees as belonging to the leisured class, preferring to see them more as a proletarian intelligentsia. (They probably did have working-class origins, but it is almost impossible to imagine them working with their hands.) The provenance of the Letter to the Hebrews, once mistakenly ascribed to Paul, is extremely tricky, as are its dating and probable audience.

Those who would pursue the New Testament connection between earthly and cosmic "powers" of evil will find no better aid than the work of Walter Wink. His influential "Powers" trilogy—*Naming the Powers, Unmasking the Powers, Engaging the Powers* (Philadelphia, 1984, 1986, 1992)—

is well recapitulated and even extended in his latest book, *The Powers That Be: Theology for a New Millennium* (New York, 1998).

IV: THE GENTILE MESSIAH

For my money, the best study of Luke is Joseph A. Fitzmyer's *The Gospel According to Luke* (New York, 1970, 1985) in two volumes of the Anchor Bible Commentaries series. Fitzmyer, perhaps our leading expert on ancient Aramaic (and one of the most important scholars to work on the DSS), has an extraordinary background in classical and ancient Near East languages and cultures; yet he is modest in his assertions and appreciative of Luke's unique qualities both as evangelist and stylist. His English translation of Luke is without peer and was most helpful to me in making my own.

Though a majority of scholars put the gospels of Matthew and Luke in the late 70s or early 80s, a preponderance of these would now place Luke a little earlier than Matthew. In my text, I suggest the opposite, but this is because Luke strikes me as more developed theologically than Matthew (and, as I say later on, halfway to the theology of John). Matthew could well have written later than Luke; but, even so, he exemplifies the earlier and less exalted Christology of Palestinian Jewish Christians.

Though I mention Jesus's provocative attitude toward the Temple, I do so only as an example of Luke's tendency to tone down instances of Jesus's anger—and Jesus's temper was definitely part of the oral tradition. For an exhaustive (and enlightening) consideration of Jesus's relationship to Temple Judaism, see Sanders (see notes to Chapter Two). For my treatment of Jesus's miracles, I am much indebted to John P. Meier's *A Marginal Jew*, volume 2:509–1038 (see notes to Chapter Two).

V: DRUNK IN THE MORNING LIGHT

Once again, Joseph Fitzmyer comes to our rescue with his Anchor Bible Commentary, in this case on *The Acts of the Apostles* (New York, 1998), an immensely learned and judicious assessment of the many (and conflicting) waves of contemporary scholarship. The picture of communistic Jerusalem Christianity painted by Luke is, like much of Luke, idealistic rather than realistic—intended as an archetype for bad times.

A small book by Raymond E. Brown was essential to my picture of the early Christians—*The Churches the Apostles Left Behind* (New York, 1984)—but others of his small books, all from Paulist Press, were also helpful, especially *Priest and Bishop* (New York, 1970) and, with John P. Meier, *Antioch and Rome* (New York, 1983). A lovely reimagining of the early Christians is presented in the first volume of Michel Clévenot's *Les hommes de la fraternité* (Paris, 1981).

The touchstone feminist study of the life of the early Christians is Elizabeth Schussler Fiorenza's *In Memory of Her: A Feminist Theological Reconstruction of Christian Origins* (New York, 1983). Though I disagree (mildly) with her in my main text on the question of who wrote Colossians, I find that her overall approach, bracing in one's first encounter, only grows in stature as this book approaches its seventeenth birthday.

The excerpt from Dorothy Day is taken from her essay "Room for Christ," collected in *By Little and By Little: The Selected Writings of Dorothy Day*, edited by Robert Ellsberg and Tamar Hennessy (New York, 1983). The poem by Emily Dickinson is number 409 in her collected poems. The lines from Gerard Manley Hopkins come from his untitled poem that begins "As kingfishers catch fire, dragonflies draw flame."

VI: The Word Made Flesh

The great interpreter of John's Gospel and letters is Raymond E. Brown, who to some extent based his studies on the seminal work of C. H. Dodd. His Anchor Bible Commentaries *The Gospel According to John* (New York, 1966, 1970), in two volumes, and *The Epistles of John* (New York, 1982) are among the most influential works of modern biblical criticism. Though Brown had hoped to revise the Gospel volumes, his untimely death has prevented that; but his treatment of John's Gospel in his final work, *An Introduction to the New Testament* (see notes to Chapter Two), gives some indication of what shape his revision might have taken. Essential to my picture of the evolution and sensitivities of the Johannine church was Brown's groundbreaking *The Community of the Beloved Disciple: The Life, Loves, and Hates of an Individual Church in New Testament Times* (New York, 1979).

Once again, there are many topics standard in scriptural studies that I fail to deal with in the main text because these have little or no bearing on our principal pursuit of establishing the impact of Jesus on our culture. One of these, which may puzzle the reader, is John's unique chronology for the Passion narrative. In Paul and the Synoptics, the Last Supper, which takes place "on the night he was betrayed," is clearly thought to have been a "Passover [meal]." In John, Jesus on the day after his betrayal comes before Pilate, and this day John describes as "the Day of Preparation [for Passover]," thus indicating that Passover is yet to take place. It is obvious that John does this for theological reasons, especially to dramatize the role of Jesus as Paschal Lamb and unleavened [i.e., incorrupt] bread, but which chronology is the correct one can probably never be settled. For a detailed study of this and similar contradictions between John and the Synoptic tradition, see Brown, *The Gospel According to John* (above).

Perhaps nothing will give readers pause so much as my failure to deal directly with the question of who killed Jesus. Once again, this question has little bearing on our principal considerations; and its function in the history of anti-Semitism has made it invidious. I actually belong to the Brown school on this one: I think (*pace* Crossan *et al.*) that the gospels are sufficiently reliable historical documents for us to conclude that some Jewish leaders whipped up popular animosity toward Jesus and used this to influence the Roman governor, who like most Roman officials needed scant provocation to execute a Jewish troublemaker. But from the perspective of cultural history, as from an informed theological perspective, such a conclusion takes us nowhere. The deep truth of the matter, both in the New Testament and in all the subsequent cultural development of the West that we can continue to cherish as valuable, is that we all killed Jesus—and are forgiven.

Contrary to my assertion at the outset of this chapter that the Jews *in the time of Jesus* were expecting only one Messiah, John J. Collins in *The Scepter and the Star* (see notes to Chapter One), 74ff., draws our attention to indications in the DSS that among the Essenes there may have been some expectation of two messiahs, a kingly one and a priestly one. But the Essenes were far removed from normal Jewish life; and we may take their (possible) expectation as the exception that proves the rule. (In earlier times, the word "messiah," or *moshiach*, had been applied to many different men, such as Saul, David, and even Cyrus the Great.)

The incomparable study of Jesus's Passion is Raymond E. Brown's *The Death of the Messiah: From Gethsemane to the Grave* (New York, 1994) in two volumes, an exquisitely detailed "commentary on the Passion narratives in the four gospels." It is Brown's masterpiece, the result of a lifetime of reflection, and I doubt it will ever be surpassed.

The most recent "Shroud" book of interest is Leoncio A. Garza-Valdes's *The DNA of God?* (New York, 1999), which proposes the bioplastic coating that confounds accurate carbon dating. But many other books have attempted to establish the Shroud's authenticity, most convincingly perhaps several books by Ian Wilson and various reports by STURP (Shroud of Turin Research Project) on research carried out in the 1970s. (Much of the essential information on this project is contained in *Report on the Shroud of Turin* by John Heller, who was professor of internal medicine at Yale, though the carbon-14 tests on the Shroud came after the work of Heller and his colleagues.) But all these texts have something of the whiff of the unhinged believer about them. The great fear that anyone must have in going near this material is to be dismissed as another "Shroudie." Though I find the data immensely intriguing and largely convincing, nothing that I have to say in this book depends on the Shroud's authenticity or would have to be altered if the Shroud were definitively proved a forgery.

The quotation toward the end of this chapter from the hymn in Paul's Letter to the Philippians, may seem to confirm that Paul, like John, held to a Christology that saw Jesus as the incarnation of God's preexistent "Word" ("Though he possessed divine estate . . ."). But it is just as legitimate to read this hymn as an example of Paul's "Adamic" Christology. Jesus, born like Adam "in the image of God," "was not jealous to retain" any of the favors of Eden but "cast off" his rightful human "inheritance," and took on "the nature of a slave"—that is, the lot of fallen humanity. Though I have chosen to explain Paul according to the "Adamic" Christology that Murphy-O'Connor and others find in his letters, a good argument can also be made for interpreting Paul along the lines of an "eternal preexistence-with-God" Christology that more closely approaches John. For an impressive defense of this second position, see John P. Meier's *A Marginal Jew* (see notes to Chapter Two), Volume 3 (forthcoming).

The full text of "Still Falls the Rain" by Edith Sitwell may be found in her *Collected Poems* (New York, 1954).

VII: YESTERDAY, TODAY, AND FOREVER

The quotations from Chaim Potok are taken from his novel *My Name Is Asher Lev* (New York, 1972). Potok has written a second book about the same character, called *The Gift of Asher Lev* (New York, 1990). Potok sets Asher Lev's experience of Michelangelo's late *Pietà* in the Duomo (or cathedral) of Florence. Since 1981, however, this sculpture has been housed in the Museo dell'Opera del Duomo behind the cathedral.

Malcolm Muggeridge expressed his fervent admiration for Mother Teresa and her nuns in *Something Beautiful for God* (San Francisco, 1971). His reflection on who runs leprosariums was first offered, I believe, in his "Seasonal Cross-Examination of Himself" in the *Observer Review* for December 15, 1968, but it is also contained in his BBC television program on the work of Mother Teresa. The Universal Declaration of Human Rights is available in many collections of documents and at www.un.org. Mohammad Yunus, founder of the Grameen Bank of Bangladesh, wrote an engrossing op-ed piece for the *New York Times* (April 2, 1990) under the headline "Credit as a Human Right." An editorial on the same subject appeared in the *New York Times* (February 16, 1997) under the headline "Micro-Loans for the Very Poor." *The Journal of Economic Issues* (June 1997) carried an excellent article on the work of the Grameen Bank under the unpromising title "The Grameen Bank as Progressive Institutional Adjustment." A brief biography of the life of Aung San Suu Kyi, who is a follower of Gandhi and daughter of Aung San, the George Washington of Burma, may be found in *Current Biography Yearbook 1992*. Her essays are collected under the title *Freedom from Fear* (London, 1991).

Donald Kagan's dazzling tour de force of historical analysis, *On the Origins of War and the Preservation of Peace* (New York, 1995), takes us from the Peloponnesian War of the fifth century B.C. to the Cuban Missile Crisis. The quotation from Yuan Zhiming is taken from "The Pilgrimage from Tiananmen Square" by Ian Buruma in the *New York Times Magazine* (April 11, 1999).

The headquarters of the Community of Sant'Egidio is Piazza di Sant'Egidio 3A, 00153 Roma. Except during August, they meet for prayer at 8:30 every evening in the basilica of Santa Maria in Trastevere, an excellent opportunity to approach a member of the community for additional information. The Friends of Saint Giles, an American offshoot of Sant'Egidio, meet for prayer every Wednesday evening at 5:45, except during August and on the day and eve of national holidays, at Saint Malachy's Church, 239 West 49th Street, New York, NY 10019.

The quotation from W. H. Auden is the ending to his verse play *For the Time Being: A Christmas Oratorio* and may be found in his *Collected Longer Poems* (New York, 1969).

In closing, I would like to give the context for the alarming assertion of Shaye Cohen with which this book began. It was delivered as part of a Jewish-Christian dialogue (with John Meier) on "The Jewishness of Jesus" at Fordham University, November 10, 1993, and is contained in *No Religion Is an Island: The Nostra Aetate Dialogues* (New York, 1998):

"The challenge that the Jewishness of Jesus brings to Christianity is that Christians must develop a non-supersessionist theology that validates the Christian message and the Christian promise without at the same time de-legitimating Judaism *for Jews*. Christians must find a way to maintain Christianity's identity and sense of purpose without at the same time denying Judaism a reason for its continued existence. That is a contemporary challenge to those who take seriously Jesus's Jewishness.

"The challenge that the Jewishness of Jesus brings to Judaism is that Jews must develop a theology of the Other, a theology that validates the Jewish way without at the same time de-legitimating the Christian message and the Christian promise *for Christians*. We Jews must realize that Christians, too, have a claim to the Old Testament (as Christians call it) and to biblical history, and that the Christian claims are no less real and no less authentic than our own. The challenge is to recognize that Christianity, too, is (or at least once was) a form of Judaism, and that we Jews must work out in our own minds a way of understanding what Christianity is, and what purpose Christianity serves in the cosmic order. As fas as I know, Jewish thinkers have barely begun to confront this challenge, but the challenge must be confronted."

We have all of us barely begun to confront the challenges Shaye Cohen rightly sets for us. But I dare to hope that this book, taken in conjunction with its predecessor, *The Gifts of the Jews*, will be seen as a step toward answering these challenges and even as an act of reconciliation.

The Books *of the* New Testament

---

*Paul's authorship rarely disputed.
†Paul's authorship universally disclaimed.

THE CATHOLIC LETTERS

(written in letter form but intended as literary documents for all, thus "catholic")

James

1 Peter

†2 Peter

1 John

2 John

3 John

†Jude

---

†Apostolic authorship universally disclaimed.

PROPHECY/APOCALYPTIC

The Revelation of John

Chronology

This is hardly a complete chronology, just a reference guide to historical dates relevant to episodes mentioned in the main text.

1010–970 B.C.   David rules the United Kingdom of Israel.

966   David's son Solomon builds the Temple in Jerusalem.

933   The United Kingdom is divided into Israel and Judah.

722/721   The Kingdom of Israel is overrun by the forces of the Assyrian king Sargon II, and its inhabitants are deported: the ten northern tribes are lost.

597   Nebuchadnezzar of Babylon captures Jerusalem, begins deporting Jews (Babylonian Captivity); he then levels Temple and city.

539   Cyrus, king of the Persians, enters Babylon.

538   The Edict of Cyrus is proclaimed, allowing the exiles to return to the Promised Land.

515   The Second Temple is completed.

336   Alexander the Great on the throne of Macedon.

332   Alexander marches through Palestine.

323   Alexander dies in Babylon; his empire is divided.

200   Greek Seleucid kings rule Palestine from Antioch.

167–164   Construction of Acra at Jerusalem; the Temple is defiled by pagans.

166   Revolt of Judas Maccabeus.

160   Death of Judas, who is succeeded by his brother Jonathan.

152   Jonathan is named high priest by the Seleucids; soon thereafter, formation of the Essene community near the Dead Sea.

63   Roman general Pompey takes Jerusalem.

48   Julius Caesar defeats Pompey, who is killed in Egypt.

37–34   Herod the Great king of Roman Judea.

31   Octavian defeats Antony and Cleopatra at the naval battle of Actium.

30   Suicides of Antony and Cleopatra.

29   Roman Senate gives Octavian the office of Imperator (Emperor); Herod builds the Antonia fortress, probable site of Jesus's trial before Pilate.

27   Senate gives Octavian the title of (Caesar) Augustus.

23–20   Herod constructs his enormous palace in Jerusalem's upper city; he begins the reconstruction of the Second Temple.

c. 6   Birth of Jesus.

4   Death of Herod.

A.D. 5–10   Birth of Saul-Paul at Tarsus in Cilicia.

14   Death of Augustus.

14–37   Tiberius emperor.

26–36   Pontius Pilate prefect of Judea.

c. 27   Herod Antipas marries his brother's wife, drawing the condemnation of John the Baptizer. The ministry of Jesus begins.

30   On Friday, the eve of Passover, "Christ condemned to death by Pontius Pilate under the Emperor Tiberius" (Tacitus, Annals).

37   Death of Tiberius.

37–41   Caligula emperor, assassinated before he can see fulfilled his order to erect his statue in the Temple in Jerusalem.

41–54   Claudius emperor; expels the Jews from Rome.

44   Herod Agrippa imprisons Peter in Jerusalem.

45–49   Paul's first missions.

c. 48   "Council" of Jerusalem declares gentile Christians exempt from the Law of Moses.

49–52   Paul's missions to Galatia, Macedonia, Athens, Corinth.

54–68   Nero emperor.

57–58   Paul writes letters to Corinthians, Galatians, Romans.

61–63   Paul in Rome, under military guard, writes letters to Colossians, Ephesians, and Philippians.

64–67   Martyrdoms of Peter and Paul at Rome. Mark's Gospel is written.

68–69   Galba emperor.

70   Destruction of Jerusalem by the Romans.

c. 80   Gospels of Matthew and Luke and the Acts of the Apostles are written.

81–96   Domitian emperor.

c. 95   Final text of the Revelation; soon thereafter, final text of John's Gospel and the three letters of John the Elder.

Acknowledgments

To friends who read the first draft of the manuscript—my wife, Susan Cahill, John E. Becker, William Cassidy, John J. Collins, Michael D. Coogan, Paul Dinter, Herman Gollob, Madeleine L'Engle, Stefani Michelson, Gary B. Ostrower, Thomas V. Peterson, Burton Visotzky, and Robert J. White—I owe much by way of corrections both small and large. But what errors and imperfections remain are mine alone.

Within Doubleday and its parent, Random House, Inc., there dwell many who deserve my gratitude, my editor and publisher, Nan A. Talese, always topping the list; but I must mention also Peter Olson, Richard Sarnoff, Katherine Trager, William G. Barry, Stephen Rubin, Jacqueline Everly, John Pitts, Sandee Yuen, Judy Jacoby, Mario Pulice, Maria Carella, and Sean McDonald. Beyond Doubleday and Random House, I owe many thanks to Marysarah Quinn, the book's designer; Kathy Kikkert, the jacket designer; my assistant, Diane Marcus; my redoubtable agent, Lynn Nesbit, and her colleagues Cullen Stanley, Tina Bennett, and Eric Simonoff; the bookseller Henry Morren (till recently) of the Union Theological Bookstore in New York City; the research librarian Andrea Ginsky of the Selby Public Library in Sarasota, Florida; and James P. McCabe, director of the libraries of Fordham University. All these have been instrumental at one time or another, in one way or another, in enabling me to get a few steps further in creating this series of books and this book in particular.

No book can reach its readers without the help of the publisher's sales force. Indeed, within the world of reading, the moment in which the sales rep tries to interest the bookshop buyer in a new title is even more crucial than the moment the reader pulls a new book off the bookshop shelf. The Doubleday sales reps have been essential to the success of The Hinges of History series, starting with the 1994 sales conference at which they insisted on tripling the initial print run for *How the Irish Saved Civilization*, thus tripling the house's expectations for this quirky little title. They deserve to be thanked individually: Robert Allen, Carlos Azula, Barbara Barr, Warren Bost, Reed Boyd, Gail Browning, Philip Canterbury, Brian Cassin, Linda Chisholm, Michael Coe, Janet Cooke, Tom Cox, Michael Croy, Deb Darrock, Bruce Dasse, Kelly Duffin, Karen Fink, Dennis Geare, Michael Gillies, David Glenn, Harvey Goodman, Ken Graham, Al Greco, Chris Grimm, Jim Hiscocks, Don Hoglund, Karen Hopkins, Evelyn Hubbard, Marian Jackson, Lauren Johnson, Sally Johnson, Constance Jump, Ann Kingman, Mary Lang, David Lappin, Scott Lepine, Britt Levine, Jerry Lex, Tom Lovett, Lisa McCormack, Marty McGrath, Constance MacKenzie, Brad Martin, Jim Masiakowski, Jay Melton, Wayne Miller, John Neale, Amy Nover, Annette Trial O'Neil, Helen Ortiz, David Persaud, Maura Phelan, David Phethean, Susan Reiheld, Ron Richardson, Heidi Sachner, Jack St. Mary, Linda Scott, Ron Shoop, Lorne Sproule, Robert Standing, Robert Trail, Alan Trask, Lahring Tribe, David Underwood, Cinda Van Deursen, Leslie Vasilio, Valerie Walley, Don Weisberg, Margaret Winter, and James Young. (Because it is all too easy to omit someone from a list this long, I beg forgiveness from anyone so omitted and rush to assure you that the omission was inadvertent.) Lastly, I would thank those whose careers have now taken them elsewhere but who were so important in setting this series on its feet: Steve Atinsky, Aileen Berg, Kip Triplett, Jacqueline Updike, and the legendary, unforgettable Bruce de Garmeaux.

Index *of*
Biblical Citations

This list, which is offered as an aid to those who would explore the Bible more fully, is confined to those biblical passages quoted in the main text that contain a full sentence or more. For those unfamiliar with the conventions of biblical citation: each citation begins with the title (sometimes in shortened form) of one of the books to be found in the Bible, followed by the chapter number, followed (after the colon) by the verse number(s).

General Index